Sublexical representations and the 'front end' of visual word recognition

Manuel Carreiras

Department of Cognitive Psychology, University of La Laguna, Spain

Jonathan Grainger

LPC-CNRS, University of Provence, France

In this introduction to the special issue on sublexical representations in visual word recognition, we briefly discuss the importance of research that attempts to describe the functional units that intervene between low-level perceptual processes and access to whole-word representations in long-term memory. We will comment on how the different contributions to this issue add to our growing knowledge of the role of orthographic, phonological, and morphological information in the overall task of assigning the appropriate meaning to a given string of letters during reading. We also show how the empirical findings reported in this special issue present a challenge for current computational models of visual word recognition.

Research on visual word recognition has occupied a central position in cognitive psychology ever since the birth of this discipline many decades ago. Research has blossomed over this period, and the field still attracts a considerable amount of attention as reflected by the number of talks on the topic at international conferences. In spite of the amount of attention that this field has received, a great deal of empirical and theoretical work is still necessary before all the intricacies of the complex process of printed word perception have been sorted out. One key issue, that we believe deserves more attention, is the role of sublexical units in the process of mapping form onto meaning with printed word stimuli. The goal of this special issue, which grew out of a symposium on sublexical units in visual word recognition organised by the first author during the 8th AMLaP

Correspondence should be addressed to Manuel Carreiras, Dept. de Psicologia Cognitiva, Universidad de la Laguna 38205, Tenerife, Spain.

© 2004 Psychology Press Ltd

http://www.tandf.co.uk/journals/pp/01690965.html   DOI: 10.1080/01690960344000288

(Architectures and Mechanisms for Language Processing) conference in Tenerife, Spain, is to highlight current progress on that issue.

Although not all researchers agree that a lexical-sublexical distinction is a necessary ingredient of a theory of printed word perception,[1] there is a general consensus that this distinction is a useful construct for interpreting data observed in this field. At the very least it allows researchers to break down the global process of visual word recognition into more manageable component parts, hence avoiding a monolithic approach. Within this general perspective, sublexical units can be further subdivided into orthographic, phonological, and morphological representations. The contributions to this special issue provide examples of research in each of these subfields.

Orthography

Most researchers in the field would agree that individual letter representations play a critical role in printed word perception in languages that have alphabetical orthographies. Printed text provides clear spacing between words, and albeit to a lesser degree, between the individual letters within a word in non-cursive script. One of the reasons why literate brains ought to take advantage of such information is that it is much more economical to solve the problem of variations in surface form at the level of individual letters, than at the level of words. Thus, rather than having separate representations for upper and lowercase versions of the same word (and other types of surface variation), we expect that abstract letter identities are mapped onto a single whole-word orthographic representation for each word. Although the precise mechanisms involved in individual letter identification are still not completely specified, assuming that the computation of letter identities represents the first major step in printed word perception then raises the tricky question as to how these individual letters are combined in the correct order. Solutions to the problem of letter position encoding vary from postulating position-specific, length-dependent letter detectors, as in the Interactive-Activation model (McClelland & Rumelhart, 1981), to a minimal specification of letter order (e.g., Shillcock, Ellison, & Monaghan, 2000). Recent empirical research suggests that the solution lies somewhere between these two extremes, with some form of approximate, relative-position information being computed.

---

[1] In fully distributed connectionist models (e.g., Plaut et al., 1996), form representations map onto meaning representations without having to assign a special status to words at any point in the process.

A recent email message about a purported experiment run at Cambridge University provides a useful illustration of this type of coarse orthographic coding. The message demonstrates that a text composed of words whose inner letters have been re-arranged can be raed wtih qutie anazimg esae! Although some of the readability of this email message is likely due to top-down factors made possible by the fact that almost 50% of the words are not mixed up, a significant part of this 'jumbled word effect' may well be due to the special way the human brain encodes the positions of letters in printed words (Grainger & Whitney, 2004). In well-controlled laboratory experimentation, masked-priming studies (Humphreys, Evett, & Quinlan, 1990; Peressotti & Grainger, 1999) have shown that target word recognition is facilitated when primes are composed of a subset of the target word's letters compared with an unrelated prime condition (even when the proportion of shared letters is quite low, and absolute, length-dependent, letter position is violated), as long as the shared letters are in the same order in prime and target stimuli. That is, priming occurs only when relative positions are respected. For example, a 6-letter word such as 'garden' is identified more rapidly when preceded by the masked prime 'grdn' compared to the unrelated condition 'pmts', and partly changing the order of letters (gdrn, nrdg) destroys the priming effect. This result would appear to be at odds with the 'jumbled word effect' mentioned above. However, when primes share all their letters with target words, priming is robust with small changes in letter order, a phenomenon referred to as transposition priming. Thus primes formed by transposing two adjacent letters in a target word (e.g., gadren-garden) facilitate word recognition compared with appropriate control primes (Perea & Lupker, 2003; Schoonbaert & Grainger, 2004 this issue).

These two phenomena, relative-position priming and transposition priming, impose considerable constraints on attempts to define the mechanisms involved in orthographic processing. Not one of the predominant computational models of visual word recognition can capture these two key phenomena. The position-specific, slot-based coding of the Interactive Activation (McClelland & Rumelhart, 1981) and Dual Route Cascaded (Coltheart, Rastle, Perry, Ziegler, & Langdon, 2001) models is inconsistent with these experimental results. Context-sensitive bigram and trigram coding, as used in the Seidenberg and McClelland (1989) model, cannot account for these effects. Neither can the vowel-centered schemes adopted in the Plaut, McClelland, Seidenberg, and Patterson (1996) or Zorzi, Houghton, and Butterworth (1998) models. In sum, until quite recently, no computational models of visual word recognition could account for these important phenomena.

These and other phenomena have led to the development of a new approach to letter position coding that involves the computation of more flexible relative-position information. The SOLAR model (Davis, 1999) uses a spatial coding scheme, such that letter order is computed on the basis of the relative activation levels of letter detector units. Whitney (2001) proposed an encoding based on ordered letter pairs (e.g., the input 'take' is represented by activation of units representing TA, TK, TE, AK, AE, and KE). These units do not contain precise information about letter position, or about which letter is next to which. The same units (dubbed 'open bigrams') were later endorsed by Grainger and van Heuven (2003). Open-bigrams provide a convenient computational mechanism for representing the relative position of letters in a string. They are directly motivated by the relative-position priming results discussed above, but also provide a quite natural explanation for effects of transposed letters, and other key data discussed by Whitney (2001).

The article by Schoonbaert and Grainger in this issue provides a further test of relative position coding schemes as used in the SOLAR model (Davis, 1999) and open-bigram coding (Grainger & van Heuven, 2003; Whitney, 2001). In Experiments 1 and 2, Schoonbaert and Grainger examined the role of letter repetition in masked orthographic priming. Although an interesting main effect of letter repetition was observed (target words that contained a repeated letter took longer to respond to than target words without a repeated letter), there was no influence of letter repetition on priming. This can be accounted for in an open-bigram scheme that limits the level of non-contiguity that is permitted. This constrained open-bigram scheme has found further support in relative-position priming experiments (Granier & Grainger, 2004) showing that level of contiguity of the subset of target letters that form the prime stimulus affects the amount of priming that is observed.

Phonology

Much prior research has been devoted to studying whether phonology is involved in visual word recognition and at what stage. There is growing evidence from a variety of paradigms suggesting that phonological information plays an early role in visual word recognition (see Frost, 1998; Rayner, 1998, for reviews). For example, using the masked prime paradigm, Ferrand and Grainger (1992, 1994), and Ziegler, Ferrand, Jacobs, Rey, and Grainger (2000) showed evidence for phonological influences on target word processing that lagged only about 20–30 ms behind orthographic influences. Frost, Ahissar, Gotesman, and Tayeb (2003) also found early phonological influences on visual word recognition, although only with quite large phonological contrasts. Frost et al. (2003) also correctly pointed out the importance of controlling for stimulus luminance in masked priming studies. Variations in the estimates of how much prime exposures is necessary for obtaining phonological priming could well be due to uncontrolled differences in luminance across different experiments.

These masked priming results suggest that the computation of phonological codes is mandatory during visual word recognition, as in the model proposed by Van Orden, Pennington, and Stone (1990), and the bi-modal interactive activation model of Grainger and Ferrand (1994). It is the fact that phonological processing lags behind orthographic processing that can explain why some experiments find no phonological effects. Furthermore, as noted by Frost et al. (2003), evidence for early phonological influences on visual word recognition is incompatible with the Dual Route Cascaded (DRC) model of Coltheart et al. (2001).

A critical issue here is the precise nature of the phonological codes that are computed from printed strings of letters, and the manner in which they connect to the phonological representations involved in spoken word recognition. Three articles in this special issue address the role of syllable-sized representations in visual word recognition. They address two key questions: is there evidence for syllable-sized representations, and if so, are these representations defined orthographically or phonologically?

The syllable

The role of the syllable as an access unit for polysyllabic words was a central issue in the work of Taft (1979) and Taft and Forster (1976). A working hypothesis at that time was that polysyllabic words are accessed via their first syllable. However, this initial interest in attempting to define the access representations for polysyllabic and polymorphemic words, using verbal theorising, was to be replaced in later computational models by a focus on the processing of simple, monosyllabic words, for reasons of tractability. Most current models of visual word recognition (e.g., Coltheart et al., 2001; Grainger & Jacobs, 1996; Plaut et al., 1996) are models of monosyllabic word recognition. To our knowledge, there is only one computational model of reading aloud that incorporates a representation of syllabic structure (Ans, Carbonnel, & Valdois, 1998), and one recent extension of the interactive-activation model includes a syllable level of representation (van Heuven, 2000).

More recently there has been a growing interest in understanding how polysyllabic words are recognised, and empirical evidence has been reported suggesting that the syllable plays an important role in visual recognition, at least in languages with clearly defined syllable boundaries (see Carreiras & Perea, 2002). In particular, a number of experiments have found that syllable frequency influences response times to words in

Spanish (e.g., Álvarez, Carreiras, & Taft, 2001; Carreiras, Álvarez, & de Vega, 1993; Perea & Carreiras, 1998). The main finding is that words with high-frequency syllables produce longer latencies than words with low-frequency syllables in the lexical decision task. This inhibitory effect of syllable frequency has been interpreted in terms of competition at the word level in an interactive activation framework (McClelland & Rumelhart, 1981). Syllabic units, extracted from the orthographic input, would activate words that contain a given syllable. When the frequency of syllables is high, more competing candidates sharing the initial syllable of a target word would be activated and thus inhibit processing of the target word, as compared with when the frequency of syllables is low. A recent ERP study provides further converging empirical evidence to this explanation (Barber, Vergara, & Carreiras, in press).

Three papers of this issue investigate whether syllables play a role in the process of visual word recognition in three different languages: German, English, and Spanish, using different methodologies. In one of the papers, Conrad and Jacobs (2004 this issue) replicated and extended the syllable frequency effect in German, a non-Romance language (see also Mathey & Zagar, 2002 for a replication of the effect in French). Conrad and Jacobs found an inhibitory effect of syllable-frequency in a lexical decision task (Experiment 1) and a perceptual identification task (Experiment 2). This finding is important because even though German, like Spanish, has a shallow orthography, other very important differences still remain, such as the number of syllables, syllable complexity, and the clarity of syllable boundaries. Therefore, the finding reinforces the role of the syllable in visual word recognition by providing evidence that this effect is neither language, nor task-specific.

Further evidence in favour of the syllable as a basic processing unit in visual word recognition has been obtained using priming paradigms in which target words are preceded by primes that share or do not share the first syllable (see Carreiras & Perea, 2002). In this issue, Ashby and Rayner examined effects of syllable compatibility in two eye movement experiments in English, using the fast priming paradigm (Experiment 1) and the parafoveal preview technique (Experiment 2). Subjects read target words that contained either CV-initial syllables or CVC-initial syllables preceded by primes that exactly matched or mismatched their initial syllable. Experiment 1 failed to find evidence for the processing of syllable information when the prime and target were presented foveally. However, in Experiment 2, Ashby and Rayner found very clear syllabic effects such that readers' first fixation durations on the target were shorter on words preceded by a matching syllable preview than a mismatching preview. In an attempt to resolve the apparent inconsistency in these results, the authors suggest that the two techniques might yield different reading environments and tap into different aspects of the word recognition process. Whatever the reasons for this discrepancy, it is important to note that syllabic effects were obtained in English, a language with less clearly defined syllable boundaries than Spanish, for example. The other important aspect to highlight is that this study provides evidence for syllabic processing during word recognition in the course of natural, silent reading of text.

The syllable and phonology

Ashby and Rayner claim that the syllabic effects they observe are phonological effects. Even though we agree with them on this point, the empirical evidence they provide does not unequivocally allow them to reject an orthographic interpretation. In this special issue, Alvarez, Carreiras, and Perea used the masked priming paradigm to offer evidence that the syllable information encoded from visually presented primes is phonological in nature. In Experiment 1, a masked prime that shared a syllable with the target produced stronger facilitation than a masked prime that did not share a syllable with the target, but had an equivalent number of shared letters (ju.nas-JU.NIO versus jun.tu-JU.NIO). Experiment 2 used an interesting property of Spanish to investigate whether this effect is orthographic or phonological. The authors compared priming from pairs that shared syllables defined phonologically and orthographically (e.g., vi.rel-VI.RUS) with priming from pairs that shared syllables defined only phonologically (e.g., bi.rel-VI.RUS). This experiment showed no extra advantage for shared orthography. A final experiment examined whether priming from the rime of the first syllable could have been responsible for the effect in Experiment 2 by comparing primes that shared their first phonological syllable with targets (e.g., bi.rel - VI.RUS) and primes that shared the rime of the first syllable (e.g., fi.rel - VI.RUS). The authors found priming only from primes that shared a syllable with the target.

Thus, it now appears critical for future research that computational models of visual word recognition provide the necessary mechanisms for processing polysyllabic words, in an attempt to account for effects that appear to be due to syllabic structure. Current models could be modified to include mechanisms such as a syllabic level of processing through which syllable effects would arise (see Carreiras et al., 1993; Carreiras & Perea, 2002, for a call in this direction). One possibility within the framework of an extension of Grainger and Ferrand's (1994) bi-modal interactive-activation model, is that syllables play a critical role at the interface between sublexical orthography and sublexical phonology (see van Heuven, 2000, for one possible implementation). The results of Alvarez et al. in this issue suggest that amodal syllable representations may be operational at this interface. Graphemic representations derived from visual input on the one hand, and phonemic representations derived from the speech input on the other hand, could converge on higher-order syllable representations that are insensitive to orthographic variation. Such developments in computational modelling ought to help explain how syllabic effects arise, and more important, they should also help explain why in certain experimental conditions syllabic effects do not arise.

Morphology

The role of morphological information in both visual and spoken word recognition is a rapidly expanding area of research that has been the focus of several special issues of this journal. The article by Krott et al. in the present issue, serves to illustrate the importance of morphology as a factor that imposes considerable constraints on the overall architecture of the processing system that extracts meaning from print.

Complex words are composed of two or more morphemes, hence such morphemic representations are by definition smaller (in number of letters) than the whole word from which they are extracted. However, this does not necessarily give morphology the same sublexical status as the sublexical orthographic and phonological representations discussed above. An on-going debate in this field opposes the hypothesis that morphology acts as an organising principle for whole-word representations (Giraudo & Grainger, 2000, 2001), with the more generally accepted hypothesis that morphemic representations provide one route to the mental lexicon (e.g., Taft, 1994). The critical difference between these two approaches is the position morphemic representations occupy in a processing hierarchy that moves from sublexical form representations to meaning via lexical (whole-word) representations. Grosso modo, in a sublexical approach, morphemic representations receive activation from sublexical orthographic or phonological representations and transfer this activation on to the appropriate whole-word representation, or directly to some form of semantic representation. On the other hand, in the supralexical approach, modality-independent morphological representations are activated by whole-word representations. In the supralexical approach, morphological representations act as an amodal interface between modality-specific whole-word representations and semantic representations.

In this issue, Krott et al. show how wellformedness decisions on existing and novel compound words with interfixes (as is common in the Dutch language) are affected by the constraints imposed by the set of compounds sharing one or the other of the compound's constituents (the left and right constituent families). Although the authors acknowledge that these results can be interpreted within either of the above approaches to morphological representation, they point to an interesting connection between the supralexical approach and the concept of paradigmatic analogy, developed initially to explain empirical data concerning the production of compound words (Krott, Baayen, & Schreuder, 2001). The basic idea is that during production and comprehension (given the results of Krott et al., 2004 this issue), the set of words that share one of the constituents of a compound word (the constituent family) are co-activated during the processing of that compound word and influence on-going processing. In comprehension, this constituent family co-activation implies some form of morphological decomposition that could occur either sublexically or supralexically. It is in future attempts to link work on language production and language comprehension that the correct solution should become obvious. Furthermore, specifying the precise mechanisms involved in paradigmatic analogy, either at the sublexical or supralexical level, should help pinpoint where morphological representations are contacted in the processing hierarchy that moves from visual features to meaning.

Conclusions

The papers included in this special issue report a series of challenging findings that cannot be ignored by current computational models of visual word. First, the letter transposition effects call for more flexible orthographic coding schemes than used in current models of visual word recognition. Second, syllable effects (syllable frequency and syllable compatibility) call for a syllabic level of representation that is absent in the vast majority of computational models. It is admittedly important to start simple in any attempt to model complex behaviour, but it could well be the case that developing models that account for processing in more complex stimuli (in terms of number of syllables and/or number of morphemes, for example) might help elucidate the more elementary processes. One major goal in future modelling work is to understand how the kind of flexible orthographic coding revealed by recent experiments can map onto phonological (syllabic and subsyllabic) representations while reading a given word, and how both orthographic and phonological representations combine to determine the morphological structure of that word.

REFERENCES

Álvarez, C.J., Carreiras, M., & Taft, M. (2001). Syllables and morphemes: Contrasting frequency effects in Spanish. *Journal of Experimental Psychology: Learning, Memory and Cognition, 27*, 545–555.

Álvarez, C.J., Carreiras, M., & Perea, M. (2004). Are syllables phonological units in visual word recognition. *Language and Cognitive Processes, 19*, 427–452.

Ans., A., Carbonnel, S., & Valdois, S. (1998). A connectionist multiple-trace memory model for polysyllabic word reading. *Psychological Review*, *105*, 678–723.

Ashby, J., & Rayner, K. (2004). Representing syllable information during silent reading: Evidence from eye movements. *Language and Cognitive Processes*, *19*, 391–426.

Barber, H., Vergara, M., & Carreiras, M. (in press). Syllable-frequency effects in visual word recognition: Evidence from ERPs. *Neuroreport*.

Carreiras, M., Álvarez, C.J., & de Vega, M. (1993). Syllable frequency and visual word recognition in Spanish. *Journal of Memory and Language*, *32*, 766–780.

Carreiras M., & Perea, M. (2002). Masked priming effects with syllabic neighbors in a lexical decision task. *Journal of Experimental Psychology: Human Perception and Performance*, *28*, 1228–1242.

Coltheart, M., Rastle, K., Perry, C., Ziegler, J., & Langdon, R. (2001). DRC: A Dual Route Cascaded model of visual word recognition and reading aloud. *Psychological Review*, *108*, 204–256.

Conrad, M., & Jacobs, A.M. (2004). Replicating syllable frequency effects in Spanish in German: One more challenge to computational models of visual word recognition. *Language and Cognitive Processes*, *19*, 369–390.

Davis, C.J. (1999). *The Self-Organising Lexical Acquisition and Recognition (SOLAR) model of visual word recognition*. Unpublished doctoral dissertation, University of New South Wales, Australia.

Ferrand, L., & Grainger, J. (1992). Phonology and orthography in visual word recognition: Evidence from masked nonword priming. *Quarterly Journal of Experimental Psychology*, *45A*, 353–372.

Ferrand, L., & Grainger, J. (1994). Effects of orthography are independent of phonology in masked form priming. *Quarterly Journal of Experimental Psychology*, *47A*, 365–382.

Frost, R. (1998). Towards a strong phonological theory of visual word recognition: True issues and false trails. *Psychological Bulletin*, *123*, 71–99.

Frost, R., Ahissar, M., Gotesman, R., & Tayeb, S. (2003). Are phonological effects fragile? The effect of luminance and exposure duration on form priming and phonological priming. *Journal of Memory and Language*, *48*, 346–378.

Giraudo, H., & Grainger, J. (2000). Effects of prime word frequency and cumulative root frequency in masked morphological priming. *Language and Cognitive Processes*, *15*, 421–444.

Giraudo, H., & Grainger, J. (2001). Priming complex words: Evidence for supralexical representation of morphology. *Psychonomic Bulletin and Review*, *8*, 127–131.

Grainger, J., & Ferrand, L. (1994). Phonology and orthography in visual word recognition: Effects of masked homophone primes. *Journal of Memory and Language*, *33*, 218–233.

Grainger, J., & Jacobs, A.M. (1996). Orthographic processing in visual word recognition: A multiple read-out model. *Psychological Review*, *103*, 518–565.

Grainger, J., & van Heuven, W.J.B. (2003). Modeling letter position coding in printed word perception. In P. Bonin (Ed.), *The mental lexicon* (pp. 1–24). New York: Nova Science.

Grainger, J., & Whitney, C. (2004). Can the huamn mnid raed words as a wlohe? *Trends in Cognitive Sciences*, in press.

Granier, J.P. & Grainger, J. (2004). *Letter position information and printed word perception: The relative-position priming constraint*. Manuscript submitted for publication.

Humphreys, G.W., Evett, L.J., & Quinlan, P.T. (1990) Orthographic processing in visual word identification. *Cognitive Psychology*, *22*, 517–560.

Krott, A., Baayen, R.H., & Schreuder, R. (2001). Analogy in morphology: modeling the choice of linking morphemes in Dutch. *Linguistics*, *39*, 51–93.

Krott, A., Hagoort, P., & Baayen, R.H. (2004). Sublexical units and supralexical combinatorics in the processing of interfixed Dutch compounds. *Language and Cognitive Processes, 19*, 453–471.

Mathey, S., & Zagar, D. (2002). Lexical similarity in visual word recognition: The effect of syllabic neighborhood in French. *Current Psychology Letters, 8*, 107–121.

McClelland, J.L., & Rumelhart, D.E. (1981). An interactive activation model of context effects in letter perception: Part 1. An account of basic findings. *Psychological Review, 88*, 375–407.

Perea, M., & Carreiras, M. (1998). Effects of syllable frequency and neighborhood syllable frequency in visual word recognition. *Journal of Experimental Psychology: Human Perception and Performance, 24*, 1–11.

Perea, M., & Lupker, S.J. (2003). Transposed-letter confusability effects in masked form priming. In S. Kinoshita and S.J. Lupker (Eds.), *Masked priming: State of the art* (pp. 97–120). Hove, UK: Psychology Press.

Peressotti, F., & Grainger, J. (1999) The role of letter identity and letter position in orthographic priming. *Perception and Psychophysics, 61*, 691–706.

Plaut, D.C., McClelland, J.L., Seidenberg, M.S., & Patterson, K. (1996). Understanding normal and impaired word reading: Computational principles in quasi-regular domains. *Psychological Review, 103*, 56–115.

Rayner, K. (1998). Eye movements in reading and information processing: 20 years of research. *Psychological Bulletin, 124*, 372–422.

Schoonbaert, S., & Grainger, J. (2004). Letter position coding in printed word perception: Effects of repeated and transposed letters. *Language and Cognitive Processes, 19*, 333–367.

Seidenberg, M.S., & McClelland, J.L. (1989). A distributed, developmental model of word recognition and naming. *Psychological Review, 96*, 523–568.

Shillcock, R., Ellison, T.M., & Monaghan, P. (2000). Eye-fixation behavior, lexical storage, and visual word recognition in a split processing model. *Psychological Review, 107*, 824–851.

Taft, M. (1979). Lexical access via an orthographic code: the BOSS. *Journal of Verbal Learning and Verbal Behavior, 18*, 21–39.

Taft, M. (1994). Interactive-activation as a framework for understanding morphological processing. *Language and Cognitive Processes, 9*, 271–294.

Taft, M., & Forster, K.I. (1976). Lexical storage and retrieval of polymorphemic and polysyllabic words. *Journal of Verbal Learning and Verbal Behavior, 15*, 607–620.

Van Heuven, W.J.B. (2000). *Visual word recognition in monolingual and bilingual readers.* Unpublished doctoral dissertation, University of Nijmegen, The Netherlands.

Van Orden, G.C., Pennington, B.F., & Stone, G.O. (1990). Word identification in reading and the promise of subsymbolic psycholinguistics. *Psychological Review, 97*, 488–522.

Whitney, C. (2001). How the brain encodes the order of letters in a printed word: The SERIOL model and selective literature review. *Psychonomic Bulletin and Review, 8*, 221–243.

Ziegler, J.C., Ferrand, L., Jacobs, A.M., Rey, A., & Grainger, J. (2000). Visual and phonological codes in letter and word recognition: Evidence from incremental priming. *Quarterly Journal of Experimental Psychology, 53A*, 671–692.

Zorzi, M., Houghton, G., & Butterworth, B. (1998) Two routes or one in reading aloud? A connectionist dual-process model. *Journal of Experimental Psychology: Human Perception and Performance, 24*, 1131–1161.

LANGUAGE AND COGNITIVE PROCESSES, 2004, *19* (3), 333–367

Letter position coding in printed word perception: Effects of repeated and transposed letters

Sofie Schoonbaert

Ghent University, Ghent, Belgium

Jonathan Grainger

CNRS and University of Provence, Aix-en-Provence, France

We report four experiments investigating the effects of repeated and transposed letters in orthographic processing. Orthographically related primes were formed by removing one letter from the target word, by transposing two adjacent letters, or by replacing two adjacent letters with different letters. Robust masked priming in a lexical decision task was found for primes formed by removing a single letter (e.g., *mircle*-MIRACLE), and this was not influenced by whether or not the prime contained a letter repetition (e.g., *balace* vs. *balnce* as a prime for BALANCE). Target words containing a repeated letter tended to be harder to respond to than words without a letter repetition, but the nonwords formed by removing a repeated letter (e.g., BALNCE) were no harder to reject than nonwords formed by removing a non-repeated letter (e.g., MIRCLE, BALACE). Significant transposition priming effects were found for 7-letter words (e.g., *sevrice*-SERVICE), and these priming effects did not vary as a function of the position of the transposition (initial, final, or inner letter pair). Priming effects disappeared when primes were formed by replacing the two transposed letters with different letters (e.g., *sedlice*-SERVICE), and five-letter words only showed priming effects with inner letter transpositions (e.g.,

Correspondence should be addressed to Jonathan Grainger, Laboratoire de Psychologie Cognitive, Université de Provence, 29 av. Robert Schuman, 13621 Aix-en-Provence, France. Email: grainger@up.univ-mrs.fr

The research reported in this article was performed while the first author was visiting the Laboratoire de Psychologie Cognitive during a Socrates exchange program between the University of Provence and Ghent University. We thank André Vandierendonck for his help in arranging this visit.

http://www.tandf.co.uk/journals/pp/01690965.html   DOI: 10.1080/01690960344000198

ponit-POINT). We present a revised "open-bigram" scheme for letter position coding that accounts for these data.

If there is one aspect of sublexical processing in visual word recognition for which there exists a general consensus among researchers working on the topic, this must be the role of individual letters. It is generally assumed that the recognition of a printed word during reading is mediated by some minimal orthographic processing that involves the word's component letters, at least in languages that use an alphabetic orthography. Although there is some evidence for the operation of more holistic information, such as word shape or contour (Perea & Rosa, 2002), this is generally considered as supplementary to letter-based orthographic processing. In the vast majority of accounts of visual word recognition, the individual letter is thought to be the unit that provides information input to more complex sublexical and lexical processes, such as phonological and morphological processing. More precisely, the input is generally thought to be an ordered set of letter identities, but exactly how the order information is computed is still not clearly understood.

The present study provides a modest contribution to this less-investigated component of orthographic processing. We first describe current theoretical positions concerning how letter position information is processed during printed word perception. Then we present some recent orthographic priming data that limit the number of viable possibilities. Then we discuss the case of repeated letters, which is the focus of Experiments 1 and 2. Following Experiment 2, we examine the case of letter transpositions, to be studied in the last two experiments.

LETTER POSITION CODING

Current theoretical approaches to coding the position of letters in a string of letters can be classified into three major kinds: slot-based coding, local context-sensitive coding, and spatial coding. *Slot-based coding* involves units that code letter identity and position together, such that a given letter is tagged to a specified location in the string. The different possible locations are the slots to which the different letters can be associated. For example, in the interactive activation model of McClelland and Rumelhart (1981), letter strings are processed in parallel by a set of length-dependent, position-specific letter detectors. This means, for example, that there is a processing unit for the letter T as the first letter of a 4-letter word, a different unit for T as the second letter of a 4-letter word, and a different unit for the letter T as the first letter of a 5-letter word. This is the most efficient means of coding letter position information, but efficiency is bought at great cost: a large number (n + n−1 + n−2 . . . + 1) of duplications of the alphabet are necessary in order to code all positions in letter strings of up to length N.

Relative-position coding can be introduced into slot-based coding schemes by adding anchor points. Letter position is then defined relative to the given anchor point(s). In recent modelling work extending the original interactive activation model (Coltheart, Curtis, Atkins, & Haller, 1993; Jacobs, Rey, Ziegler, & Grainger, 1998) two different relative-position coding schemes have been proposed that adopt one or more anchor points. Coltheart et al. adopted a left-to-right length-independent coding scheme. Letter position is coded relative to the beginning of the string such that the third letter in a 4-letter string is coded as being in the same position as the third letter of a 7-letter string (see also Coltheart, Rastle, Perry, Ziegler, & Langdon, 2001). Jacobs et al. (1998) used the beginning and end points of a letter string as two anchor points for relative-position coding. Thus the following string "BLACK" was coded as I = "B"; I + 1 = "L"; I + 2 = F − 2 = "A"; F − 1 = "C"; F = "K", where I stands for initial letter and F for final letter in the string. The major motivation for adopting either of these two coding schemes was to implement a single coding scheme and a single lexicon for words of varying length in an interactive activation model of visual word recognition.

In recent computational models of reading aloud, a more minimalist slot-based coding scheme has been used to deal with monosyllabic words (Harm & Seidenberg, 1999; Plaut, McClelland, Seidenberg, & Patterson, 1996). Three positions are defined relative to the orthographic onset, nucleus, and coda of the word, and letters are assigned to one of these three positions. Such schemes provide a quite accurate means of coding of letter position for word stimuli since there is hardly any ambiguity in the position of a given set of letters assigned to one of these positions (e.g., given T, S, and R assigned to the onset position, there is only one possible order of these letters as the onset of an English monosyllabic word: STR). However, this coding scheme begs the question as to why a normal reader of English does not misinterpret RTSING as STRING? Obviously the order of letters within each position slot needs to be represented. This is the case in the solution adopted by Zorzi, Houghton, and Butterworth (1998). In this scheme, letter position in monosyllabic words is coded relative to the orthographic onset and rime. The authors defined three onset positions (O1, O2, O3) and five rime positions (R1, R2, R3, R4, R5) in order to specify the order of letters within each segment. It should be noted that coding schemes such as these using sub-syllabic structure to code letter location, require a pre-classification of letters as consonants and vowels before position coding can begin.

Finally, the minimalist slot-based scheme (excluding a one-slot scheme which is tantamount to not coding for position at all) was proposed by Shillcock, Ellison, and Monaghan (2000) in their split-fovea model of visual word recognition. Letters are assigned to one of two possible positions: left and right of the point of eye fixation in the word. Letters falling to the left of fixation are sent to the right hemisphere and processed as an unordered set of letters in that position, while letters to the right of fixation are sent to the left hemisphere forming an unordered set of letters in that location. Shillcock et al. (2000) showed that 98.6% of all the words in the CELEX database were uniquely identified by the two sets of unordered letters generated by a central/centre-left split. However, for 4-letter words this figure dropped somewhat, with 4.7% of these words being ambiguous. Shillcock et al. solved this problem by specifying the identity of the first and last letter, thus assigning a special role to exterior letters in orthographic processing. Thus, in this particular version of the split-fovea model, letter identities are in fact assigned to one of four possible positions: first letter, last letter, inner letter left, inner letter right. However, more recent implemented versions of this model (e.g., Shillcock & Monaghan, 2001) have adopted a multiple slot-based coding scheme that provides information about the relative position of letters in the right and left visual hemifields. We will return to this model in the section on relative-position priming.

The inspiration for letter position coding schemes that use *local-context* comes from the work of Wickelgren (1969) who introduced the concept of a "wickelphone" as a means for encoding phoneme positions in speech. This scheme was adapted by Seidenberg and McClelland (1989) in the form of "wickelgraphs" or letter triples. Thus the word BLACK is coded as an unordered set of letter triples: #BL, BLA, LAC, CK, CK# (where # represents a space). Wickelgraphs code local context in that only information about the relative position of adjacent letters is directly computed. In general, however, a given set of letter triples has only one possible ordering for a given language (e.g., the five wickelgraphs for the word BLACK cannot be re-arranged to form another English word). A more elaborate local-context scheme was proposed by Mozer (1987) in his BLIRNET model. Again, letter triples form the basis of local-context coding in this model, but the scheme is enhanced by the use of what we will refer to as "open-trigrams". In Mozer's model such open-trigrams could be formed by inserting a letter between the first and the second, or between the second and the third letter of each letter triple. So the word BLACK contains the letter triple BLA (and other letter triples as above) plus the open trigrams BL_A and B_LA associated with this triple. The underscore signifies that any letter can be inserted in this position. The idea of coding the relative position of non-adjacent letters has been used in two more recent accounts of letter position coding (Grainger & van Heuven, 2003; Whitney, 2001). In the model of letter position coding proposed by Whitney (2001), we find a clear illustration of how open-bigrams can be used in orthographic processing. In Whitney's (2001) example, the word CART is coded as the following set of bigrams: CA, CR, CT, AR, AT, RT. Thus bigrams are formed across adjacent and non-adjacent letters in the correct order, the basis of what we refer to as open-bigram coding. In Whitney's model, the correct bigrams are activated on the basis of position information provided in a locational gradient at the level of letter representations. In this respect Whitney's model can also be categorised as a spatial coding scheme using an activation gradient to derive letter positions.

The notion of *spatial coding* was developed by S. Grossberg (e.g., Grossberg, 1978), and forms the basis of two recent accounts of letter position coding: the SERIOL model (Whitney, 2001) and the SOLAR model (Davis, 1999). The relative position of spatially distributed items is coded in terms of their relative activation level. This is best achieved when the items in the list form a monotonically increasing or decreasing set of activation values, referred to as an activation gradient. For the purposes of letter position coding, the activation gradient must form a monotonically decreasing activation function across letter position with the highest value for initial letters and the lowest value for the final letter of the string. Whitney (2001) describes a method for translating acuity-dependent activations into the desired monotonically decreasing gradient. As mentioned above, the SERIOL model transforms relative activation at the letter level to activation of ordered bigram units (open-bigrams).

The starting point for processing in the SOLAR model (Davis, 1999) is a set of letter identities that provide serial, left-to-right input to the orthographic processing system, one letter at a time. Since there is only one node for each letter in the letter identification system, letter repetitions cannot be represented at this level. The SOLAR model handles letter repetitions via a latch-field that mediates between letter input and nodes in the orthographic processing module. The latch-field controls the timing of information transfer from the sequential letter input to the spatial orthographic code. Each letter node is connected to four latch-nodes that represent the maximum number of repetitions of a letter in an English word. In this way different nodes handle repeated letters giving them practically the same status as non-repeated letters. Thus, the word BANANA would be represented in the orthographic processing layer as the nodes B1, A1, N1, A2, N2, and A3, with monotonically decreasing activation levels across these six nodes. Activity in these orthographic input nodes is then fed onto a layer representing sequences (lists) of letters, that may correspond to whole-words, or to frequently occurring parts of words such as affixes and bound stems.

RELATIVE-POSITION PRIMING

The vast majority of the above-mentioned coding schemes fail to account for a now well-established result obtained with the masked priming paradigm. Using a four-field variant of this technique with briefly presented primes and targets, Humphreys, Evett, and Quinlan (1990) investigated orthographic priming by varying the number of letters shared by prime and target and the relative position of letters in primes and targets. We will follow the notation of Humphreys et al. in describing different types of orthographic prime. When no specific example is given, a prime condition is described using the numbered letters of the target (e.g., 12345 for a 5-letter target) to indicate which of the target letters appeared in the prime and in which location they appeared. Letters that are present in the prime stimulus but are not present in the target are indicated by the letter "d" (for different). So the prime 1d3d5 indicates that primes shared the first, third, and fifth letters with targets and had two unrelated letters placed in the second and fourth positions.

One key result reported by Humphreys et al. (1990) involves what they referred to as relative-position priming. In this situation, primes and targets differ in length so that absolute position information changes, while the relative order of letters in primes and targets is maintained. Using the above-mentioned notation for describing orthographic primes, for a 5-letter target (12345), a 5-letter prime stimulus such as 12d45 contains letters that have the same absolute position in prime and target, while a 4-letter prime such as 1245 contains letters that preserve their relative order in prime and target but not their precise length-dependent position. Humphreys et al. (1990, Experiment 4) found significant priming for primes sharing four out of five of the target's letters in the same relative position (1245) compared with both a cross-position condition (1425) and an outer-letter only condition (1dd5).

More evidence for effects of relative-position priming was provided by Peressotti and Grainger (1999). With 6-letter target words, relative-position primes (1346) produced significant priming compared with unrelated primes (dddd). Inserting filler letters or characters (e.g., 1d34d6, 1-34-6) to provide absolute position information never led to significantly larger priming effects in this study. Violating the relative position of letters across prime and target (e.g., 1436, 6341) cancelled priming effects relative to all different letter primes (dddd). These relative-position priming effects have found further support in some unpublished work from our laboratory (Granier & Grainger, 2004). Using 7-letter

French words, significant priming relative to an all-different letter prime condition was obtained for primes formed by the first, last, and three central letters (13457), but no priming was obtained for primes where the order of the three central letters was reversed (15437), or where the first and last letter were transposed (73451). Using Italian 9-letter stimuli, Pesciarelli, Peressotti, and Grainger (2001) found significant priming for 5-letter primes sharing the first, last, and a combination of three inner letters of target words (e.g., 12349, 16789, 14569, 13579). Finally, Granier and Grainger (2003) compared effects for primes sharing initial letters with 7 and 9-letter targets (12345) compared with primes sharing final letters (34567, 56789). These conditions were found to generate about the same amount of priming, and stronger priming than a condition maintaining both of the target's outer letters (13457, 14569). It should be noted that this result is particularly damaging for the version of the split-fovea model of letter position coding described in Shillcock et al. (2000), since for example, for a 9-letter word, a 14569 prime correctly assigns all letters to the left and right of a central fixation point, whereas 12345 and 56789 primes clearly do not. However, it remains to be seen whether later versions of this model can accommodate relative-position priming effects. Shillcock and Monaghan (2001) used a staggered presentation technique to simulate the variable viewing positions that are encountered during normal reading. The model is trained to "recognise" the same word at different viewing positions, and given the split-fovea architecture, the hidden units in the model will "learn" to represent the different letter clusters that are formed by a staggered presentation. The shift-invariant mapping that the model learns should allow it to capture priming effects obtained with consecutive letter primes (e.g., 56789), but might run into trouble with priming effects from non-adjacent letter combinations (e.g., 13579).

These relative-position priming effects probably provide the single most constraining set of data for any model of orthographic processing (another critical set of results concerns letter transposition effects, to be summarised in the introduction to Experiment 3). Practically all of the above letter position coding schemes fail to account for these effects. Here we will examine three models that can account for relative-position priming effects. These are Davis' (1999) SOLAR model, Whitney's (2001) SERIOL model, and the open-bigram scheme of Grainger and van Heuven (2003). The present study provides a further test of these specific coding schemes. One point on which these schemes differ, concerns the presence or absence of positional biases in orthographic priming. This is examined in the second part of the study where we focus on the role of transposed letters. The first part of the present study (Experiments 1 and 2) focuses on the role of repeated letters in orthographic processing.

REPEATED LETTERS

Repeated letters are problematic for any relative position-coding scheme. As noted above, this led Davis (1999) to introduce a special means for dealing with repeated letters in his SOLAR model. An additional representational layer, called a latch-field, is introduced to record letter repetitions, such that on presentation of the word BANANA, only a single letter A exists at the item level, but the different occurrences of letter A (A1, A2, and A3), are represented in the latch-field. This means that repeated letters are handled just like unrepeated letters, and should not affect processing of a stimulus. In models using 'open bigram' coding schemes (Grainger & van Heuven, 2003; Whitney, 2001), letter repetition implies repetition at the bigram level. Thus words containing a repeated letter will activate fewer bigrams than words without a letter repetition. For example, the word BALANCE has 21 bigram units: BA, BL, *BA*, BN, BC, BE, AL, AA, AN, AC, AE, LA, LN, LC, LE, *AN*, *AC*, *AE*, NC, NE, CE. Four of these bigrams are presented twice (the repetitions are in italics), which means that there are only 17 unique bigram codes. Thus, for a fixed word length in letters (and fixed viewing conditions), words with a repeated letter should be harder to recognise than words with no repeated letters.

Most critical for the present study, the open-bigram scheme also predicts that creating a nonword prime for the target BALANCE by omitting the second occurrence of the repeated letter (e.g., balnce), would produce significantly more priming than a nonword prime such as *balace*, which is created by omitting a unique letter of the target word.[1] According to the open-bigram coding scheme, the following bigrams would be generated for a prime like *balnce*: BA, BL, BN, BC, BE, AL, AN, AC, AE, LN, LC, LE, NC, NE, CE. Fifteen of the seventeen unique bigrams of BALANCE are present. On the other hand, in a prime like *balace* there are three repeated bigrams, so in comparison with the prime *balace*, it has three unique bigrams less, and hence should produce less priming. Given our prior work on orthographic priming, both of these conditions are expected to produce significant priming effects relative to an unrelated condition, where no letters are shared between prime and target (Granier & Grainger, 2004).

---

[1] In this example, removing a vowel or a consonant affects the pronounceability of the resulting nonword prime. The possible consequences of this were examined in post-hoc analyses to be discussed following Experiment 1.

EXPERIMENT 1

Experiment 1 presents a relative-position priming manipulation (primes are formed by removing one of the target's letters) that examines the role of repeated letters in orthographic processing. Summarising the predictions for Experiment 1, the open-bigram scheme (Grainger & van Heuven, 2003; Whitney, 2001) predicts that primes formed by removing one of the repeated letters of a target word should be more effective than primes formed by removing a non-repeated letter. Furthermore, targets containing a repeated letter should be harder to identify than words without any repeated letters. On the other hand, the special scheme implemented in the SOLAR model in order to handle repeated letters (Davis, 1999) leads the model to predict that stimuli with repeated letters will be processed with approximately the same ease as stimuli with non-repeated letters. Experiment 1 puts these two alternatives to the test.

Method

Participants.   Forty-four psychology students at the University of Provence participated in the experiment and received course credit in exchange. In this and the following experiments, all of the participants were native speakers of French who reported having normal or corrected-to-normal vision. All participants took part in one experiment only.

Stimuli and design.   Forty-five French 7-letter words were selected as critical targets in a masked priming lexical decision experiment (Appendix 1). Their mean printed frequency was 41 per million, and ranged from 10 to 290 (New, Pallier, Ferrand, & Matos, 2001). All of these critical target words contained one letter that was repeated just once (e.g., *BALANCE* but not *CASCADE, nor INITIAL*). Care was taken so that the repeated letter did not appear on the first, nor the last position of the word (e.g., *BALANCE* but not *AISANCE*, or *SILENCE*, or *ENFANCE*). Furthermore, there was at least one intervening letter between the first and the second appearance of the repeated letter (e.g., *BALANCE* but not *COLLINE*). These constraints were used because outer letters and adjacent repeated letters (i.e., geminates) could possibly act as special cases. Plurals, feminine forms, and conjugated verbs were excluded. For all of these targets, three different types of 6-letter nonword primes were constructed (see Table 1, for an overview): (1) a related prime which was formed by omitting the second appearance of the repeated letter (omitted repeat condition, e.g., *balnce* as a prime for *BALANCE*), (2) a related prime in which the letter before or after the repeated letter was omitted (omitted unique condition, e.g., *balace-BALANCE*), and (3) an unrelated prime which had no letters in common with the target and had the same

TABLE 1
Matched variables and examples of stimuli (in parentheses) for the different conditions
tested in Experiments 1, 3, and 4

Target type	Freq	N (target)	Prime type	N (prime)
Experiment 1				
Repeat	40.6	1.1	Omitted repeat (balnce)	.33
(BALANCE)			Omitted unique (balace)	.40
			Unrelated (fodiru)	.36
Control	36.0	1.2	Omitted repeat* (mircle)	.42
(MIRACLE)			Omitted unique (mirale)	.40
			Unrelated (bentho)	.36
Experiment 3				
5 letters	84.5	3.34	TL-initial (rdoit)	.03
(DROIT)			TL-inner (dorit)	.03
			TL-final (droti)	.03
			Unrelated (cegnu)	.05
7 letters	79.5	1.2	TL-initial (esrvice)	.03
(SERVICE)			TL-inner (sevrice)	.02
			TL-final (serviec)	.05
			Unrelated (notould)	.07
Experiment 4				
5 letters	84.5	3.34	OC-initial (sfoit)	.05
(DROIT)			OC-inner (dafit)	.05
			OC-final (dronu)	.03
			Unrelated (cegnu)	.05
7 letters	79.5	1.2	OC-initial (atrvice)	.03
(SERVICE)			OC-inner (sedlice)	.02
			OC-final (serviom)	.03
			Unrelated (notould)	.07

* Labelled as "Omitted repeat" to match the corresponding experimental condition.
N: mean number of orthographic neighbours.
Freq: Mean printed frequency per million.

CV-structure as one of the two related primes (unrelated condition, e.g.,
fodiru-BALANCE).[2] The three types of prime were all closely matched on
number of orthographic neighbours. The measure used was Coltheart's N,
defined as the number of words differing by a single letter from the
stimulus, preserving letter positions (e.g., worse, and house are both
orthographic neighbours of horse; Coltheart, Davelaar, Jonasson, &
Besner, 1977). Additionally, 45 control target words (also French 7-letter
words with a mean printed frequency of 36 per million; range: 10–127)
were selected. These control words did not contain a repeated letter, had

---

[2] As indicated in Appendix 1, by error two unrelated primes did not have the same CV-
structure as one of the corresponding related primes. Excluding these two items did not affect
any of the results to be presented here.

the same CV-structure as their corresponding critical target and were also matched overall on frequency and number of orthographic neighbours with the critical words. Three different prime types were constructed in the same way as for the critical target words. However, because there was no repeated letter in these control words, we omitted the letter in the same position as the omitted letter in the corresponding critical target, for all prime types respectively. This allowed us to control for any possible effect of the position of the letter that was removed to form the prime stimulus. Thus the experiment involved a 2 (Type of target: Repeat vs. Control) × 3 (Prime type: omitted repeat vs. omitted unique vs. unrelated) design for the participants analyses. All of these were within-participant factors. Prime-target pairing was counterbalanced using a Latin-square design. Each participant saw all targets once only in one of the three prime conditions for the two types of target, and target words were tested in all prime conditions across different participants. In the item analyses Type of target was treated as a between-items factor and Prime type was a within-items factor. In addition to the selection of ninety target words, ninety 7-letter nonwords were constructed as filler items (since the task was lexical decision). Half of these nonwords had a repeated letter, whereas the other half did not (Appendix 2). These two subgroups were matched on number of orthographic neighbours and CV-structure. Primes were constructed for the nonword targets following the same procedure as for the words. In fact, the design for nonword targets mirrored that of the words.

Procedure.   Each trial consisted of a sequence of four visual events. The first was a row of nine hash marks (#########), which served as a forward mask, and was presented for 500 ms together with two vertical lines positioned above and below the centre of the mask and serving as a fixation mark. Second, the prime was displayed on the screen for 53 ms and was followed immediately by a backward mask for 13 ms. Finally, the target was presented for a maximum duration of 4000 ms, or until participant's response. Each stimulus appeared in the centre of the screen. The intertrial interval was 523 ms. Stimulus presentation and response collection were controlled by DMDX and TimeDX software Version 3.02 (Forster & Forster, 2003). All stimuli were presented on a standard 15" VGA colour monitor (with a 13.32 ms refresh rate) in fixed-width 'Courier New' font, as white characters on a black background. Primes appeared in lower case (font size 12), whereas targets were presented in upper case (font size 16). For the masks, the same font size as for the primes was used. The presentation of all trials was randomised with a different order for each participant. Participants were asked to focus on the centre of the row of hash marks (indicated by the two vertical lines) and to decide as quickly and accurately as possible if the stimulus in upper case was a French word

TABLE 2
Mean RT (ms) and error percentage for each experimental condition tested in Experiment 1

		Type of target			
		Repeat		Control	
	Type of prime	Mean RT	Errors	Mean RT	Errors
Words	Omitted repeat	565***	3%	560***	2%
	Omitted unique	572***	3%	561***	2%
	Unrelated	607	6%	597	3%
Nonwords	Omitted repeat	695	5%	677***	5%
	Omitted unique	686	6%	670	4%
	Unrelated	691	6%	672	4%

***$p < .001$: significant differences relative to the unrelated condition.

or not. The two possible response buttons were the right control key (for a 'Yes' response) and the left control key (for a 'No' response) of a standard PC keyboard. The assignment of responses was reversed for left-handed participants. None of the participants was informed about the presence of a prime.

Results

Mean response times and percentage error are presented in Table 2. Only correct responses were analysed after removing outliers (RTs greater than 250 ms or less than 1500 ms). This procedure affected less than 1% of all data for correct responses. ANOVAs were carried out with participants (F_1) and items (F_2) as random variables. In the participants analyses List was included as a between-participants factor, and figured as a between-item factor in the item analyses. For all experiments reported in the present study, this same procedure of analysis was used.

Word analyses. An ANOVA on mean RTs showed that targets containing a repeated letter took longer to respond to than targets without a repeated letter, $F_1(1, 41) = 7.38$, $p < .05$, although this effect was not significant in the items analysis, $F_2(1, 84) = 0.97$.[3] There was a main effect of Prime type, $F_1(1, 82) = 46.29$, $p < .001$, $F_2(2, 168) = 49.74$, $p < .001$. The interaction between Target type and Prime type was not significant. Planned comparisons between the different prime conditions indicated that the related prime condition produced significantly faster RTs than the

---

[3] Further item analyses were performed including log word frequency as a covariate. This did not change the significance level of any of the results reported here.

unrelated prime condition: $F_1(1, 41) = 59.64, p < .001, F_2(1, 84) = 67.32$, $p < .001$, for the omitted repeat condition, and $F_1(1, 41) = 60.47, p < .001, F_2(1, 84) = 31.94, p < .001$, for the omitted unique condition. A planned comparison for the repeat targets only, showed that the difference between the two related prime conditions (i.e., omitted repeat vs. omitted unique) was not significant. An ANOVA conducted on error percentages to word targets yielded a significant main effect of Target type, $F_1(1, 41) = 10.16, p < .01, F_2(1, 84) = 4.79, p < .05$. Accuracy was lower for words containing a repeated letter.

Nonword analyses. An ANOVA conducted with RT as dependent variable, revealed a main effect of Target type, $F_1(1, 41) = 18.45, p < .01$, that was not significant in the item analysis, $F_2(1, 84) = 2.07$. In the accuracy analysis, the main effect of Target type was also significant in the participants analysis, $F_1(1, 41) = 6.62, p < .05$, but not in the item analysis, $F_2(1, 84) = 1.44$. Nonword targets without a repeated letter tended to generate faster RTs and less errors than nonword targets containing a repeated letter.

Discussion

The results of Experiment 1 provide mixed support for both the SOLAR model (Davis, 1999) and open-bigram accounts of letter position coding (Grainger & van Heuven, 2003; Whitney, 2001). The fact that primes formed by removing a repeated letter in the target word were not more effective than other orthographically related primes contradicts the predictions of the open-bigram scheme. This absence of an influence of letter repetition on orthographic priming was further explored with post-hoc analyses examining whether the CV-status of the removed letter affected priming. Priming effects were compared for primes formed by removing a consonant vs. primes formed by removing a vowel. Separate analyses were performed for the omitted repeat and omitted unique priming conditions. These analyses showed significant priming effects for omitted repeat, $F(1, 82) = 17.01, p < .01$, and omitted unique primes, $F(1, 82) = 47.25, p < .001$, that did not interact with the CV-status of the letter that was removed to form the related prime, $F(1, 82) = 1.22$ and $F < 1$ respectively. There was a 32 ms priming effect for primes formed by removing a consonant and a 42 ms effect for primes formed by removing a vowel. Furthermore, a direct comparison of the two types of prime revealed no significant difference. The CV-status of the letter that was removed to form a related prime in Experiment 1, did not affect the amount of priming that was obtained.

The open-bigram model correctly predicted the main effect of target type observed in Experiment 1: targets containing a repeated letter were harder to respond to (more errors and slower RTs) than targets without a repeated letter. This repeated-letter effect was observed for both word and nonword stimuli. This is, to our knowledge, the first report of an influence of repeated letters on printed word perception. Nevertheless, the fact that the effect in RTs to word targets failed to reach significance in the item analyses suggests that further research is necessary to consolidate this potentially critical finding.

The priming effects observed in Experiment 1, or rather the lack of an influence of the repeated-letter manipulation in prime stimuli, contradicts the open-bigram model. According to this model, primes generated by removing one of a repeated letter pair in a target word share more bigrams with the target word than primes generated by removing a non-repeated letter. This priming condition should therefore have generated stronger priming effects. The fact that this did not occur is more in line with the predictions of the SOLAR model (Davis, 1999). However, one means of saving the open-bigram model would be to argue that the masked priming paradigm is not sensitive enough to detect the rather subtle manipulation of prime type in Experiment 1. If nonword primes formed by removing a repeated letter from a given word provide more activation input to their corresponding base-word than nonwords formed by removing a non-repeated letter, then these nonwords should be harder to reject as targets in an unprimed lexical decision task. This was tested in Experiment 2.

EXPERIMENT 2

Experiment 2 is an unprimed lexical decision experiment where the critical targets are the nonword primes from Experiment 1.

Method

Participants.   Forty psychology students at the University of Provence participated in this experiment for course credit.

Stimuli and design.   Stimuli were the 270 six-letter nonwords that had served as primes for word targets in Experiment 1, and 90 six-letter word targets. The latter were used as filler items for the lexical decision task (here the focus was on performance to nonword targets), and had a mean printed frequency of 26 per million (New et al., 2001). There was no experimental manipulation of the word stimuli. Critical targets were therefore 135 nonword targets derived from words with repeated letters (45 repeat word targets from Experiment 1 $\times$ 3 prime types) and 135 control nonword targets, based on words without a repeated letter. Following the counterbalancing of Experiment 1, three lists were generated, each containing 90 critical nonword targets and 90 word

targets. This gave a 2 (Type of base-word: Repeated letter vs. Control) ×
3 (Target type: Omitted repeat vs. Omitted unique vs. Unrelated) design
for the participants analyses. Both of these factors were manipulated
within-participants. The same design was used in the item analyses, where
both factors were between-items factors.

Procedure.   Each trial consisted of a simple sequence of two events, as
used in standard lexical decision. A fixation point (*) appeared initially in
the centre of the screen, and was replaced by the target after 500 ms. The
target itself was presented for a maximum duration of 4000 ms, or until
participant's response. Targets appeared in lower case, fixed-width
'Courier New' font (font size 12). In general, the same procedure as in
Experiment 1 was used for stimulus presentation and data collection
(except for the differences mentioned above).

Results

Mean response times and percentage of errors are presented in Table 3.
Outliers were removed as in Experiment 1. An ANOVA conducted on
responses to nonword targets with RT as dependent variable, revealed no
main effect of Type of base-word, but a significant main effect of Target
type, $F_1(2, 74) = 74.48$, $p < .001$, $F_2(2, 252) = 39.10$, $p < .001$. The
interaction was not significant. Planned comparisons between the different
target conditions showed that the main effect of Target type was due to
significantly slower RTs for the two categories of nonwords generated by
removing a letter from a real word (omitted repeat and omitted unique) as
opposed to the unrelated condition, respectively $F_1(1, 37) = 51.47$, $p <
.001$, $F_2(1, 252) = 30.80$, $p < .001$, and $F_1(1, 37) = 130.71$, $p < .001$, $F_2(1,
252) = 76.34$, $p < .001$. An ANOVA on percentages of error also revealed
a significant main effect of Target type, $F_1(2, 74) = 39.16$, $p < .001$, $F_2(2,
252) = 17.30$, $p < .001$, no effect of Type of base-word, and no interaction.

TABLE 3
Mean RT (ms) and error percentage for the six types of nonword target tested in
Experiment 2

| Type of target | Type of base word | | | |
| | Repeat | | Control | |
	Mean RT	Errors	Mean RT	Errors
Omitted repeat	714***	11%***	694***	10%***
Omitted unique	736***	9%***	736***	11%***
Unrelated	659	2%	646	1%

*** $p < .001$: significant differences relative to the unrelated condition.

Planned comparisons between the different target conditions indicated that the error percentages were significantly higher for the two categories of nonwords derived by removing a letter from a real word as opposed to unrelated nonwords, respectively $F_1(1, 37) = 57.34, p < .001, F_2(1, 252) = 27.83, p < .001$ for the omitted repeat nonwords, and $F_1(1, 37) = 68.88, p < .001, F_2(1, 252) = 23.91, p < .001$, for the omitted unique nonwords. No other significant differences were found.

Discussion

The results of Experiment 2 provide a further demonstration of how similarity with a real word can influence responses to nonword targets in the lexical decision task. Nonwords formed by removing a letter from a real word were harder to reject (more errors and slower RTs) than nonwords that were matched in terms of number of orthographic neighbours (Coltheart et al., 1977). However, contrary to the predictions of the open-bigram model, nonwords formed by removing a repeated letter (e.g., BALNCE from BALANCE) were not harder to respond to than nonwords formed by removing a non-repeated letter (e.g., BALACE from BALANCE, or MIRCLE from MIRACLE). This result is in line with models of orthographic processing that have a specific mechanism for dealing with letter repetitions, such as the SOLAR model (Davis, 1999).

However, there is one very simple, and theoretically justified modification of the open-bigram model that allows it to capture the general pattern of results obtained in Experiments 1 and 2. This involves imposing a limit on the number of letters that can be inserted in between the two letters that form the open-bigram. This amounts to imposing a limit on the degree of "coarseness" of the coding scheme. We are not the first to suggest such a constraint on open-bigram coding. Humphreys et al. (1990), when discussing Mozer's BLIRNET model in the light of their own data, suggested that the model could be refined such that "... the degree to which input activates cluster units decreases as the distance between letters increases (p. 550)." And Whitney (2001) states that "The activation of a bigram node depends on the activation of the letter nodes representing its constituent letters (increasing activation with increasing input levels) and the time separation between the firing of those letter nodes (decreasing activation with increasing separation) (p. 227)."

Although we completely adhere to a graded activation approach as suggested by Humphreys et al. (1990) and Whitney (2001), for simplicity we will assume an arbitrary limit of two intervening letters beyond which no bigrams are formed. This allows us to generate albeit approximate predictions from the revised model, without having to implement graded activation input from peripheral letter representations. Thus the open-bigrams for the word BALANCE are now limited to: BA, BL, (BA), AL, AA, AN, LA, LN, LC, AN, AC, AE, NC, NE, CE. This scheme still predicts that words with repeated letters should be handicapped relative to words without repeated letters. More important, it now accounts for the lack of an effect of the nonword manipulation in Experiment 1 (as primes) and Experiment 2 (as targets). Both types of prime now generate an equivalent number of overlapping bigrams with the target (10 bigrams for the nonword BALNCE: BA, BL, (BN), AL, AN, AC, LN, LC, (LE), NC, NE, CE. Ten bigrams for the nonword BALACE: BA, BL, AL, AA, AC, LA, LC, (LE), AC, AE, CE).

This constrained version of the open-bigram model was directly motivated by the results of Experiments 1 and 2 of the present study. However, it is important to note that this critical modification of the open-bigram model has since been successfully applied to a large set of relative-position priming results described in Grainger and van Heuven (2003) and Granier and Grainger (2004). The new version of the model provides a complete account of these data, that the old version could only partly account for (we will return to this point in the general discussion). One interesting consequence of the new coding scheme is that stimulus length now influences the extent to which open-bigrams cover all possible ordered letter combinations that can be generated by a given stimulus. As stimulus length increases, the proportion of bigrams that are computed in the new scheme will diminish relative to the complete set of unconstrained bigrams. This leads to length-dependent predictions concerning effects of transposed letters, to be examined in Experiment 3.

EXPERIMENT 3

Experiment 3 examines the influence of transposed letters in the masked priming paradigm. This has been the subject of a recent study published by Perea and Lupker (2003), who provide an excellent summary of research on this topic. Here we first summarise results obtained using the masked priming paradigm, before presenting the predictions of the models that are to be put to test.

Letter transposition priming

In standard masked priming with the lexical decision task and relatively long target words, Forster, Davis, Schoknecht, and Carter (1987) found that effects of transposed letter primes (e.g., salior-SAILOR) were practically the same as identity primes (e.g., sailor-SAILOR). With shorter words (Humphreys et al., 1990), or when primes do not contain all of the target's letters (Peressotti & Grainger, 1999), then transposition priming is greatly diminished. Using their 4-field masking procedure and perceptual identification responses to targets, Humphreys et al. (1990) found only a non-significant 3.1% increase in response accuracy for transposed letter primes (e.g., snad-SAND) compared with primes sharing two out of four letters with targets (e.g., smed-SAND). Similarly, Peressotti and Grainger (1999, Experiment 3a) observed a non-significant 5 ms advantage relative to all different primes when the inner letters were transposed in primes sharing four out of six letters with targets (e.g., bcln-BALCON).

More recent work on transposed letter priming by Perea and Lupker (2003) has provided support to the initial observation of Forster et al. (1987), and helped clarify the precise conditions in which these effects are obtained. In Perea and Lupker's study, transposed letter primes were formed by exchanging two of the target's inner letters (inner transposition; e.g., uhser-USHER) or by exchanging the last two letters of the target (final transposition; e.g., ushre-USHER). Effects of transposition primes were evaluated against an all-different letter prime or an orthographic control prime where the two transposed letters were replaced by letters not in the target (e.g., ufner, ushno). In 5- and 6-letter words, priming effects relative to the unrelated condition did not vary as a function of position of the transposition. However, when measured relative to orthographic control primes, Perea and Lupker (2003) report a significant effect for inner transposition primes that greatly diminishes for the final transposition condition.

Predictions for Experiment 3

Here we will briefly summarise the predictions of three models of letter position coding that provide the focus of the present study. The SOLAR model (Davis, 1999), the SERIOL model (Whitney, 2001), and the new version of the open-bigram scheme presented above, all predict effects of transposed letter primes in the masked priming paradigm. One potential difference between activation gradient accounts of letter position coding (Davis, 1999; Whitney, 2001) and parallel activation accounts (Grainger & van Heuven, 2003; Mozer, 1987) are their predictions concerning effects of positional bias in transposition priming. However, the activation gradient used to generate a spatial orthographic code does not necessarily translate into a straightforward beginning-to-end positional bias at higher-level representations. The equations used in the SOLAR model (Davis, 1999) actually lead it to predict no positional biases in transposition priming.[4] In the SERIOL model (Whitney, 2001), the activation profile of bigram units does not decrease monotonically from beginning to end. This model does

---

[4] We thank Colin Davis for having pointed this out.

nevertheless predict that least priming should be obtained when an initial bigram is modified in the prime. This is because the initial bigram carries the most activation in the SERIOL model, as can be seen in the equations and the examples provided in Whitney and Berndt (1999).

The new version of the parallel open-bigram scheme makes an interesting prediction concerning variations in positional bias as a function of word length. The predictions of the new open-bigram scheme (with maximum two intervening letters) for the three types of related prime and the two word lengths tested in Experiment 3 are as follows. For 5-letter words, initial and final transposition primes share 7 out of 9 bigrams with targets, while inner transposition primes share 8 bigrams with targets. For 7-letter words, all three types of prime share 13 out of 15 bigrams with targets. Thus, the model predicts an inner letter transposition advantage (relative to initial and final transpositions) for 5-letter words, and equivalent priming effects for all three types of prime with 7-letter words. Experiment 3 tests for such positional biases by using primes formed by transposing two adjacent letters at the beginning, in the middle, or at the end of a given target word.

Method

Participants. Thirty-seven psychology students at the University of Provence participated in the experiment for course credit.

Stimuli and Design. A set of 120 items were selected to be used as word targets (Appendix 3). Sixty words of 5-letters (mean printed frequency 85 per million; range 10–452, New et al., 2001) and sixty words of 7-letters (mean printed frequency 80 per million; range 10–353) were included. Four types of prime were created for all targets (see Table 1). These primes were formed by (1) transposing the first two letters of targets (TL-initial, e.g., *rdoit* as prime for DROIT); (2) transposing the two middle letters of targets, i.e., the second and third position or third and fourth position for 5-letter words, and the third and fourth, or fourth and fifth position for 7-letter words (TL-inner, e.g., *dorit*-DROIT); (3) transposing the two final letters of targets (TL-final, e.g., *droti*-DROIT); or were (4) unrelated to targets (e.g., cegnu-DROIT). All these prime types were closely matched on number of orthographic neighbours (Coltheart et al., 1977), and all were nonwords. Thus a 2 (Stimulus length: 5 letters vs. 7 letters) × 4 (Prime type: TL-begin vs. TL-inner vs. TL-final vs. unrelated) repeated measures design was used in the participants analyses. For the item analyses, the same design was used but Stimulus length was treated as a between-items factor. Additionally, 120 nonwords (sixty 5-letter and sixty 7-letter nonwords) were created as filler items for the lexical decision task. The manipulation of the nonword targets was the same as for the word targets. A Latin-square was used to create four completely counterbalanced presentation lists, with each list containing all 240 targets. The primes in the four lists were again matched on number of orthographic neighbours. All participants were exposed to only one presentation list, and given the counterbalancing, each participant was tested in all experimental conditions with a given target presented only once.

Procedure.   The same masked priming procedure as Experiment 1 was used here, except that different font sizes were used.[5] Primes were presented in lowercase (font size 16), and targets in uppercase (font size 12). The forward mask had the same font size as the primes. The different size and case used for prime and target stimuli minimizes visual overlap in the related prime condition when primes and targets have the same length in letters.

Results

Mean response times and percentage error are presented in Table 4. Outliers were removed as in the previous analyses. However, a preliminary analysis showed mean error rates higher than 40% on two 5-letter words, two 7-letter words, and one seven-letter nonword. These items were excluded from further analysis.

Word analyses.   An ANOVA on mean RTs revealed significant main effects of Stimulus length and Prime type, respectively $F_1(1, 33) = 679.42$, $p < .001$, $F_2(1, 109) = 3.76$, $p < .06$, and $F_1(3, 99) = 9.78$, $p < .001$, $F_2(3, 327) = 6.92$, $p < .001$. Their interaction was marginally significant in the participants analysis, $F_1(3, 99) = 2.61$, $p < .06$, and significant in the item analysis $F_2(3, 327) = 2.97$, $p < .05$. This trend to an interaction reflects the greater magnitude of priming effects with 7-letter words compared with 5-letter words. Planned comparisons for the 5-letter words indicated that TL-inner primes produced significantly shorter RTs compared with the unrelated prime condition, $F_1(1, 33) = 8.90$, $p < .01$, $F_2(1, 109) = 4.36$, $p < .05$. The TL-initial and TL-final prime conditions did not differ significantly from the unrelated prime condition with 5-letter words. For 7-letter words, planned comparisons showed that all related (TL) prime conditions were faster than the unrelated condition: TL-initial

---

[5] The reason for this change is that in pilot experimentation with transposed-letter primes we had found stronger priming effects with this particular combination of prime and target sizes.

TABLE 4
Mean RT (ms) and error percentage for the different experimental condition tested in Experiment 3 with transposed letter primes and 5-letter and 7-letter targets

		5 Letters		7 Letters	
	Prime type	Mean RT	Errors	Mean RT	Errors
Words	1. Initial	616	6%	590**	2%
	2. Inner	597**	8%	587***	3%
	3. Final	613	9%	587***	1%
	4. Unrelated	621	7%	623	3%
Nonwords	1. Initial	706	8%	717	4%
	2. Inner	693*	7%	715	2%
	3. Final	715	7%	705	3%
	4. Unrelated	721	7%	705	4%

*$p < .05$; **$p < .01$; ***$p < .001$; significant differences relative to the unrelated condition.

primes, $F_1(1, 33) = 10.75, p < .01, F_2(1, 109) = 20.40, p < .001$, TL-inner primes, $F_1(1, 33) = 14.92, p < .001, F_2(1, 109) = 15.13, p < .001$, and TL-final primes, $F_1(1, 33) = 21.83, p < .001, F_2(1, 109) = 14.86, p < .001$.

An ANOVA with percentage of error as dependent variable revealed a significant main effect of Stimulus length $F_1(1, 33) = 47.50, p < .001, F_2(1, 109) = 15.52, p < .001$. Five-letters words produced more errors than seven-letter words. The main effect of Prime type was not significant. The interaction between Stimulus length and Prime type was significant in the participant analysis, $F_1(3, 99) = 2.98, p < .05$, but failed to reach significance in the item analysis, $F_2(3, 327) = 1.85, p < .07$.

Nonword analyses. An ANOVA on mean RTs revealed a significant interaction between Stimulus length and Prime type, $F_1(3, 99) = 3.63, p < .05, F_2(3, 333) = 2.83, p < .05$. No main effects were significant. Planned comparisons for the 5-letter nonwords showed that TL-inner primes produced significantly shorter RTs compared to the unrelated prime condition, $F_1(1, 33) = 8.90, p < .01, F_2(1, 111) = 9.86, p < .01$. None of the other prime conditions differed significantly from the unrelated condition in either 5-letter or 7-letter nonwords. An ANOVA conducted on the mean percentage of errors revealed a main effect of Stimulus length, $F_1(1, 33) = 29.30, p < .001, F_2(1, 111) = 13.44, p < .001$. Five-letter nonwords produced significantly more errors than 7-letter nonwords. There was no effect of Prime type, and no interaction.

Discussion

Consistent with the predictions of the new open-bigram scheme for letter position coding, 7-letter words showed equivalent effects from primes generated by transposing the first two letters (TL-initial), the last two letters (TL-final), and an inner letter pair (TL-inner). Again consistent with the predictions of the new coding scheme, 5-letter words showed significant priming only from TL-inner primes. The fact that a positional bias was observed with 5-letter words is not consistent with the predictions of the SOLAR model (Davis, 1999). Furthermore, there was no evidence for reduced priming with initial letter transpositions compared with final letter transpositions, as predicted by the SERIOL model (Whitney, 2001).

The results for 5-letter words replicate and extend those reported in Perea and Lupker (2003). However, Perea and Lupker found a similar pattern of priming effects for 6-letter words, while our results for 7-letter words did not show the expected inner letter transposition advantage relative to TL-final primes (Perea & Lupker did not test for TL-initial primes). It is interesting to note that in Perea and Lupker's study, TL-inner and TL-final primes generated very similar RTs (529 ms vs. 534 ms) which is perfectly consistent with the results of the 7-letter words in our Experiment 3. The difference in priming effects in their study only arose in a comparison with orthographic control primes. The orthographic control involved substituting the two critical letters of a given TL prime with two unrelated letters (e.g., TRANI (TL) and TRAPO (control) for the target TRAIN). In Perea and Lupker's study, orthographic control primes involving a substitution of inner letters produced longer RTs than orthographic controls involving final letter substitution (hence the stronger priming effect for TL-inner primes). Experiment 4 examines priming effects for 2-letter substitution primes (following Perea & Lupker, 2003) matched to the TL primes tested in Experiment 3. The new open-bigram scheme predicts no effects of 2-letter substitution primes relative to unrelated primes, given the very low degree of overlap with targets (3 out of 9 bigrams for 5-letter words, and 9 out of 15 for 7-letter words).

EXPERIMENT 4

Method

Participants. Thirty-nine psychology students at the University of Provence participated in the experiment for course credits.

Stimuli and design. The target stimuli of Experiment 3 were used again. Three new prime types, which served as orthographic controls for the transposed letter primes of Experiment 3, were created for the purpose of the present experiment (Appendix 3). The orthographic controls (OC) were identical to the TL primes except that the transposed letters were now replaced by two other letters. The three types were: (1) OC-initial, e.g., *sfoit* (instead of *rdoit*) as prime for DROIT; (2) OC-inner, e.g., *dafit*-DROIT (instead of *dorit*-DROIT); and (3) OC-final, e.g., *dronu*-DROIT (instead of *droti*-DROIT). The unrelated prime condition (e.g., cegnu-DROIT) was the same as for Experiment 3 (see Table 1, for an overview). All these prime types were closely matched on number of orthographic neighbours (Coltheart et al., 1977). The same procedure for construction of orthographic control primes was used for the nonword targets. The primes in the four lists were again matched on number of orthographic neighbours. The experiment involved a 2 (Stimulus length; 5 letters vs. 7 letters) × 4 (Prime type; OC-begin vs. OC-inner vs. OC-final vs. unrelated) repeated-measures design in the participants analyses, with counterbalanced lists as in Experiment 3.

Procedure.   The procedure was the same as for Experiment 3.

Results

Mean response times and percentage errors are presented in Table 5. Outliers were removed as in the previous analyses. The same items that were removed from the analyses in Experiment 3, were once again the items that generated the highest error rates. They were excluded from further analysis.

TABLE 5
Mean RT (ms) and error percentage for the different experimental conditions tested in Experiment 4, with orthographic control primes and 5-letter and 7-letter targets

		5 Letters		7 Letters	
	Prime type	Mean RT	Errors	Mean RT	Errors
Words	1. Initial	622	5%	605	2%
	2. Inner	626	5%	606	3%
	3. Final	620	5%	592*	2%
	4. Unrelated	623	5%	608	2%
Nonwords	1. Initial	729	6%	729	2%
	2. Inner	725	6%	728	3%
	3. Final	735	8%	733	3%
	4. Unrelated	740	8%	731	3%

*$p < .05$; significant differences relative to the unrelated condition.

Word analyses.   An ANOVA on mean RTs revealed a significant main effect of Stimulus length, $F_1(1, 35) = 24.11$, $p < .001$, $F_2(1, 108) = 6.48$, $p < .05$. Seven-letter words produced significantly faster RTs than five-letter words. Neither the main effect of Prime type, nor the interaction between Stimulus length and Prime type were significant. An ANOVA on percentage of error revealed a significant main effect of Stimulus length, $F_1(1, 35) = 30.21$, $p < .001$, $F_2(1, 108) = 8.43$, $p < .01$. Five-letter words produced significantly more errors than seven-letter words. No other significant effects were found. The only planned comparison (against the unrelated prime condition) to reach significance was the effect of OC-final primes for 7-letter targets, $F_1(1, 35) = 6.48$, $p < .05$, $F_2(1, 108) = 5.16$, $p < .05$.

Nonword analyses.   The only main effect to reach significance in the latency and accuracy analyses for nonwords, was the effect of Stimulus length in the accuracy analysis, $F_1(1, 35) = 34.78$, $p < .001$, $F_2(1, 111) = 14.30$, $p < .001$. Five-letters nonwords produced significantly more errors than 7-letter nonwords.

Discussion

The results of Experiment 4 show that the level of orthographic overlap across prime and target with 2-letter substitution primes is not great enough to significantly affect performance relative to the unrelated prime condition. There is, however, some evidence for a positional bias in the results for 7-letter words. The substitution primes involving the two last letters of target words produced a 16 ms facilitation relative to the unrelated prime condition. Although somewhat smaller than the 31 ms effect reported by Perea and Lupker (2003), it is in the same direction. This result lends some support to Perea and Lupker's argument that, when compared with orthographic control primes (with two adjacent letters substituted), then transposition priming effects may be stronger when the transposition involves two inner letters compared with when it involves the two last letters. Most important, however, is the fact that there was no difference between the initial letter and inner letter substitution conditions in Experiment 4. This implies that the results for initial letter and inner letter transposition primes in Experiment 3 are due to the transposition manipulation and not to the other letters shared by prime and target. This therefore consolidates the critical pattern showing an inner letter transposition advantage for 5-letter words that disappears with 7-letter targets. This pattern was predicted by the new version of the open-bigram coding scheme involving a constraint on the number of possible intervening letters.

GENERAL DISCUSSION

The results of the present study were designed to test three recent models of letter position coding that appeared particularly promising in the light of recent data obtained with the masked priming paradigm. These are Davis' (1999) SOLAR model, Whitney's (2001) SERIOL model, and the open-bigram model developed conjointly by Grainger and van Heuven (2003) and the present authors. These particular models can account for relative-position priming effects, where prime stimuli sharing letters in the same relative position as target words (e.g., 13457, for a 7-letter word) facilitate target processing to the same extent as primes sharing letters in the same absolute position as targets (Granier & Grainger, 2004; Humphreys et al., 1990; Pesciarelli et al., 2001; Peressotti & Grainger, 1999). These three models were put to further test in the present study by manipulating the presence or not of repeated letters in prime and target stimuli, and by testing stimuli with transposed letters in the masked priming paradigm.

Repeated letters

In Experiments 1 and 2 of the present study, a repeated letter manipulation was used, such that target words containing a repeated letter (e.g., BALANCE) were primed by stimuli formed either by removing one of the repeated letters (balnce), or by removing one of the non-repeated letters (balace). Priming effects were compared with those obtained with target words without repeated letters. In line with the predictions of both the SERIOL model (Whitney, 2001) and Grainger and van Heuven's (2003) open-bigram model, and contrary to the predictions of the SOLAR model (Davis, 1999), words with repeated letters were harder to process than words without repeated letters. However, in line with the SOLAR model and contrary to the other two models, the status of repeated letters had no influence whatsoever on priming effects. Experiment 2 tested the nonword primes of Experiment 1 as targets in an unprimed lexical decision task. Nonwords created by removing a letter from a real word were harder to reject than control nonwords. However, once again the status of repeated letters had no influence on the processing of such stimuli.

Open-bigram coding schemes predicted an influence of repeated letters at all levels of performance (as a main effect on target processing, and as a modulator of priming effects). Letter repetition leads to the generation of a smaller number of bigrams, hence lower-levels of activation input to lexical representations (for a fixed level of activation in more peripheral letter representations), and lower levels of orthographic overlap across prime and target stimuli in a priming situation. However, the prediction that maintaining repeated letters in a prime stimulus (e.g., balace, for the target BALANCE) should lead to less priming than when one of the repeated letters is removed (e.g., balnce), only holds when open-bigrams are formed across all letters in the stimulus with an unlimited number of intervening letters. When the number of intervening letters is limited to two, then this prediction no longer holds (see discussion of Experiment 2).

This modified open-bigram scheme forms the basis of a model that has been conjointly developed and tested by Grainger and van Heuven (2003). A further motivation for the new coding scheme was found in some relative-position priming experiments. These experiments examined the effects of 5-letter relative-position primes on the processing of 7-letter target words, with primes formed by the first and last letter of target words plus varying combinations of three inner letters. In one critical experiment, three conditions produced significant facilitation relative to an all-different letter prime (ddddd). These were prime conditions 12457, 13457, and 13467. Three conditions failed to generate significant facilitation relative to unrelated primes. These were prime conditions 12367, 12467, and 12567. The original open-bigram scheme could not account for these differences. The new scheme does. Prime conditions 12457, 13457, and 13467, share seven out of nine bigrams with their corresponding targets (readers are invited to check this for themselves). On the other hand, prime conditions 12367, 12467, and 12567, share only five or six out of the target's nine bigrams. If the minimum orthographic overlap required to observe significant priming is seven out of nine, then the new coding scheme captures this complex pattern of priming effects.

Transposed letters

A further significant test of the new open-bigram coding scheme was provided in Experiment 3, where letter transposition was manipulated across prime and target. Letter transposition effects provide a strong test of models of letter position coding. The three models that served as the theoretical focus of the present study can account for priming effects obtained when primes are created by transposing two of the target word's letters (Forster et al., 1987; Perea & Lupker, 2003). All slot-based coding schemes fail on this test, except for those using staggered presentation techniques (Shillcock & Monaghan, 2001). Standard bigram or trigram schemes (e.g., Seidenberg & McClelland, 1987) also fail, since letter transposition disrupts the number of correct n-grams in the prime stimulus (for example, the prime BLCAK retains only one trigram from the target BLACK: #BL, and only two bigrams: #B, and BL).

The SOLAR model (Davis, 1999), the SERIOL model (Whitney, 2001), and the open-bigram model (Grainger & van Heuven, 2003), can all account for priming effects obtained with letter transpositions. However, only the new version of the open-bigram model, motivated by the results of Experiments 1 and 2 of the present study plus the relative-position priming data of Granier and Grainger (2004), could predict the specific pattern of results obtained in Experiment 3. In this experiment, transposed letter primes only facilitated performance to 5-letter targets when the transposition involved inner letters. Initial and final-letter transposition did not facilitate target processing relative to unrelated primes in 5-letter target words. With 7-letter target words, priming effects were obtained independently of the position of transposition (initial, inner, final). SERIOL predicted a disadvantage for initial-letter transpositions that was not observed, while SOLAR predicted no positional biases in transposition priming. As noted by Perea and Lupker (2003), however, in one version of the SOLAR model, an advantage has been given to final letter activation such that inner-letter transpositions could actually generate more priming than final letter transpositions. Nevertheless, this version of the SOLAR model would still have difficulty in accommodating the fact that the inner-letter transposition advantage was length dependent, only occurring for 5-letter words.

Further evidence against any beginning-to-end bias in orthographic processing was presented in the introduction to the present study.[6] We noted some recent work on relative-position priming that provides converging evidence against any form of beginning-to-end positional bias in orthographic priming. Granier and Grainger (2004) compared relative-position primes formed by the first letters of targets, the last letters, or a combination of the first, last, and some inner letters. The results are most striking for 9-letter targets. Prime conditions 12345 and 56789 generated equivalent amounts of priming, and stronger priming than the 14569 prime condition. The new open-bigram scheme captures this pattern of priming effects, whereas this pattern was not predicted by either SERIOL or SOLAR. It should be noted, however, that positional biases can arise via other factors such as variations in letter visibility and lexical constraint (Clark & O'Regan, 1999; Grainger & Jacobs, 1993; Stevens & Grainger, 2003). Only further experimentation will allow us to separate out the effects due to a particular form of orthographic coding from the influences of other possible factors.

---

[6] We acknowledge the evidence in favour of serial processing during reading aloud (e.g., Rastle & Coltheart, 1999), but would argue that this is specific to the act of articulation which requires a serial output.

Conclusions

The present study provides a modest contribution to a fast developing area of research using (mostly, but not exclusively) the masked priming paradigm to investigate early orthographic processing in printed word perception. Several studies have shown that the orthographic code for printed strings of letters involves some form of relative-position information for a set of letter identities (Forster et al., 1987; Granier & Grainger, 2003; Humphreys et al., 1990; Perea & Lupker, 2003; Peressotti & Grainger, 1999; Pesciarelli et al., 2001). Adopting a relative-position code implies that the processing system has knowledge about order information of the type "B is after A and before C", and that this will be true for the string ABC and also for the string AGBMC. The notion of "open-bigram" was introduced to capture the essence of this type of coding. The present study provides further evidence in favor of such relative-position coding of printed strings of letters, and suggests that there is a constraint on the number of possible intervening letters in open-bigram coding. Future research will provide further tests of this approach to letter position coding.

REFERENCES

Clark, J.J., & O'Regan, J.K. (1999). Word ambiguity and the optimal viewing position in reading. *Vision Research, 39*, 843–857.

Coltheart, M., Curtis, B., Atkins, P., & Haller M. (1993). Models of reading aloud—Dual Route and parallel distributed processing approaches. *Psychological Review, 100*, 589–608.

Coltheart, M., Davelaar, E., Jonassan, J.F., & Besner, D. (1977). Access to the internal lexicon. In S. Dornic (Ed.), *Attention and performance VI* (pp. 535–555). Hillsdale, NJ: Lawrence Erlbaum Associates Inc.

Coltheart, M., Rastle, K., Perry, C., Ziegler, J., & Langdon, R. (2001). DRC: A dual route cascaded model of visual word recognition and reading aloud. *Psychological Review, 108*, 204–256.

Davis, C.J. (1999). *The self-organising lexical acquisition and recognition (SOLAR) model of visual word recognition*. Unpublished doctoral dissertation, University of New South Wales, Australia.

Forster, K.I., Davis, C., Schoknecht, C., & Carter, R. (1987). Masked priming with graphemically related forms—repetition or partial activation. *Quarterly Journal of Experimental Psychology, 39*, 211–251.

Forster, K.I., & Forster, J. (2003). DMDX: A Windows display program with millisecond accuracy. *Behavioral Research Methods: Instruments and Computers, 35*, 116–124.

Grainger, J. & Jacobs, A.M. (1993). Masked partial-word priming in visual word recognition: Effects of positional letter frequency. *Journal of Experimental Psychology: Human Perception and Performance, 19*, 951–964.

Grainger, J., & van Heuven, W. (2003). Modeling letter position coding in printed word perception. In P. Bonin (Ed.), *The mental lexicon*. New York: Nova Science.

Granier, J.P. & Grainger, J. (2004). *Letter position coding in printed word perception: Evidence from relative-position priming.* Manuscript submitted for publication.

Grossberg, S. (1978). A theory of human memory: Self-organization and performance of sensory-motor codes, maps, and plans. In R. Rosen & F. Snell (Eds.), *Progress in theoretical biology* (Vol 5, pp. 233–374). New York: Academic Press.

Harm, M.W., & Seidenberg, M.S. (1999). Phonology, reading acquisition, and dyslexia: Insights from connectionist models. *Psychological Review, 106,* 491–528.

Humphreys, G.W., Evett, L.J., & Quinlan, P.T. (1990). Orthographic processing in visual word recognition. *Cognitive Psychology, 22,* 517–560.

Jacobs, A.M., Rey, A., Ziegler, J.C., & Grainger, J. (1998). MROM-p: An Interactive activation, multiple read-out model of orthographic and phonological processes in visual word recognition. In J. Grainger & A.M. Jacobs (Eds.), *Localist connectionist approaches to human cognition* (pp. 147–188). Mahwah, NJ: Lawrence Erlbaum Associates Inc.

McClelland, J.L., & Rumelhart, D.E. (1981). An interactive activation model of context effects in letter perception: I. An account of basic findings. *Psychological Review, 88,* 375–407.

Mozer, M. (1987). Early parallel processing in reading: A connectionist approach. In M. Coltheart (Ed.), *Attention and Performance XII: The psychology of reading* (pp. 83–104). Hove, UK: Lawrence Erlbaum Associates Ltd.

New B., Pallier C., Ferrand L., & Matos, R. (2001) Une base de données lexicales du français contemporain sur internet: LEXIQUE, *L'Année Psychologique, 101,* 447–462.

Paap, K.R., Newsome, S.L., McDonald, J.E., & Schvaneveldt, R.W. (1982). An activation-verification model for letter and word recognition: The word-superiority effect. *Psychological Review, 89,* 573–594.

Perea, M., & Lupker, S.J. (2003). Transposed-letter confusability effects in masked form priming. In S. Kinoshita and S.J. Lupker (Eds.), *Masked priming: State of the art.* Hove, UK: Psychology Press.

Perea, M., & Rosa, E. (2002). Does "whole-word shape" play a role in visual word recognition? *Perception and Psychophysics, 64,* 785–794.

Peressotti, F., & Grainger, J. (1999). The role of letter identity and letter position in orthographic priming. *Perception and Psychophysics, 61,* 691–706.

Pesciarelli, F., Peressotti, F., & Grainger, J. (2001). Processing external and middle letters in printed word perception. *Proceedings of the XIIth Conference of the European Society for Cognitive Psychology,* Edinburgh, September.

Plaut, D.C., McClelland, J.L., Seidenberg, M.S., & Patterson, K. (1996). Understanding normal and impaired word reading: Computational principles in quasi-regular domains. *Psychological Review, 103,* 56–115.

Rastle, K., & Coltheart, M. (1999). Serial and strategic effects in reading aloud. *Journal of Experimental Psychology: Human Perception and Performance, 25,* 482–503.

Seidenberg, M.S., & McClelland, J.L. (1989). A distributed, developmental model of word recognition and naming. *Psychological Review, 96,* 523–568.

Shillcock, R.C., Ellison, T.M., & Monaghan, P. (2000). Eye-fixation behavior, lexical storage, and visual word recognition in a split processing model. *Psychological Review, 107,* 824–851.

Shillcock, R.C. & Monaghan, P. (2001). The computational exploration of visual word recognition in a split model. *Neural Computation, 13,* 1171–1198.

Stevens, M., & Grainger, J. (2003). Letter visibility and the viewing position effect in visual word recognition. *Perception and Psychophysics, 65,* 133–151.

Whitney, C. (2001). How the brain encodes the order of letters in a printed word: The SERIOL model and selective literature review. *Psychonomic Bulletin and Review, 8,* 221–243.

Whitney, C. & Berndt, R.S. (1999). A new model of letter string encoding: simulating right neglect dyslexia. In J.A. Reggia, E. Ruppin, & D. Glanzman (Eds.), *Progress in Brain Research* (Vol. 121, pp. 143–163). Amsterdam: Elsevier.

Wickelgren, W. (1969). Context-sensitive coding, associative memory, and serial order in (speech) behavior. *Psychological Review, 76,* 1–15.

Zorzi, M., Houghton, G., & Butterworth, B. (1998). Two routes or one in reading aloud? A connectionist dual-process model. *Journal of Experimental Psychology: Human Perception and Performance, 24,* 1131–1161.

Appendix 1
Word targets and the corresponding nonword primes tested in Experiment 1

Repeat Target	Omitted Repeat	Omitted Unique	Unrelated	Control Target	Omitted Unique	Omitted Unique	Unrelated
PROGRÈS	progès	progrs	blumit	CHARBON	charon	charbn	plevus
PLACARD	placrd	placad	thonis	PRUDENT	prudnt	prudet	chabol
PROFOND	profnd	profod	blameg	PLAFOND	plafnd	plafod	brivet
CRAVATE	cravte	cravae	spiglo	FROMAGE	fromge	fromae	thulin*
GLOBALE	globae	globle	fristu	FRAGILE	fragie	fragle	chontu
CHINOIS	chinos	chinis	trubal	SPÉCIAL	spécil	spécal	grunot
STATION	staion	staton	drugel	CHALEUR	chaeur	chalur	stinod
TRAVAIL	travil	traval	snedum	PRODUIT	prodit	produt	snavel
SERGENT	sergnt	serget	balzuc	MÉCHANT	méchnt	méchat	virdus
CONTENU	conteu	contnu	palgri	FORTUNE	fortue	fortne	gemais*
CULTURE	cultre	cultue	fondia	MACHINE	machne	machie	sergou
DIGNITÉ	dignté	dignié	normau	COSTUME	costme	costue	mendai
HORLOGE	horlge	horloe	mantui	DIPLÔME	diplme	diplôe	genrau
VICTIME	victme	victie	narsou	SYMBOLE	symble	symboe	burdai
VITRINE	vitrne	vitrie	colmau	BAGNOLE	bagnle	bagnoe	perdui
BONJOUR	bonjur	bonjor	methis	SECTION	secton	sectin	gardul
BONSOIR	bonsir	bonsor	pamlet	GARDIEN	garden	gardin	pulmos
LECTEUR	lectur	lecter	bongad	FACTEUR	factur	facter	molsin
NERVEUX	nervux	nervex	bachol	MONDIAL	mondal	mondil	verbut
SECTEUR	sectur	secter	dalfin	MALHEUR	malhur	malher	cofnis
MANTEAU	manteu	mantau	sucroi	MORCEAU	morceu	morcau	fulnoi
BALANCE	balnce	balace	fodiru	MIRACLE	mircle	mirale	bentho
CADAVRE	cadvre	cadare	solumi	DURABLE	durble	durale	vesigo
CAPABLE	capble	capale	tisuno	RACONTE	racnte	racote	simplu
VISIBLE	visble	visile	garuno	PÉNIBLE	pénble	pénile	fumato
VOLONTÉ	volnté	voloté	muzaci	FACULTÉ	faclté	facuté	merodi
CAPITAL	capitl	capial	nomeur	HÔPITAL	hôpitl	hôpial	vareud
DÉCISIF	décisf	déciif	logunt	DÉLICAT	délict	déliat	moguns
DÉFICIT	défict	défiit	palons	HABITER	habitr	habier	gemoul
DEVENIR	devnir	deveir	gazoul	NATUREL	natrel	natuel	jochis
LIMITER	limter	limier	machon	DOMINER	domner	domier	sachut
MAGASIN	magsin	magain	geroud	CABINET	cabnet	cabiet	bordul
MATELAS	matels	mateas	vunord	ROBINET	robint	robiet	camuld
POSITIF	positf	posiif	camund	RELATIF	relatf	relaif	mibous
MALADIE	maldie	malaie	bernou	FATIGUE	fatgue	fatiue	modrai
MUSIQUE	musiqe	musiue	negato	LOGIQUE	logiqe	logiue	betani
MARIAGE	marige	mariae	voluna	DOMAINE	domine	domaie	begulo
SALAIRE	salire	salare	bonuda	SOLAIRE	solire	solare	penugo
JUMEAUX	jumeax	jumeux	tadois	CITOYEN	citoyn	citoen	resaud
DIAMANT	diamnt	diamat	tuires	COUVERT	couvrt	couvet	maidon
COUTUME	coutme	coutue	geisna	COURAGE	courge	courae	heilbo
CUISINE	cuisne	cuisie	boelda	VOITURE	voitre	voitue	laucho
PAYSAGE	paysge	paysae	hedroi	QUALITÉ	qualté	qualié	boinsu
BOUQUET	bouqet	bouqut	paimon	SOUTIEN	souten	soutin	vailod
ARTISTE	artise	artite	elbugo	ARTICLE	artice	artile	onsudi

* Not matched in CV structure.

Appendix 2

Nonword targets and the corresponding nonword primes tested in Experiment 1

Repeat Target	Omitted Repeat	Omitted Unique	Unrelated	Control Target	Omitted Repeat	Omitted Unique	Unrelated
TOMBOUX	tombux	tombox	saltin	CADRIEM	cadrem	cadrim	goslun
NOLMOIR	nolmir	nolmor	bastud	ZARDEIN	zardin	zarden	buchot
JULNUIT	julnit	julnut	gerdof	GÉVRIOT	gévrot	gévrit	madlus
JONPOIR	jonpir	jonpor	maglet	NARTUIL	nartil	nartul	cespog
CARTAOL	cartol	cartal	bindus	FURTAIM	furtim	furtam	zondel
TAURIAL	tauril	taural	neimog	MAILOUR	mailor	mailur	veudas
RUITEUX	ruitex	ruitux	peolas	GAIROUL	gairol	gairul	nuedat
REPTIEL	reptil	reptel	gandum	MALTIER	maltir	malter	ponsud
HARIANS	harins	harans	lezoct	LORIANS	lorins	lorans	fudech
ROITRIN	roitrn	roitin	peulag	JUINVER	juinvr	juiner	deatol
PLINOIR	plinor	plinir	staged	CHOLAIN	cholan	cholin	bruget
UVIPLIT	uviplt	uvipit	eborac	ÉMOGRIS	émogrs	émogis	ilatun
VUGRAUS	vugras	vugrus	mintod	MODRAUL	modral	modrul	hespin
VAINTIR	vaintr	vainir	peugom	COINTER	cointr	coiner	jeunal
VESTELD	vestld	vested	harmon	MICHONT	michnt	michot	lavrec
VÉRMART	vérmat	vérmrt	goldif	HULDONS	huldos	huldns	gabrit
VATRIAL	vatril	vatral	zochen	HARZOIL	harzol	harzil	budgen
TROPOND	tropnd	tropod	blages	FRIGONT	frignt	frigot	slubam
TINSUNÉ	tinsué	tinsné	hemgra	COLFAME	colfae	colfme	nudroi
TIMBAID	timbad	timbid	selnop	PALNOUD	palnod	palnud	cestif
SULTALÉ	sultaé	sultlé	jindou	MURTILÉ	murtié	murtlé	bachno
SAMPLAT	samplt	sampat	lovrid	ZOLDRIN	zoldrn	zoldin	pascet
PRANAUX	pranux	pranax	stifeg	TRÔLAIN	trôlin	trôlan	spavuc
PHARAIN	pharin	pharan	glumod	BRINEUD	brinud	brined	thogam
PAUBLAN	paubln	pauban	coiget	MOUCHÉT	moucht	moucét	lieban
MORPERD	morped	morprd	giblut	VOSLIRD	voslid	voslrd	bunget
MOLOIND	molind	molond	parets	HELOIRG	helirg	helorg	vunamp
STONIOD	stonid	stonod	bralum	VREMOIS	vremis	vremis	bladun
MINIEUX	mineux	miniux	polaid	PORIEUL	poreul	poriul	muhait
LAUPRUN	lauprn	laupun	ziebom	SUITRÈL	suitrl	suitèl	geoman
JARMORT	jarmot	jarmrt	denfus	GOLMARD	golmad	golmrd	lestin
HINTOIR	hintor	hintir	machud	BONGAIL	bongal	bongil	hemdut
FARMAUX	farmux	farmax	sontig	PORLAIS	porlis	porlas	cugnet
STONTIR	stonir	stotir	clamed	VLAGRET	vlaget	vlaret	plumos
MANATOR	mantor	manaor	luspeg	BALIVER	balver	balier	nuchod
DOINPIR	doinpr	doinir	vaumel	SOILGER	soilgr	soilet	neutad
ACULNAR	aculnr	acular	ohizet	ÔNTEGIS	ôntegs	ônteis	imavut
BRARIUT	braiut	brarut	plemon	STURIOL	stuiol	sturol	cheman
BRONOMÉ	bronmé	bronoé	fludai	DRAGUME	dragme	dramue	glonsi
BERMEUX	bermux	bermex	cagnot	JOLRAIN	jolrin	jolran	humlet
BRIPARD	bripad	briprd	slumon	TRUDINT	trudit	trudnt	chelam
STIALIN	stialn	stiain	vroemd	BRAICEL	braicl	braiel	thouns
GRALAND	gralnd	gralad	chomus	SLUMOCH	slumch	slumoh	branet
FRIOGON	friogn	frioon	psauld	STUIGEL	stuigl	stuiel	choarm
GENCHEL	genchl	gencel	tolhad	DOMCHAR	domchr	domcar	bunges

Appendix 3
Word targets and the corresponding transposed letter, orthographic control, and unrelated primes tested in Experiments 3 and 4

5 Letters	TL Initial	OC Initial	TL Inner	OC Inner	TL Final	OC Final	Unrelated
POINT	opint	azint	ponit	pazit	poitn	poigr	bleau
ENFIN	nefin	tufin	enifn	enabn	enfni	enfto	sormo
MIEUX	imeux	oleux	miuex	mioax	miexu	mieco	nalor
SAINT	asint	emint	sanit	samet	saitn	saifl	belmu
DROIT	rdoit	sfoit	dorit	dofat	droti	dronu	cegnu
ABORD	baord	cuord	abrod	abcud	abodr	abopl	neilo
AMOUR	maour	peour	amuor	ameir	amoru	amopa	penbi
VIEUX	iveux	ozeux	veiux	vaoux	viexu	vieta	holaf
AUCUN	uacun	eicun	acuun	aliun	aucnu	aucvi	rtiel
SELON	eslon	iplon	sleon	smaon	selno	seldi	ahrbe
PLEIN	lpein	rmein	pelin	pocin	pleni	plegu	rabdu
BLANC	lbanc	tsanc	balnc	bisnc	blacn	blatf	omute
ENVIE	nevie	guvie	enive	enume	envei	envao	afcat
IMAGE	miage	coage	iamge	iosge	imaeg	imauc	uclon
QUANT	uqant	egant	qunat	qumit	quatn	quadg	rcope
GESTE	egste	inste	getse	gepde	geset	gesan	abuni
HAUTE	ahute	opute	hatue	hagoe	hauet	hauop	gopis
JOUER	ojuer	ibuer	joeur	joiar	joure	jousi	gatil
POIDS	opids	egids	podis	pozus	poisd	poitm	gubne
ODEUR	doeur	paeur	oedur	oimur	oderu	odeha	nacil
CHOIX	hcoix	rgoix	cohix	cazix	choxi	chozu	srube
COURT	ocurt	imurt	corut	cohat	coutr	couml	pelab
CHAUD	hcaud	rtaud	cahud	cifud	chadu	chaco	irpne
POCHE	opche	ibche	pcohe	pgahe	poceh	pocag	sualf
CROIX	rcoix	rtoix	corix	cadix	croxi	cropa	gapme
TEXTE	etxte	acxte	txete	tfite	texet	texip	aplol
STYLE	tsyle	rzyle	sytle	sihre	styel	styad	lopba
TOTAL	ottal	iptal	toatl	toepl	totla	totbi	herri
ROMAN	orman	ivman	rmoan	rtean	romna	romci	gehid
HERBE	ehrbe	ajrbe	hrebe	hsibe	hereb	herav	damto
SOUPE	osupe	ivupe	sopue	sogye	souep	souat	vrabi
PUITS	upits	enits	putis	pugos	puist	puirg	omleg
FRANC	rfanc	lpanc	farnc	filnc	fracn	fradl	doipe
PLOMB	lpomb	rfomb	polmb	pasmb	plobm	plofr	agurd
ATOME	taome	fuome	atmoe	atvue	atoem	atois	hripu
DEUIL	eduil	afuil	dueil	daoil	deuli	deumo	sarbo
POMPE	opmpe	ibmpe	pmope	psupe	pomep	pomal	nutia
SOURD	osurd	iturd	sorud	somed	soudr	soulm	nielc
BOEUF	obeuf	ileuf	beouf	baiuf	boefu	boeji	lviam
SAUTE	asute	inute	satue	simae	sauet	sauim	olrid
SUBIT	usbit	egbit	suibt	suomt	subti	subno	vamre
GENOU	egnou	isnou	gneou	gsiou	genuo	gesan	abist
FINAL	ifnal	ugnal	fnial	fgeal	finla	fingu	hemuo
GUISE	ugise	onise	gusie	gumae	guies	guiaf	clato
BARON	abron	upron	braon	bleon	barno	barsy	pievu
RURAL	urral	itral	ruarl	ruefl	rurla	rurso	ogmie
JEUDI	ejudi	oludi	jedui	jeboi	jeuid	jeual	proac

5 Letters	TL Initial	OC Initial	TL Inner	OC Inner	TL Final	OC Final	Unrelated
ISLAM	silam	delam	isalm	isorm	islma	islge	buvop
AZOTE	zaote	vuote	aztoe	azmie	azoet	azoic	uhbin
SIEUR	iseur	aneur	seiur	syour	sieru	sielo	acmot
FICHE	ifche	owche	fcihe	ftahe	ficeh	ficam	dlapu
ROBIN	orbin	ulbin	rboin	rdain	robni	robme	mevau
LOGIS	olgis	urgis	loigs	loafs	logsi	logfu	menra
RUBAN	urban	wiban	rbuan	rsoan	rubna	rubti	coerl
SERGE	esrge	alrge	srege	sqoge	sereg	seruc	ahuda
WAGON	awgon	upgon	waogn	waudn	wagno	wagpe	umbie
TRIBU	rtibu	lfibu	tirbu	tolbu	triub	triop	hacno
NOEUD	oneud	ateud	neoud	naiud	noedu	noega	ibale
ULTRA	lutra	hetra	ulrta	ulsga	ultar	ultem	cegin
LAPIN	alpin	espin	laipn	laern	lapni	lapho	udrce

7 Letters	TL Initial	OC Initial	TL Inner	OC Inner	TL Final	OC Final	Unrelated
PREMIER	rpemier	tsemier	preimer	preaner	premire	premiso	gluaval
PRESQUE	rpesque	lgesque	preqsue	prectue	presqeu	presqio	baudlan
SURTOUT	usrtout	ebrtout	surotut	suridut	surtotu	surtopi	canlima
PARFOIS	aprfois	ilrfois	parofis	parevis	parfosi	parfovu	chempel
POUVOIR	opuvoir	anuvoir	povuoir	potaoir	pouvori	pouvoma	sendans
CHAMBRE	hcambre	lpambre	chabmre	chalgre	chamber	chambut	juliong
DEMANDE	edmande	osmande	demnade	demside	demaned	demanot	sucolit
INSTANT	nistant	gastant	intsant	inlpant	instatn	instagr	effolud
SILENCE	islence	oblence	sielnce	siabnce	silenec	silenov	grumiut
DERNIER	edrnier	ufrnier	denrier	delsier	dernire	dernigu	valtaul
SERVICE	esrvice	atrvice	sevrice	sedlice	serviec	serviom	notould
CONSEIL	ocnseil	ivnseil	conesil	conapil	conseli	consefa	trahmud
SOURIRE	osurire	anurire	soruire	sogaire	sourier	sourial	gletalo
PLAISIR	lpaisir	rmaisir	pliasir	plousir	plaisri	plaiste	steonem
SECONDE	esconde	arconde	secnode	seclade	seconed	seconat	jalumat
BONHEUR	obnheur	ednheur	bohneur	bopzeur	bonheru	bonhemi	stamild
JOURNAL	ojurnal	icurnal	jorunal	johinal	journla	journpi	chimdet
TABLEAU	atbleau	erbleau	talbeau	tarheau	tableua	tableio	vompind
ARTICLE	raticle	foticle	aritcle	arufcle	articel	articod	ephomdi
MAUVAIS	amuvais	ocuvais	mavuais	madoais	mauvasi	mauvajo	loidone
SURFACE	usrface	iqrface	surafce	surimce	surfaec	surfaol	plognit
LANGAGE	alngage	ohngage	lagnage	lamsage	langaeg	langaif	sorimot
ABSENCE	basence	vusence	absnece	absmoce	absenec	absenom	utriumo
UNIVERS	nuivers	foivers	unviers	unpaers	inuvesr	inuvelp	elomact
ENFANCE	nefance	wofance	enfnace	enfmuce	enfanec	enfanum	ploirit
SEMAINE	esmaine	ulmaine	seamine	seopine	semaien	semaiot	troupol
CONTACT	ocntact	isntact	conatct	conesct	contatc	contafr	grerung
ENDROIT	nedroit	hudroit	endorit	endagit	endroti	endrola	alsmube
VOULOIR	ovuloir	ixuloir	voluoir	vowaoir	voulori	voulome	gaitame
DOCTEUR	odcteur	urcteur	docetur	docaxur	docteru	docteni	munisal
VALABLE	avlable	eblable	valbale	valzile	valabel	valaboh	jotomin
AMPLEUR	mapleur	nipleur	ampelur	ampihur	ampleru	ampleni	nochias
DIZAINE	idzaine	epzaine	diazine	diugine	dizaien	dizaiom	moulogi
BRUSQUE	rbusque	lfusque	bruqsue	bruplue	brusqeu	brusqao	vlichan

7 Letters	TL Initial	OC Initial	TL Inner	OC Inner	TL Final	OC Final	Unrelated
MANQUER	amnquer	opnquer	manuqer	manider	manqure	manqulo	tolipas
CONCERT	ocncert	uqncert	conecrt	conafrt	concetr	concesp	slaglim
SURPLUS	usrplus	imrplus	surlpus	surftus	surplsu	surplge	gomdage
ANTIQUE	natique	zetique	anitque	anodque	antiqeu	antiqoa	elosmai
CRISTAL	rcistal	mpistal	critsal	crifmal	cristla	cristho	pechbun
PASTEUR	apsteur	ocsteur	pasetur	pasodur	pasteru	pastemo	clondim
VERTIGE	evrtige	abrtige	veritge	verasge	vertieg	vertiha	dosquol
LARGEUR	alrgeur	idrgeur	lagreur	lasmeur	largeru	largebi	stinpon
TROMPER	rtomper	lgomper	tropmer	trolger	trompre	trompdu	blandis
FRONTIN	rfontin	ldontin	frotnin	frosdin	frontni	frontma	glamuld
PANIQUE	apnique	ernique	panqiue	panvoue	paniqeu	paniqao	bermold
GALERIE	aglerie	udlerie	gaelrie	gaocrie	galerei	galerou	notufod
VIOLENT	ivolent	udolent	viloent	vidaent	violetn	violehr	churamp
POIGNET	opignet	ecignet	poginet	powanet	poignte	poigndu	vumbals
SPECTRE	psectre	zdectre	spetcre	spedzre	specter	spectil	vlamang
CONFIER	ocnfier	elnfier	conifer	conumer	confire	confimu	geltaud
STUPIDE	tsupide	grupide	stuipde	stuogde	stupied	stupial	velambo
GRIMACE	rgimace	ltimace	griamce	griunce	grimaec	grimaos	steboum
ADOPTER	daopter	buopter	adotper	adogler	adoptre	adopthu	geuflin
AISANCE	iasance	ousance	aisnace	aismoce	aisanec	aisanuv	oudromi
EXPOSER	xeposer	ziposer	expsoer	expzier	exposre	exposga	camudat
HOSTILE	ohstile	uvstile	hosilte	hosarle	hostiel	hostipu	vemardu
VERSION	evrsion	ohrsion	verison	veruton	versino	versima	mulbade
PLANCHE	lpanche	smanche	plnache	plsoche	planceh	plancog	fromtis
HABITER	ahbiter	onbiter	habtier	habloer	habitre	habitfu	megnous
SOIGNER	osigner	amigner	soginer	sohamer	soignre	soignta	velumat

LANGUAGE AND COGNITIVE PROCESSES, 2004, *19* (3), 369–390

Replicating syllable frequency effects in Spanish in German: One more challenge to computational models of visual word recognition

Markus Conrad and Arthur M. Jacobs

Catholic University of Eichstaett-Ingolstadt, Eichstaett, Germany

Two experiments tested the role of syllable frequency in word recognition, recently suggested in Spanish, in another shallow orthography, German. Like in Spanish, word recognition performance was inhibited in a lexical decision and a perceptual identification task when the first syllable of a word was of high frequency. Given this replication of the inhibitory effect of syllable frequency in a second language, we discuss the issue whether and how computational models of word recognition would have to represent a word's syllabic structure in order to accurately describe processing of polysyllabic words.

Several results from recent work on word recognition in Spanish suggest that "any model of lexical access has to incorporate a syllabic level of representations or include the syllable as a sublexical unit of processing in Spanish" (Álvarez, Carreiras, & de Vega, 2000; Álvarez, Carreiras, & Taft, 2001; Álvarez, de Vega, & Carreiras, 1998; Carreiras, Álvarez, & de Vega, 1993; Carreiras & Perea, 2002; Dominguez, de Vega, & Cuetos, 1997; Perea & Carreiras, 1995, 1996, 1998). As noted by these authors, this conclusion might be generalisable to other Romance languages with well-defined syllable boundaries, such as Italian, but not to English. In English, lexical access based on syllables might not be functional, because of its relatively high inconsistency (Ziegler, Stone, & Jacobs, 1997) and its relatively ill-defined syllable boundaries (Álvarez et al., 2001).

Correspondence should be addressed to Arthur M. Jacobs, Department of Psychology, Catholic University Eichstaett-Ingolstadt, Ostenstr. 26, D-85072 Eichstaett, Germany. Email: ajacobs@zedat.fu-berlin.de.

This research was supported by two grants of the Deutsche Forschungsgemeinschaft (DFG-Forschergruppe: "Dynamik kognitiver Repräsentationen", TP 7/Jacobs "Zur Rolle phonologischer Prozesse beim Lesen", TP 8/Jacobs,Gauggel "Zur Rolle des visuellen Wortformsystems beim Lesen"; Philipps-University Marburg).

http://www.tandf.co.uk/journals/pp/01690965.html   DOI: 10.1080/01690960344000224

Whereas there is longstanding evidence for the role of syllabic structure in the perception and production of speech in several languages (e.g., Carreiras & Perea, in press; Ferrand, Seguí, & Humphreys, 1997; Morais, Content, Cary, Mehler, & Seguí, 1989; Sebastián-Gallés, Dupoux, Seguí, & Mehler, 1992), the detection of an inhibitory effect of the positional frequency of the first syllable[1] in tasks in which no overt perception or production of speech is needed is a recent discovery, limited to the Spanish language. This is theoretically challenging, because no computational account of this effect has yet been offered. In a lexical decision task response times to bisyllabic Spanish words were longer when their first syllable was of high positional frequency than when it was of low frequency (Perea & Carreiras, 1998). This inhibitory effect of syllable frequency was more pronounced for low-frequency words. While Perea and Carreiras (1995) reported a similar pattern of results for a perceptual identification task, more recently Álvarez et al. (2001) could show that this inhibitory effect of syllable frequency is not confounded with the possible influence of another sublexical structure, the basic orthographic syllable structure or BOSS (Taft, 1979).

Frequencies of morphologically defined sublexical units like stems that are often highly positively correlated with the frequency of a word's first syllable, seem to facilitate lexical access (de Jong, Schreuder, & Baayen, 2000). Therefore, the pattern of results reported by Perea and Carreiras (1998) is likely to be related only to the phonologically defined syllabic structure of words. However, in contrast to perceptual identification and lexical decision tasks, the naming task has been shown to produce a facilitatory effect of the frequency of the first syllable in Spanish (Perea & Carreiras, 1996, 1998).

How can models of visual word recognition account for these findings suggesting a functional role of syllabic structure? As a matter of fact, none of the currently used computational models of word recognition (Coltheart, Rastle, Perry, Langdon, & Ziegler, 2001; Grainger & Jacobs, 1996; Jacobs, Graf, & Kinder, 2003; Ziegler, Perry, & Coltheart, 2000; Zorzi, Houghton, Butterworth, 1998) has yet been shown to (re)produce an inhibitory syllable frequency effect. The simple reason is that all of these models exclusively deal with the processing of monosyllabic words (see Ans, Carbonnel, & Valdois, 1998, for a model of naming polysyllabic words). As far as monosyllabic words are concerned, the general pattern of results is that when sublexical units are of high frequency, then word recognition performance is facilitated compared with when words have

---

[1] The positional frequency of a syllable can be understood as the number of words that share a given syllable in the same position (e.g., first or second syllable of the word) or as the cumulated word frequency of those words.

sublexical units of low frequency. Examples are bigram frequency (Massaro & Cohen, 1994; but see Paap & Johansen, 1994), positional letter frequency (Grainger & Jacobs, 1993), trigram frequency (Seidenberg, 1987), or subcomponent frequency (Nuerk, Rey, Graf, & Jacobs, 2000).

Basically, the above-mentioned computational models account for such facilitatory effects of the frequency of sublexical units by assuming that either sublexical or lexical processing units (or connections between units) are frequency-sensitive, higher levels of frequency being correlated with either lower activation thresholds or higher resting activation levels. To account for inhibitory effects of the frequency of words or their parts, current localist connectionist models such as the Multiple Read-Out Model (MROM; Grainger & Jacobs, 1996; Jacobs et al., 2003) or the revised dual-route cascaded model (DRC; Coltheart et al., 2001) make use of the inhibitory connections between lexical units. However, to be able to deal with inhibitory effects of sublexical units, such as syllables, these models presumably must be revised by including a new level of representation, namely syllabic units. This is the approach taken by Carreiras et al. (1993), Carreiras and Perea (2002), Perea and Carreiras (1998), or Álvarez et al. (1998, 2000, 2001) who interpret their results in the light of a prequantitative (verbal) version of an interactive activation model (see General Discussion).

In the present study we asked whether the inhibitory effects of syllable frequency reported for the Spanish language could be generalised to a non-Romance language having a shallow orthography, German. If so, the case for a new round of revision in current computational models of word recognition would be strengthened and theoreticians would have to consider the question of including syllabic units into their models or other structures able to account for such a general effect.

Although both Spanish and German have a shallow orthography, the assumption that German readers might rely in the same way on the syllabic structure of words as Spanish readers apparently do, is not obvious. Syllables in Spanish tend to be relatively short, about 70% of all existing syllables following a simple CV (consonant-vocal) – or CVC-structure. Altogether, there are approximately 3250 Spanish syllables (Carreiras & Perea, 2003; Dominguez et al., 1997). This is not the case in German where one syllable in the extreme case can be up to 10 letters long (as in the word SCHRUMPFST, meaning 'you shrink'). Moreover, there are about three times more syllables in German than in Spanish and less than 30% of the approximately 6000 German syllables belong to the CV or CVC class. Thus, a hypothetical mental syllabary in German would be both bigger and less consistent than its Spanish counterpart. Third, German linguists still debate about the clarity of syllabic boundaries, given that written and spoken syllables are often not identical. "While the number of syllables (of a German word) is usually obvious, the precise position of the syllable break is much harder to determine" (Wiese, 1996). Finally, there is ample evidence that German readers use subsyllabic units (graphemes and phonemes) when processing monosyllabic words (Nuerk et al., 2000; Wimmer & Goswami, 1994; Ziegler, Perry, Jacobs, & Braun, 2001; see Rey, Ziegler, & Jacobs, 2000, for compatible findings in English and French). Thus one might doubt that it is an efficient strategy for German readers to automatically retrieve syllable information from a hypothetical store containing about 6000 entries of very diverse length and structure when reading a word.

In other words, a syllable frequency effect might be special to word processing in Spanish or similar Romance languages, because of the high simplicity and clearness of syllabic structure in this language. On the other hand, if effects of syllable frequency also show up in experiments using the German language, this would support the hypothesis that effects observed in experiments using monosyllabic words cannot simply be generalised to the processing of polysyllabic words and strengthen the need for a revision of current computational models of visual word recognition.

EXPERIMENT 1: LEXICAL DECISION

Experiments that examined the effects of syllabic structure in Spanish consistently revealed an inhibitory effect of syllable frequency – at least as concerns the first syllable of bisyllabic words – when a lexical decision was required. In the first of these studies, the latencies of responses to bisyllabic words were found to be longer when the average of the positional frequency of both their syllables was high (Carreiras et al., 1993). In subsequent research the operationalisation of syllable frequency was restricted to the positional frequency of the first syllable (Perea & Carreiras, 1995, 1996, 1998). Again, in a lexical decision task Perea and Carreiras (1998, Experiment 1) reported an inhibitory effect of syllable frequency that was more pronounced for low-frequency words. For high-frequency words, there was no significant effect of syllable frequency. In a regression analysis of their data Perea and Carreiras (1998) could show that the number of higher-frequency syllabic neighbours was strongly related to the inhibitory effect of syllable frequency. Also, the number of higher-frequency syllabic neighbours itself, manipulated as an independent variable, produced an inhibitory effect (Perea & Carreiras, 1998, Experiment 3).

Because in the study of Perea and Carreiras (1998) the syllable of interest was the first, other studies focused on the role of subsequent syllables. Interestingly, when the positional frequency of a word's second syllable was manipulated, this yielded a facilitatory tendency (Álvarez et al., 2000, Experiment 3). However, these authors also reported an inhibitory effect of the frequency of the second syllable for pseudowords. In pseudowords that were composed of two syllables, each of them of either high or low frequency, the frequency of both syllables caused an inhibitory effect. In contrast, when the stimulus was a word, especially a word with a first syllable of low frequency, response times tended to be shorter when the frequency of the second syllable was high. To interpret these findings, Álvarez et al. (2000) chose a sort of serial (activation-selection) processing account: polysyllabic word representations are activated via their first syllable whereas the second syllable is important for the selection of the correct candidate amongst this activated set or cohort. As concerns pseudowords, a correct candidate cannot be found because they are not listed in the mental lexicon. Therefore, the frequency of the second syllable may prolong the selection process because more candidates could be generated depending on their similarity to the second syllable of the pseudoword. Concerning the role of subsequent syllables more empirical support for the assumption of serial processing was found by Álvarez et al. (1998) who manipulated the frequency of trisyllabic words and pseudowords. They reported significant facilitatory effects of the frequency of the second and the third syllable of words in a lexical decision task, whereas in pseudowords syllable frequency effects of an inhibitory nature were found for all three syllables.

Method

Participants.   Twenty-nine students from the Catholic University of Eichstaett-Ingolstadt participated in the experiment. Their participation was rewarded with course credits. All were native speakers of German and had normal or corrected-to-normal vision.

Design and stimuli.   A set of 112 bisyllabic German words of five and six letters in length were selected from the CELEX-database (Baayen, Piepenbrock, & van Rijn, 1993) according to the orthogonal combination of two factors in a within-participant 2×2 design: word frequency and positional frequency of the first syllable. Syllable frequency was defined as token frequency and computed by cumulating the frequencies of all words that contain a given syllable in the first position. A word was considered of high frequency when its cited frequency of occurrence in the CELEX-Database was greater or equal to 100/million, and of low frequency when the same measure did not pass 10/million. A syllable was considered of low frequency when it had a maximum token positional frequency of occurrence of 800/million. The minimum value for a high frequency syllable was set at 2600/million. Words were matched across the four experimental conditions for length, number of orthographic neighbours and positional frequency of the second syllable. None of the words had orthographic neighbours of higher word frequency. The items used in the word conditions are listed in the Appendix. Characteristics for words in Experiment 1 are shown in Table 1. In addition, 112 nonwords were constructed combining two strings of letters (each two or three letters long) that exist as the first or second syllable of a real word. The syllables used for these nonwords belonged to the extreme ranges of syllable frequency. Controlling for the number of possible orthographic neighbours and length (all nonwords were five or six letters long), nonwords were organised in four groups, forming a 2 × 2 design according to the orthogonal combination of the factors positional frequency of the first and positional frequency of the second syllable.

Apparatus and Procedure.   Stimuli were presented in uppercase letters using Courier 24 type font on a 17″ ProNitron colour monitor (resolution 1024 × 768 pixel, 75 Hz) driven by an Umax Pulsar computer. Stimulus presentation and response recording was controlled by PsyScope software (V. 1.2.4 PPC; Cohen & MacWhinney, 1993). At the utilised viewing distance of 50 cm the stimuli subtended a visual angle of approximately 1.7 degrees. Each trial was initiated by a fixation point appearing at the centre of the screen for 500 ms. The fixation point was then replaced by a blank screen (0 ms), followed by the word or nonword stimulus that remained visible until participants pressed a button indicating their decision concerning the lexicality ('yes'-button for a word; 'no'-button for a

TABLE 1

Characteristics of words used in Experiment 1. Means (M) and ranges of the independent variables word frequency (WF) and frequency of the first syllable (SF1). Means and ranges of variables that were held constant: frequency of the second syllable (SF2), density of orthographic neighbourhood (N) and mean word length (L)

| Word class | WF | | SF1 | | SF2 | | N | | L |
	M	Range	M	Range	M	Range	M	Range	M
High WF High SF	185	101–373	12711	3333–21,921	810	108–4742	1.14	0–5	5.71
High WF Low SF	176	110–480	353	125–786	1075	131–3400	1.25	0–4	5.68
Low WF High SF	3.13	0.17–9	15610	2642–110,013	1193	1–16,350	1.07	0–6	5.71
Low WF Low SF	3.46	0–8.17	176	2–573	450	3–789	1.04	0–6	5.71

nonword) of the stimulus. The time between the onset of stimulus presentation and the response was measured as the dependent variable. There were also ten initial training trials. Participants were tested individually in a quiet room.

Results and Discussion

Mean response latencies and error rates for words and nonwords in Experiment 1 are shown in Table 2.

Words. Mean correct response latencies and error percentages (see Table 2) were submitted to separate analyses of variance (ANOVAs) by participants and by items (F_1 and F_2, respectively). Concerning response times, the analyses revealed significant main effects of both word frequency and syllable frequency. High-frequency words were responded to 170 ms faster than low-frequency words, $F_1(1, 28) = 158.30, p \leq .0001$; $F_2(1, 108) = 57.09, p \leq .0001$, whereas the frequency of a word's first syllable caused a delay of 120 ms in the latencies, $F_1(1, 28) = 39.50, p \leq .0001$; $F_2(1, 108) = 28.82, p \leq .0001$. The interaction between word frequency and syllable frequency was also significant, $F_1(1, 28) = 20.09, p \leq .0001$; $F_2(1, 108) = 9.98, p \leq .002$, the inhibitory effect of syllable frequency being stronger for low-frequency words (191 ms), than for high-frequency words (49 ms). Still, also for high-frequency words only, the inhibitory

TABLE 2

Mean reaction times (RT; in ms), standard deviation (SD) of reaction times (ms) and percentage of errors for words and nonwords in Experiment 1

Words	Word frequency					
	High			Low		
Syllable frequency	RT	SD	% error	RT	SD	% error
High	671	104	4.7	911	166	25.6
Low	622	71	0.9	720	112	11.1

Nonwords	SF1					
	High			Low		
SF2	RT	SD	% error	RT	SD	% error
High	833	86	3.3	825	169	2.73
Low	846	140	3.6	796	107	1.9

Note: SF1 and SF2 = Frequency of the first and the second syllable respectively of nonwords.

effect of syllable frequency remained statistically significant, $F_1(1, 28) =$ 18.94, $p \leq .0002$; $F_2(1, 54) = 4.33$, $p \leq .05$.

The error data mirrored this pattern of results, showing a facilitatory effect of word frequency with 2.7% errors for high-frequency words vs. 18.4% for low-frequency words, $F_1(1, 28) = 99.29$, $p \leq .0001$; $F_2(1, 108) =$ 30.59, $p \leq .0001$, and an inhibitory effect of syllable frequency with 15.2% errors vs. 5.9% for high vs. low syllable frequency, respectively, $F_1(1, 28) =$ 94.01, $p \leq .0001$; $F_2(1, 108) = 26.09$, $p \leq .0001$. The interaction between the two factors also reached statistical significance, high syllable frequency provoking more errors in low-frequency words than in high-frequency words, $F_1(1, 28) = 84.87$, $p \leq .0001$; $F_2(1, 108) = 12.02$, $p \leq .0008$.

Considering the fact that the error rates for words, especially for the condition with low-frequency words and high-frequency syllables, are relatively high, we conducted some further analyses of variance in order to verify if the inhibitory effects of syllable frequency would hold when error-prone words are excluded. We set a maximum error rate of 30% as a criterion for words to enter in these analyses. Ten words amongst the 112 stimuli were excluded from the analyses. All effects of syllable frequency remained statistically significant. The frequency of the first syllable now caused a delay of 78 ms in the latencies, $F_1(1, 28) = 39.47$, $p = \leq .0001$; $F_2(1, 98) = 19.34$, $p \leq .0001$. The interaction between the factors syllable frequency and word frequency remained statistically significant, $F_1(1, 28)$ $= 11.94$, $p \leq .002$; $F_2(1, 98) = 5.48$, $p \leq .03$.

Error rates still were increased for words with high-frequency syllables with 8.8% errors vs. 2.4% for high vs. low syllable frequency, respectively, $F_1(1, 28) = 31.42$, $p \leq .0001$; $F_2(1, 98) = 38.44$, $p \leq .0001$. The interaction between the factors syllable frequency and word frequency remained statistically significant, $F_1(1, 28) = 18.34$, $p \leq .0002$; $F_2(1, 98) = 14.59$, $p \leq$ .0002).

In sum, all effects reported as results of the analyses based on all 112 stimuli remained statistically significant after the exclusion criterion had been applied so that they cannot be attributed to the specific contribution of error-prone words.

Nonwords.   As concerns response times to nonwords there was one significant main effect, an inhibition due to the frequency of the first syllable, yet only in the participants' analysis, $F_1(1, 28) = 5.93$, $p \leq .03$. Nonwords with a low-frequency first syllable were responded to 29 ms faster than when the first syllable was of high frequency. The frequency of the second syllable did not produce a significant main effect. But the interaction between first and second syllable frequency was significant in the participants' analysis, $F_1(1, 28) = 4.68$, $p \leq .04$. The tendency for second syllable frequency was facilitatory when first syllable frequency was high, but inhibitory for low first syllable frequency. In one of the four conditions, response latencies were shorter than in the three others: Nonwords that had two syllables of low frequency were responded to 38 ms faster than the other nonwords, $F_1(1, 28) = 14.07$, $p \leq .0008$.

In the error data, a significant inhibitory effect of first syllable frequency emerged, $F_1(1, 28) = 8.32$, $p \leq .01$, with 3.5% errors for high first syllable frequency vs. 2.4% for low. No main effect for second syllable frequency was obtained, but a significant interaction between first and second syllable frequency, $F_1(1, 28) = 4.68$, $p \leq .04$, with high frequency of the second syllable provoking more errors when the frequency of the first syllable was low, as well as a significant effect when nonwords that contained no syllable of high frequency were compared with those in which at least one syllable was of high frequency, $F_1(1, 28) = 10.07$, $p \leq .004$, with 3.6% errors for nonwords with at least one syllable of high frequency vs. 1.9% for completely low syllable frequency nonwords.

The important finding of Experiment 1 is that the frequency of the first syllable clearly inhibited the processing of bisyllabic German words. This inhibition appeared not only in a significant effect on response times, but also in increased error rates for words with high-frequency first syllables. Although the inhibitory effect was more pronounced for words of low frequency, it was also significant for high-frequency words, both in the F_1 and F_2 analysis. This is a notable difference as compared with the results reported for the Spanish language: there, the syllable frequency effect was significant only in the F_1 analysis and not for high-frequency words (e.g., Perea & Carreiras, 1998).

Perhaps this difference with regard to the Spanish studies is due to the way syllable frequency was calculated in our study. Whereas Álvarez et al. (2001) had used a type measure, we used the token frequency of a syllable as an independent variable. Álvarez et al. (2001) argued that a type measure (the number of words that share a given syllable in identical position) should be a more adequate way to calculate syllable frequency than a token measure (calculated as the summed frequency of all words sharing a syllable in the same position), because the type measure directly refers to the number of syllabic neighbours of a word which are supposed to be responsible for the delay in the processing of polysyllabic words (Álvarez et al., 1998, 2000, 2001; Carreiras et al., 1993; Perea & Carreiras, 1998).

Yet, in German this argument may fail. While in all Romance languages a relation between two nouns or between a verb and a noun is expressed most of the time by the use of prepositions (e.g., *the captain of the ship*), in German two words are most often simply combined to compounds (e.g., Schiffskapitän). The possible dimensions of these German compounds are enormous: they often include four normally independent single words and more than 15 letters. Thus a frequent syllable can be part of a great number of words that are rarely used in everyday language. Use of a token measure of syllable frequency thus assigns a stronger weight to the real frequency of occurrence of a syllable. Still, there is a notable correlation between the two different measures ($r = .58$ for all bisyllabic German words of five and six letters length), and because both of them have been shown to produce inhibitory effects, at current we see no theoretical reason for preferring one over the other.

Our nonword data are consistent with the view that the frequency of the first syllable inhibits lexical access, because the first syllable activates a set of lexical candidates (Álvarez et al., 2000). The inhibitory effect of a nonword's first syllable's frequency thus might reflect the fact that more word units are preactivated and competing for lexical selection than in the case of a nonword with a low-frequency first syllable. The activation of lexical candidates might in principle also be provoked by the second syllable as suggested by our result that second syllable frequency had an inhibitory effect when first syllable frequency was low in nonwords. However, because a main effect of second syllable frequency did not appear in the data, the first syllable seems to play a stronger role for this hypothetical activation of lexical candidates. This finding thus is compatible with the serial (activation-selection) account of Álvarez et al. (1998, 2000) on polysyllabic word processing.

Reanalysis of Experiment 1

The results of Experiment 1 seem to provide evidence for the automatic computation of syllabic codes in the processing of polysyllabic words. However, the frequencies of other sublexical components that do not rely on syllabic structure might also have been influential in the present experiment given their strong correlation with syllable frequency. For example, the frequencies of the first two or three letters of words are automatically increased when the frequency of the first syllable is high. Thus, one might argue that the inhibitory effect in Experiment 1 was not necessarily driven by syllabic structure but due to purely orthographic factors, such as the positional frequency of bigrams or trigrams at the beginning of a word. Analogously, the cohort size of some number of initial phonemes could also have played a role in our experimental effects. To strengthen the theoretical assumption that the inhibitory effect in Experiment 1 is caused by inhibition from a set of competing word representations that is activated by a word's first syllable, we thus had to check the likeliness of these alternative accounts.

For words, like those used in Experiment 1, whose first syllable contains either two or three letters, the correlation between syllable frequency and the frequency of the first two or three letters is too strong to be experimentally disentangled. Therefore, we ran a multiple regression analysis on the data of Experiment 1, using six predictors for the obtained response times: word frequency, frequency of the first syllable, positional frequency of the first bigram, positional frequency of the first trigram, cohort size of the first two phonemes and cohort size of the first three phonemes. Bigram and trigram frequency were calculated analogously to the computation of syllable frequency as the cumulated frequencies of all words containing this combination of letters at their beginning. Cohort size of the first two or three phonemes was calculated as the number of words containing the same number of phonemes and sharing the same initial two or three phonemes. This analysis showed a significant facilitatory effect of word frequency on response times, $F(1, 105) = 31.14$, $p \leq .0001$, and a significant inhibitory effect of syllable frequency, $F(1, 105) = 4.32, p \leq .05$. For none of the other predictors was a significant effect obtained. The only other measure than syllable frequency that at least a predictive tendency could be reported for was the frequency of the first trigram, $F(1, 105) = 2.78, p \leq .09$. Yet, this tendency had a facilitatory direction, so that the influence of the frequency of a word's first three letters, being positively correlated with syllable frequency, cannot be held responsible for the inhibitory effect obtained in Experiment 1. Coefficients of simple and multiple correlations between predictors and response times are given in Table 3.

In sum, the results of Experiment 1 are compatible with the results reported for the Spanish language and generalise them as far as the functional role of syllabic structure for lexical access to bisyllabic words is concerned. Although the hypothetical mental syllabary is much larger in German than in Spanish, although German syllable units are much more variable, longer and have unclearer boundaries than Spanish ones, and although the high consistency of the German orthography provides no a priori reason for using higher-level units such as syllables in reading, the

TABLE 3
Pearson product-moment (r) and partial correlations (pr) between reaction times and six predictors in Experiment 1

Predictor	r	pr
Word frequency	−.458	−.478*
Positional frequency of the first syllable	.392	.199*
Positional frequency of the first two letters	.371	.058
Positional frequency of the first three letters	.245	−.161
Cohort size of the first two phonemes	.079	−.025
Cohort size of the first	.058	.071

*$p \leq .05$.

present results lend support to the notion that information about syllables is automatically computed when processing polysyllabic written words.

Still, before drawing such a conclusion, one should attempt to demonstrate that the effect is not a mere by-product of task-specific processes, following the logic of functional overlap modelling formulated by Jacobs (1994; see also Grainger & Jacobs, 1996; Jacobs & Grainger, 1994; Jacobs, Rey, Ziegler, & Grainger, 1998). Only an effect that emerged as the common output of experiments using similar designs and stimuli but different tasks should be considered as reliable evidence for motivating a round of revision in successful computational models of visual word recognition. Experiment 2 addressed this issue.

EXPERIMENT 2: PERCEPTUAL IDENTIFICATION

Whereas the inhibitory effect of first syllable frequency in Spanish is well documented for the lexical decision task, there is less evidence for it to appear in experiments using a perceptual identification task. We know of only one study, in which Perea and Carreiras (1995) reported an inhibitory effect of syllable frequency in a progressive demasking task. For low-frequency words there was a significant inhibitory effect of syllable frequency whereas for high-frequency words syllable frequency caused a facilitatory tendency. Perea and Carreiras (1995) pointed out that low-frequency words are, during a longer time, the object of inhibition from competing word candidates and that this time could be prolonged when identification is made difficult as in perceptual identification tasks. However, while a superiority of the effect for low-frequency words might be explained in this way, if the opposite direction of the effect for low- and high-frequency words they reported in their experiment was real, this would create serious problems for this account. Such a possible opposite direction of the influence of syllable frequency in low- and high-frequency words also seems incompatible with the theoretical framework proposed by Carreiras et al. (1993), accounting for the effect by the amount of inhibition caused by competing word candidates as determined by their syllable frequency.

Perhaps, this somewhat strange result might be attributed to task-specific processes induced by the progressive demasking procedure. When presentation time for a stimulus is very short (the duration of the first unmasked presentation of a word in the experiment of Perea and Carreiras (1995) was only 16 ms) only parts of the whole word will probably be recognised. Considering that the optimal viewing position for word recognition is located slightly left of a word's centre (Nazir, Jacobs, & O'Regan, 1998; O'Regan & Jacobs, 1992), in the progressive demasking task the first part of a polysyllabic word to be recognised may often be the first syllable. Now, in the case of low-frequency words, after an early recognition of the first syllable, before the rest of the word is available for further processing, this syllable may activate other word units that could interfere with the processing of the target, because their frequency is superior to the frequency of the target word. High-frequency words are less likely to possess such higher-frequency syllabic neighbours. Yet, it can be assumed that apart from the inhibitory effect of syllable frequency due to lateral inhibition occurring at a lexical level of word processing (Carreiras et al., 1993), the processing of a syllable itself should be enhanced by its frequency. In the progressive demasking task, the high frequency of the first syllable can be an advantage for high-frequency words when this syllable is recognised more easily than a low-frequency syllable. The processing of high-frequency words, which are likely not to have higher-frequency syllabic neighbours, would thus be especially enhanced when the frequency of their first syllable is high. The corresponding word units could thus be quickly activated due to an early availability of their first syllable and would not suffer any inhibition because of the absence of higher-frequency syllabic neighbours.

To avoid such potential problems, we decided to use the fragmentation procedure, as a perceptual identification task that is both widely used in fundamental and applied research (Nuerk, Graf, Boecker, Gauggel & Jacobs, 2002; Snodgrass & Vanderwart, 1980; Snodgrass & Poster, 1992) and well-understood from a computational modelling point of view (Ziegler, Rey, & Jacobs, 1998). In this task, identification of the stimulus is made difficult by fragmentation of all of a word's letters and there is no risk of some parts of a word being systematically available (or processed) before the others, since presentation duration is participant-controlled. If syllable frequency inhibits lexical access, then words with high-frequency syllables should be recognised at later levels of (de)fragmentation than words with low-frequency syllables.

Method

Participants. Twenty-nine students of the Catholic University of Eichstaett-Ingolstadt participated in the experiment to partially fulfil a course requirement. All were native speakers of German and had normal or corrected-to-normal vision.

Design and Materials. The design was the same as in Experiment 1, but another set of 88 stimuli was selected. This modification and reduction of the size of the item set was necessary because an additional variable, letter confusability, had to be controlled for. Depending on a letter's visual features, the levels at which participants are able to identify a single letter when it is presented in the fragmentation test, differ considerably. Ziegler et al. (1998) showed that the mean confusability of all the letters of a word significantly influences the level of identification of whole words. Words are identified on an earlier level when the mean letter confusability is low. To obtain a reliable index of confusability in our presentation conditions using the word fragmentation test, we ran a pre-experiment. Ten subjects identified single letters in the word fragmentation test, each letter being presented ten times in a pseudorandomised order. The resulting mean level of identification for each letter was used as a confusability index to calculate the mean confusability of the stimuli in Experiment 2. With respect to Experiment 1 the ranges defining a syllable as high- or low-frequent were modified. The maximum of frequency of occurrence was now set at 500/million for low-frequency syllables, the minimum value for high-frequency syllables at 3500/million. The range of the levels of the factor word frequency was the same as in Experiment 1 and all variables that had been held constant in Experiment 1 were also controlled for in Experiment 2. The stimuli of Experiment 2 are listed in the Appendix. Characteristics for words in Experiment 2 are given in Table 4.

Procedure.   Participants were seated approximately 50 cm in front of a computer screen, while being tested individually in a quiet room. There were six practice trials before the experiment started. Stimuli were presented in uppercase letters. At the beginning of each trial, only 12% of the visual features of each stimulus were visible on the computer screen. All stimulus words had been subjected to a randomised fragmentation procedure. Participants were instructed to activate more parts of each word's visual features by pressing a key, if necessary for identification. Every time they did this, another 12% of the whole word's visual features

TABLE 4
Characteristics of words used in Experiment 2

| Word class | WF | | SF1 | | SF2 | | N | | L |
	M	Range	M	Range	M	Range	M	Range	M
High WF High SF	219	101–709	12225	4066–21,921	1708	234–16,350	1.18	0–5	5.73
High WF Low SF	190	115–392	285	125–488	1905	132–4237	1.86	0–6	5.68
Low WF High SF	3.55	0–9.83	17326	3527–110,013	1158	28–16,350	1.45	0–6	5.68
Low WF Low SF	3.58	0–8	226	58–488	1509	105–4405	1.50	0–4	5.68

Means (M) and ranges of the independent variables word frequency (WF) and frequency of the first syllable (SF1). Means and ranges of variables that were held constant: frequency of the second syllable (SF2), density of orthographic neighbourhood (N) and mean word length (L).

appeared on the screen, until it became fully available on the eighth level of defragmentation. Once a word was identified, it had to be entered into the keyboard. The level, at which this typing response occurred, was recorded as the dependent variable.

Results and Discussion

Mean levels of fragmentation corresponding to correct identifications and error data were submitted to separate ANOVAs. The analysis of the response levels revealed a significant main effect of word frequency, $F_1(1, 28) = 78.34, p \leq .0001; F_2(1, 84) = 12.83, p \leq .0006$. High-frequency words were identified at an earlier level of fragmentation (4.64) than low-frequency words (5.14). More importantly, there also was a significant main effect of syllable frequency in the participant analysis. More defragmentation was necessary to identify words with high-frequency syllables, $F_1(1, 28) = 15.46, p \leq .0005; F_2(1, 84) = 1.69, p \leq .2$; level 4.98 for high, level 4.80 for low syllable frequency. There was no significant interaction between word and syllable frequency. Neither were there any significant effects in the analysis of the error data. There was a tendency for words to provoke more incorrect responses when word frequency was low, with 9.0% errors for words with high word frequency vs. 10.7% errors for low-frequency words. Similarly an inhibitory tendency was caused by syllable frequency with 10.4% errors for words with high-frequency syllables vs. 9.3% errors for low syllable frequency words. Mean levels of identification and percentage of errors for words in Experiment 2 are given in Table 5.

Replicating the main result of the lexical decision task used in Experiment 1, the frequency of a word's first syllable inhibited the process of recognition in the present perceptual identification task, thus generalising the inhibitory effect of syllable frequency reported for the Spanish language to another language and another task environment. Interestingly, this inhibitory effect also appeared in the data for high-frequency words, which had not been the case when Perea and Carreiras (1995) presented

TABLE 5

Mean levels of identification (LI), standard deviation of levels of identification (SD) and percentage of errors for words in Experiment 2

| Syllable frequency | Word frequency | | | | | |
| | High | | | Low | | |
	LI	SD	% error	LI	SD	% error
High	4.73	.60	9.7	5.24	.67	11.1
Low	4.56	.67	8.3	5.04	.60	10.3

Spanish words in the progressive demasking task. The fact that in the word fragmentation task all parts of a word are, if not completely, but simultaneously available might have helped to more precisely reveal the role that syllabic frequency plays for lexical access.

The fact that this inhibitory effect of syllable frequency does not appear in the error data might be due to task-specific processes. Because stimulus presentation time in this task is not limited, errors are generally less likely to occur considering that participants might exclude wrong word candidates by a more extensive analysis of the input than in other perceptual identification or speeded response tasks.

GENERAL DISCUSSION

The results of two experiments using a lexical decision and a perceptual identification task indicate that German words are recognised more slowly when their first syllable is of high frequency than when it is of low frequency. This inhibitory effect of syllable frequency is especially strong for low-frequency words. Such effects of the phonologically defined syllabic structure should only emerge if participants perform in some way a segmentation of the whole word into its phonological subcomponents, the syllables, before or while lexical access to the word is achieved.

At an abstract, information-theoretic level, the effect can be understood as being due to an increased level of uncertainty about the identity of words that start with a high-frequency syllable as compared with words that start with a low-frequency syllable: low-frequency syllables provide more information than high-frequency ones, especially if the processing of polysyllabic words is in some way biased towards their beginning or done in some serial fashion (Álvarez et al., 1998, 2000; see also Taft & Forster, 1976).

At a more algorithmic level, Carreiras et al. (1993), who discovered the syllable frequency effect in Spanish, interpret it in a similar way as a lexical access effect by help of a specific qualitative model of the interactive activation family that includes an additional level of syllabic representations. During the processing of a word, this syllabic level would receive activation from the letter level and would send out activation to all the entries in the word level that share an identified syllable in a specific position with the input. The size of this cohort of competing candidates, the syllabic neighbours, would be modified by syllable frequency. In particular, a word's higher-frequency syllabic neighbours would, by the mechanism of lateral inhibition, interfere with the processing of a target word and thus cause the experimentally observed delays in recognition latencies for words with a high-frequency first syllable. The account of the syllable frequency effect thus is analogous to Grainger and colleagues' account of the orthographic neighbourhood frequency effect (Grainger & Jacobs, 1996; Grainger, O'Regan, Jacobs, & Seguí, 1989, 1992). On the one hand one has to be suspicious when using simulation models that represent nonlinear dynamic systems, such as the interactive activation model family, for qualitative accounts of experimental effects. On the other hand the lack of any computational model that could at present simulate this effect and the intuitive appeal of Carreiras et al.'s (1993) account, which seems, at present, the most simple and straightforward one, are reasons to make us adopt this interpretation.

A first step towards implementing such a model has been made with the 'functional units model' (FUM; Rey, 1998; Richter, 1999). Based on the MROM, the FUM has an additional structure of sublexical units (i.e., graphemes) between the letter and word levels that enable it to account for the grapheme effect obtained by Rey et al. (2000). Because alternative computational models such as Zorzi et al.'s (1998) or the revised German DRC (Coltheart et al., 2001; Ziegler et al., 2000) also cannot deal with polysyllabic words, at present it seems in order not to speculate how they could possibly account for the effect (but see Ferrand & New, 2003). The only computational model which incorporates a representation of syllabic structure that we know of can simulate the process of naming of polysyllabic words (Ans et al., 1998) and could thus possibly be used to account for the facilitatory effect of first syllable frequency on naming latencies (Perea & Carreiras, 1996, 1998), but not for the inhibition due to first syllable frequency in recognition tasks. A more general problem for all computational models of word recognition that could, in principle, be modified so as to be able to simulate the present inhibitory syllable frequency effect is the question whether those revised models could still successfully simulate all the other relevant experimental effects in the word recognition field (e.g., the neighbourhood frequency effect). For instance, including a syllabic level of representations might alter the dynamics of the model in a way that requires modifications of important model parameters that were always kept constant in previous, successful simulation studies. These modifications in turn, could lead to different model predictions concerning well established effects. However, what would be gained, if, say, the revised DRC (Coltheart et al., 2001) could simulate the inhibitory syllable frequency effect after the modifications recently proposed by Ferrand and New (2003), but could no longer simulate the inhibitory neighbourhood frequency effect? Given that very little is known about the processing of polysyllabic words as compared with the processing of monosyllabic words (Carreiras & Perea, 2002; Chateau & Jared, 2003), we would like to argue that a good deal of more research should be devoted to the establishment of a set of reliable experimental effects on the processing of polysyllabic words, before intensive computational model revision studies are launched. After all, it could be that the processing of longer, complex polysyllabic words is qualitatively different from the reading of short, monosyllabic, monomorphemic words (e.g., if only because of the involvement of different eye movement patterns). If so, perhaps the development of a new generation of word recognition models would be more promising than trying to shape-up the previous generation.

To sum up, the theoretical significance of the present study can be seen in the fact that, by successfully replicating in a non-Romance language and at least one different task (fragmentation task) the inhibitory effect of syllable frequency, first described by Carreiras et al. (1993) for the Spanish language, it provides evidence for the conclusion that this effect is neither language-, nor task-specific. If so, it cannot be ignored by current computational models of visual word recognition that have been designed to describe the basic mechanisms underlying word recognition in general. Coming back to the quotation starting this paper, we would thus like to conclude that "any model of lexical access has to incorporate a syllabic level of representations or include the syllable as a sublexical unit of processing in Spanish and German". Whether the effect can also be found in other Romance or non-Romance languages is an issue for future research. Work is in progress to examine these findings in the French language, in whose historical development syllables have played a much greater role than in German, but in which there is contrasting evidence suggesting that orthographic rather than phonological word subcomponents are functional in visual word recognition (Rouibah & Taft, 2001), or the contrary (Ferrand & New, 2003).

REFERENCES

Álvarez, C.J., Carreiras, M., & De Vega, M. (2000). Syllable-frequency effect in visual word recognition: Evidence of sequential type-processing. *Psicológica, 21*, 341–374.

Álvarez, C.J., Carreiras, M., & Taft, M. (2001). Syllables and morphemes: contrasting frequency effects in spanish. *Journal of Experimental Psychology: Learning, Memory, and Cognition, 27*, 545–555.

Álvarez, C.J., De Vega, M., & Carreiras, M. (1998). La sílaba como unidad de activación lexica en la lectura de palabras trisílabas. *Psicothema, 10*, 371–386.

Ans, B., Carbonnel, S., & Valdois, S. (1998). A connectionist multiple-trace model for polysyllabic word reading. *Psychological Review, 105*, 678–723.

Baayen, R.H., Piepenbrock, R., & van Rijn, H. (1993). *The CELEX Lexikal Database (CD-ROM)*. Philadelphia, PA: Linguistic Data Consortium, University of Pennsylvania.

Carreiras, M., & Perea, M. (2002). Masked priming effects with syllabic neighbors in a lexical decision task. *Journal of Experimental Psychology: Human Perception and Performance, 28*, 1228–1242.

Carreiras, M., & Perea, M. (in press). Naming pseudowords in Spanish: Effects of syllable frequency in production. *Brain and Language*.

Carreiras, M., Álvarez, C.J., & De Vega, M. (1993). Syllable frequency and visual word recognition in spanish. *Journal of Memory and Language, 32*, 766–780.

Chateau, D., & Jared, D. (2003). Spelling–sound consistency effects in disyllabic word naming. *Journal of Memory and Language, 48*, 255–280.

Cohen, J.D., MacWhinney, B., Flatt, M. & Provost, J. (1993). PsyScope: A new graphic interactive environment for designing psychology experiments. *Behavioral Research Methods, Instruments & Computers, 25*(2), 257–271.

Coltheart, M., Rastle, K., Perry, C., Langdon, R., & Ziegler, J.C. (2001). DRC: A dual route model of visual word recognition and reading aloud. *Psychological Review, 108*, 204–256.

De Jong, N.H., Schreuder, R., & Baayen, R.H. (2000). The morphological family size effect and morphology. *Language and Cognitive Processes, 15*, 329–365.

Dominguez, A., De Vega, M., & Cuetos, F. (1997). Lexical inhibition from syllabic units in visual word recognition. *Language and Cognitive Processes, 12*, 401–422.

Ferrand, L., & New, B. (2003). Syllabic length effects in visual word recognition and naming *Acta Psychologica, 113*, 167–183.

Ferrand, L., Segui, J., & Humphreys, G.W. (1997). The syllable's role in word naming. *Memory & Cognition, 25*, 458–470.

Grainger, J., & Jacobs, A.M. (1993). Masked partial-word priming in visual word recognition: effects of positional letter frequency. *Journal of Experimental Psychology: Human Perception and Performance, 19*, 951–964.

Grainger, J., & Jacobs, A.M. (1996). Orthographic processing in visual word recognition: A multiple read-out model. *Psychological Review, 103*, 518–565.

Grainger, J., O'Regan, J.K., Jacobs, A.M., & Segui, J. (1989). On the role of competing word units in visual word recognition: the neighborhood frequency effect. *Perception and Psychophysics, 45*, 189–195.

Grainger, J., O'Regan, J.K., Jacobs, A.M., & Segui, J. (1992). Neighborhood frequency effects and letter visibility in visual word recognition. *Perception and Psychophysics, 51*, 49–56.

Jacobs, A.M. (1994). On computational theories and multilevel, multitask models of cognition: The case of word recognition. *Behavioral and Brain Sciences, 17*, 670–672.

Jacobs, A.M., Graf, R., & Kinder, A. (2003). Receiver-operating characteristics in the lexical decision task: evidence for a simple signal detection process simulated by the multiple read-out model. *Journal of Experimental Psychology: Learning, Memory, and Cognition, 29*(3), 481–488.

Jacobs, A.M., & Grainger, J. (1994). Models of visual word recognition: Sampling the state of the art. *Journal of Experimental Psychology: Human Perception and Performance, 20*, 1311–1334.

Jacobs, A.M., Rey, A., Ziegler, J.C., & Grainger, J. (1998). MROM-P: An interactive activation, multiple read-out model of orthographic and phonological processes in visual word recognition. In J. Grainger, & A.M. Jacobs (Eds.), *Localist connectionist approaches to human cognition*, (pp. 147–187). Mahwah, NJ: Lawrence Erlbaum Associates, Inc.

Massaro, D.W., & Cohen, M. (1994). Visual, orthographic, phonological, and lexical influences in reading. *Journal of Experimental Psychology: Human Perception and Performance, 20*, 1107–1128.

Morais, J., Content, A., Cary, L., Mehler, J., & Seguí, J. (1989). Syllabic segmentation and literacy. *Language and Cognitive Processes, 4*, 57–67.

Nazir, T.A., Jacobs, A.M., & O'Regan, J.K. (1998). Letter legibility and visual word recognition. *Memory and Cognition, 26*, 810–821.

Nuerk, H.C., Rey, A., Graf, R., & Jacobs, A.M. (2000). Phonographic sublexical units in visual word recognition. *Current Psychology Letters, 2*, 25–36.

Nuerk, H.-C., Graf, R., Boecker, M., Gauggel, S., & Jacobs, A.M. (2002). Der Wortfragmentationstest FRAG als computergestütztes Verfahren zur Erfassung der visuellen Worterkennung bei aphasischen und nicht-aphasischen Patienten. *Zeitschrift für Neuropsychologie, 13,* 3–18.

O'Regan, J.K., & Jacobs, A.M. (1992). Optimal viewing position effect in word recognition: A challenge to current theory. *Journal of Experimental Psychology: Human Perception and Performance, 18,* 185–197.

Paap, K.R., & Johansen, L.S. (1994). The case of the vanishing frequency effect. *Journal of Experimental Psychology: Human Perception and Performance, 20,* 1129–1157.

Perea, M., & Carreiras, M. (1995). Efectos de frecuencia silábica en tareas de identificación. *Psicológica, 16,* 483–496.

Perea, M., & Carreiras, M. (1996). Efectos de frecuencia silábica y vecindad ortográfica en la pronunciación de palabras y pseudopalabras. *Psicológica, 17,* 425–440.

Perea, M., & Carreiras, M. (1998). Effects of syllable frequency and syllable neighborhood frequency in visual word recognition. *Journal of Experimental Psychology: Human Perception and Performance, 24,* 134–144.

Rey, A. (1998). *Orthographie et Phonologie dans la Perception des Mots écrits.* Doctoral Dissertation, Université de Provence Aix, Marseille.

Rey, A., Ziegler, J.C., & Jacobs, A.M. (2000). Graphemes are perceptual reading units. *Cognition, 75,* B1–B12.

Richter, K. (1999). *A functional units model of visual word recognition.* Masters thesis, Philipps-University, Marburg.

Rouibah, A., & Taft, M. (2001). The role of syllabic structure in French visual word recognition. *Memory and Cognition, 29,* 373–381.

Sebastián-Gallés, N., Dupoux, E., Seguí, J., & Mehler, J. (1992). Contrasting syllabic effects in Catalan and Spanish. *Journal of Memory and Language, 31,* 18–32.

Seidenberg, M.S. (1987). Sublexical structures in visual word recognition: Access units or orthographic redundancy? In M. Coltheart (Ed.), *Attention and performance XII: The psychology of reading.* Hove, UK: Lawrence Erlbaum Associates Ltd.

Snodgrass, J.G., & Poster, M. (1992). Visual-word recognition thresholds for screen fragmented names of the Snodgrass and Vanderwart pictures. *Behaviour Research Methods, Instruments, and Computers, 24,* 1–15.

Snodgrass, J.G., & Vanderwart, M. (1980). A standardized set of 260 pictures: Norms for name agreement, image agreement, familiarity and visual complexity. *Journal of Experimental Psychology: Human Perception and Performance, 6,* 174–215.

Taft, M. (1979). Lexical access via an orthographic code: The basic orthographic syllable structure (BOSS). *Journal of Verbal Learning and Verbal Behaviour, 18,* 21–39.

Taft, M., & Forster, K.I. (1976). Lexical storage and retrieval of polymorphemic and polysyllabic words. *Journal of Verbal Learning and Verbal Behaviour, 15,* 638–647.

Wiese, R. (1996). *The phonology of German.* Oxford: Clarendon Press.

Wimmer, H., & Goswami, U. (1994). The influence of orthographic consistency on reading development: Word recognition in English and German children. *Cognition, 51,* 91–103.

Ziegler, J.C., Perry, C., & Coltheart, M. (2000). The DRC model of visual word recognition and reading aloud: An extension to German. *European Journal of Cognitive Psychology, 12,* 413–430.

Ziegler, J.C., Perry, C., Jacobs, A.M., & Braun, M. (2001). Identical words are read differently in different languages. *Psychological Science, 27,* 547–559.

Ziegler, J.C., Rey, A., & Jacobs, A.M. (1998). Simulating individual word identification thresholds and errors in the fragmentation task. *Memory and Cognition, 26,* 490–501.

Ziegler, J.C., Stone, G.O., & Jacobs, A.M. (1997). What's the pronounciation for _OUGH and the Spelling for /u/? A database for computing feedforward and feedback consistency in English. *Behavior Research Methods, Instruments, and Computers, 29,* 600–618.

Zorzi, M., Houghton, G., & Butterworth, B. (1998). Two routes or one in reading aloud? A connectionist dual-process model. *Journal of Experimental Psychology: Human Perception and Performance*, 24, 1131–1161.

APPENDIX

Words for Experiments 1 and 2

List of words used in Experiment 1, differing in word frequency and frequency of the first syllable

High word frequency		Low word frequency	
SF high	*SF low*	*SF high*	*SF low*
ANDERS	DIREKT	ADELN	ACHSEL
ANFANG	DOLLAR	ALSTER	BAGGER
AUFBAU	FAHREN	ALTERS	BISON
BEGINN	FIRMA	ANBEI	DIPLOM
BEREIT	GRENZE	ANHAND	ELSTER
BESUCH	GRUPPE	ANTUN	EXTERN
BEVOR	HANDEL	AUFTUN	EXTRA
BEZIRK	HELFEN	BEHEND	FAHRIG
DAHER	HILFE	BESAGT	FASELN
EINIG	HOFFEN	DERLEI	GEISEL
EINZIG	HOTEL	EINHER	GEIZIG
ERFOLG	KIRCHE	ERBEN	GLATZE
GEBIET	KLASSE	ERDIG	GOLFER
GEFAHR	KOSTEN	ERDUNG	GUMMI
GENAU	LEHRER	ERWEIS	HARZIG
GERING	MONTAG	GEDEIH	HECKE
GESAMT	MUSIK	GESELL	KIEFER
GESETZ	NUTZEN	HABIT	MENSA
GEWALT	OPFER	HAPERN	MUSKEL
INDEM	PARIS	INBILD	ORGEL
MITTE	PARTEI	MITHIN	PILGER
MITTEL	PERSON	UMHIN	PINSEL
RECHEN	RUHIG	UNWEIT	PUMPEN
SOGAR	STIMME	VORDEM	TADELN
SOWIE	SYSTEM	WIRBEL	TIGER
UMSATZ	THEMA	WIRTIN	ZIEGEL
VORHER	WARUM	ZUBER	ZIRKA
WIRKEN	ZIMMER	ZULIEB	ZIRKUS

Note: SF = frequency of the first syllable.

List of words used in Experiment 2, differing in word frequency and frequency of the first syllable

High word frequency		Low word frequency	
SF high	*SF low*	*SF high*	*SF low*
ANFANG	BITTEN	ABTEI	ACHSEL
AUFBAU	DOLLAR	ABWURF	BLUTEN
BEREIT	FIRMA	ANHAND	DICHTE
BESUCH	GELTEN	AUFTUN	DONNER
BEVOR	GRENZE	BECHER	FUNKEN
DAMALS	GRUPPE	BELEG	GEISEL
DAVON	HILFE	DERLEI	HONIG
DIENEN	KIRCHE	EICHE	LAUNIG
EINIG	LEHRER	EINHER	MALMEN
EINMAL	MONTAG	EINZEL	MENTAL
EINZIG	MUSIK	ERBEN	MUTTI
ERFOLG	ROLLE	ERDUNG	ORGEL
GEBIET	RUFEN	ERKER	PLANE
GENAU	RUHIG	GESELL	RADLER
GESETZ	SCHULE	HAPERN	ROSTIG
INDEM	STIMME	INTUS	RUDERN
MITTEL	SYSTEM	UNMUT	SENKE
SIEBEN	THEMA	UNWEIT	TANGO
SOGAR	TRETEN	VORWEG	TAUMEL
SOWOHL	WARTEN	WIRBEL	TIGER
UMSATZ	ZIEHEN	ZULAUF	TONLOS
WIRKEN	ZIMMER	ZUSATZ	ZIMBEL

Note: SF = frequency of the first syllable.

LANGUAGE AND COGNITIVE PROCESSES, 2004, *19* (3), 391–426

Representing syllable information during silent reading: Evidence from eye movements

Jane Ashby and Keith Rayner

University of Massachusetts, Amherst, USA

Two eye movement experiments investigated the nature of the phonological representations used in reading English. Each tested whether sublexical, syllable information is part of that representation. Target words with CV-initial syllables (DE.MAND) or CVC-initial syllables (LAN.TERN) were preceded by primes that exactly matched or mismatched their initial syllable. In Experiment 1, the primes were presented foveally using a fast-priming technique. Target words of both types were read faster when preceded by a three-letter than a two-letter prime, and no effect of matching syllable information was observed. In Experiment 2, primes were presented parafoveally using a preview technique. First fixation durations were shorter on words which were preceded by a matching syllable preview than a mismatching preview. These results indicate that proficient readers do process sublexical, syllable information while reading, which provides evidence for a multi-layered phonological representation. The results of Experiments 1 and 2 suggest that syllable information is encoded as part of the memory processes that preserve information across saccades.

This paper presents two experiments that investigate the phonological processes used by proficient readers while reading sentences for comprehension. Specifically, we wanted to examine the nature of the

Correspondence should be addressed to Jane Ashby, Department of Psychology, University of Massachusetts, Amherst, MA 01003, USA. Email: ashby@psych.umass.edu.

The research reported here formed part of the first author's master's thesis at the University of Massachusetts. She was supported by Training Grant (MH16745) from the National Institute of Mental Health and by a Training Grant (HD07327) from the National Institute of Health. The research was also supported by Grants HD17246 and HD26765 from the National Institute of Health. We thank the other members of the master's committee (Alexander Pollatsek and John Kingston), Charles Clifton, and two anonymous reviewers for helpful comments on an earlier version of this paper. Portions of the data were presented at the 2002 AMLAP Meeting and the 2002 Psychonomic Society Meeting.

http://www.tandf.co.uk/journals/pp/01690965.html   DOI: 10.1080/01690960344000233

phonological representations used during reading in English, and test whether these representations consist solely of strings of constituent phonemes. Alternatively, it is possible that the phonological representations used during reading contain layers of sublexical information, such as syllable structure, in addition to phoneme information. These experiments utilised a display-change technique in order to provide readers with advance information (in the form of a prime or preview) about the initial segments of a target word. This advance information consisted of the initial two or three segments of the target word, and was either identical to the first syllable of the target (congruent) or not (incongruent). In the incongruent conditions, the preview also shared initial segments with the target word, but contained either one segment more or less than the target's initial syllable. We asked the following question. If readers were supplied with advance information about the initial syllable of the target, would they use this information to recognise it? If so, then we would expect a word to be read more quickly when it was preceded by a syllabically congruent prime than when it was preceded by an incongruent prime. Such a finding would suggest that the phonological representation is multi-layered, since it can encode syllable as well as phoneme information. If, on the other hand, readers only used segment information to identify a target word, then a word should be read faster when it is preceded by a three segment prime than a two segment prime, irrespective of whether that prime is syllabically congruent.

Eye movement experiments have examined the role of phonology in reading by using homophone and pseudohomophone stimuli within parafoveal preview and fast-priming paradigms (Henderson, Dixon, Petersen, Twilley, & Ferreira, 1995; Lesch & Pollatsek, 1998; Lima, 1987; Pollatsek, Lesch, Morris & Rayner, 1992; Rayner, Sereno, Lesch & Pollatsek, 1995). Recent experiments have contrasted phonological and orthographic processing to describe the time course of each process during word recognition (Lee, Rayner & Pollatsek, 1999). Collectively, these experiments (and numerous others) found evidence of pre-lexical phonological processes operating at the letter/phoneme level in reading, irrespective of which experimental paradigm was used. Although this research has helped to establish a central role for phonological processes, it has not specified the form of phonological representations, their use, or when they are created.

Regarding the form of phonological representations, one basic question is whether reading and speech share the same representational structure. Perfetti, Zhang, and Berent (1992) are among the many reading researchers who contend that the pervasiveness of phonological processes indicates that reading makes use of pre-existent, oral language processes. Surprisingly, only a few investigators have invoked the phonological principles of spoken language in order to further understand the nature of phonological representations in reading and writing (Berent, Bouissa, & Tuller, 2001; Berent & Perfetti, 1995; Berent, Shimron & Vaknin, 2001; Birch, Pollatsek, & Kingston, 1998; Caramazza & Miceli, 1990). As a result, there remains much to be learned about the points of overlap between the phonological representations used in reading and in spoken language. For example, do phonological representations consist solely of phonemes? Or do they carry several layers of sublexical phonological information?

Currently, many reading researchers conceptualise phonological representations as strings of phonemes, but linguistic evidence offers an alternative description of phonological representations as multi-layered, dimensional structures. Linguistic models of phonology share a core concept: phonological representation consists of a hierarchical structure (Clements & Keyser, 1983; Selkirk, 1982; Treiman, Fowler, Gross, Berch, & Weatherston, 1995). In a chapter reviewing lexical phonology, Frauenfelder and Lahiri (1989) described a multidimensional model from Clements and Keyser (1983) that includes three layers of representation: a prosodic level that indicates the number of syllables in a word; a skeletal level which codes the consonant/vowel pattern; and a melodic (phonetic) level that describes the actual speech sounds.

Recently, some researchers have applied this linguistic perspective to study phonological representation during isolated word reading. Berent, Bouissa, and Tuller (2001) and Berent, Shimron, and Vaknin (2001) used the hierarchical view as a theoretical base for investigating word recognition in English and Hebrew, respectively. In these papers, Berent and colleagues confined their attention to the basic, skeletal level of the representation since that layer was most relevant to their specific hypotheses. The present research takes a somewhat different approach, focusing on the syllable level of phonological representation.

These experiments are the first to seek evidence for the use of syllable information during word recognition in the course of natural, silent reading of text. Evidence for the use of syllable information would indicate that the phonological representation is hierarchically structured, suggest-

TABLE 1
Hierarchical phonological representation

Word	CANDY				
Prosodic level		δ			δ
Skeletal level	C	V	C	C	V
Melodic level	[k	ae	n	d	i]

ing that reading and spoken language representations carry similar types of phonological information in a similar structure. That finding would suggest an early coupling of reading with spoken language processes. On the other hand, if these experiments fail to find evidence for the use of syllable information, and detect only the use of phoneme or grapheme information, then the data would offer some support for a linear, one-dimensional structure in reading.

Several naming and lexical decision experiments have examined the role of syllables in reading single words in English, but the results have been inconsistent. Although the current experiments concern word recognition during silent reading, we include results from naming experiments in the following discussion for several reasons. Historically, nearly all of the findings from naming experiments have been replicated by eye movement studies, which suggests that the naming paradigm taps word recognition processes. Also, the particular naming experiments that we describe provided some of the earliest evidence for syllable effects in English and, thus, influenced the design of the current experiments. Later, we contrast these data with the data from lexical decision experiments, which tap word recognition processes without involving any observable speech production processes.

Naming experiments.   Several early experiments investigated the role of syllables in word recognition by contrasting the naming latency for monosyllabic and polysyllabic words. The findings were inconsistent, with some studies reporting an effect of number of syllables on naming time (Butler & Hains, 1979; Eriksen, Pollack, & Montague, 1970; Klapp, Anderson, & Berrian 1973) while other studies found no effect (Forster & Chambers, 1973; Frederiksen & Kroll, 1976).

More recently, Jared and Seidenberg (1990) found that a greater number of syllables extended the naming latencies for low frequency words (but not high frequency words). This interaction of syllable number and frequency was replicated with French speakers in Ferrand (2000). As Jared and Seidenberg (1990) suggested, it appears that a failure to control for word frequency can account for the divergent findings of the experiments conducted in the 1970s. However, they did not find evidence that participants divide low-frequency words into syllables in order to name them. In their final discussion, Jared and Seidenberg pointed out that even though readers may not explicitly syllabify words, syllables may act as perceptual units in word recognition because of their phonological and orthographic properties (see Prinzmetal, Treiman, & Rho, 1986).

Ferrand, Segui, and Humphreys (1997) conducted a provocative series of naming experiments in English, in which they used a masked priming paradigm to investigate the role of syllables in speech production. The stimuli were pairs of words with clear syllable boundaries which shared the same initial three phonemes. Experiments 1 and 5 used target words with a clear CVC pattern in the first syllable or a clear CV pattern in the first syllable, respectively. Words of these two types were preceded by both CVC%%% and CV%%%% primes, so that each participant saw each target type with each type of prime. Participants saw a forward mask, followed by the presentation of the prime for 29 ms (SAL%%%% or SA%%%%), followed by a backward mask before the target word (SALVAGE) was displayed. Results from these naming experiments demonstrated shorter latencies when primes constituted the first syllable of the target. Since the CV primes were more effective than the CVC primes in facilitating naming of CV targets in Experiment 5, the syllable effect was not attributed to the degree of phonemic/ orthographic overlap between prime and target. Ferrand et al. (1997) claimed that the appearance of syllabic effects at such a brief prime duration indicated that syllable information is encoded early in word recognition. Thus, these naming experiments offer some evidence for the early availability of syllabic information during visual word recognition when production processes are involved.

When Schiller (2000) attempted to replicate the results from Ferrand et al.'s Experiment 5, he failed to do so. Schiller used the same English materials, design, and procedure in his Experiment 1A, but did not find any effects of syllable structure. The reason for this failure to replicate Ferrand et al. (1997) is open to question, however. One serious concern arises from the comparison of mean naming times for targets preceded by neutral primes with the means for those preceded by letter primes. The mean for the neutral prime condition (%%%) was a scant millisecond faster than either the two-letter or three-letter prime conditions. The failure to demonstrate a consistent advantage for letter primes compared with non-letter primes across all groups of participants, could cast doubt on the findings of this first experiment.

In his second failure to replicate Ferrand et al., Schiller used a modified design in which each participant named every target word six times to increase statistical power (Experiment 1B). Despite this increased power, only one of the comparisons of non-letter primes versus letter primes reached significance both by items and participants. Targets preceded by incongruent three-letter primes were named 4 ms faster on average than those preceded by congruent two-letter primes. Schiller interpreted these results as evidence for segment effects. Yet, the data fail to demonstrate that any significant benefit was derived from two-letter primes as compared with non-letter primes.

In sum, Schiller's experiments 1A and 1B did not replicate Ferrand et al.'s (1997) results, nor did they yield a clear pattern of data with which to challenge those results. Schiller's later experiments obtained stronger results to support the segment theory of word production, but he used very different stimuli from Ferrand et al. in order to do so. For example, CV targets with initial syllable stress were used in Experiment 3, although previous studies had failed to find syllable effects in the perception of spoken words with initial syllable stress (Finney, Protopapas & Eimas, 1996; Cutler, Mehler, Norris & Segui, 1986). Schiller's Experiment 4 used high frequency words (occurring several hundred times per million) instead of the mid-to-low frequency words used by Ferrand et al. In sum, Schiller's experiments clearly indicate that syllable structure is not necessarily represented during naming tasks. These experiments do not, however, eliminate the possibility that syllable structure *can* be included in the early phonological representation of a written word.

Lexical decision experiments.   Despite the ubiquity of lexical decision experiments in word recognition research, few have investigated the salience of the syllable in word recognition in English. Those that did, such as Cutler and Clifton (1984), failed to demonstrate effects of number of syllables on reaction times.

Ferrand et al. (1997) conducted one lexical decision experiment, in addition to the series of naming experiments described above, to examine the priming effects of syllable structure on word recognition. The data from the lexical decision experiment did not demonstrate priming effects, although the naming experiments did. Based on the restriction of syllabic priming effects to word recognition that involved naming, Ferrand et al. concluded that although syllable information is detected early in word recognition (i.e., at short prime durations), it is the units involved in speech production which are structured syllabically.

Although lexical decision experiments in English have failed to find effects for syllable number and syllable structure in word recognition, such studies in other languages have found evidence of syllable information in word recognition. In an experiment with French speakers, Ferrand and New (2003) reported slower lexical decision times for 3-syllable low frequency words than for 2-syllable low frequency words. Carreiras and Perea (2002) conducted a series of lexical decision experiments in Spanish. In Experiments 1–3, Carreiras and Perea found faster reaction times to targets which were primed by whole words that shared an identical initial syllable, rather than one phoneme more or less. In Experiment 4, they used the Ferrand et al. (1997) procedure to present syllabically congruent and incongruent sublexical primes before CV and CVC targets. Prime durations were longer in this experiment (116 ms and 160 ms) than in Ferrand et al. (29 ms), and the data clearly show faster reaction times when the prime was syllabically congruent to the target.

To summarise, then, the naming and lexical decision experiments that found effects of syllable structure during single word reading suggest that these effects function post-lexically in the preparation of articulatory codes. It is unclear, then, how the representation of syllable structure would support reading processes, since normal (silent) reading does not appear to involve the assembly of a production code (Rayner & Balota, 1989). Yet, reading comprehension processes do seem to use post-lexical articulatory codes (Slowiaczek & Clifton, 1980). The most obvious post-lexical role for syllable structure would be to retain identified words in the phonological loop of short-term memory (for a further discussion of this see Besner, 1987). The next section describes linguistic evidence for the role of syllables in post-lexical memory processes.

Tasks that require memory processes. Fowler, Treiman, and Gross (1993) conducted a series of experiments that required participants to move phonemes between pairs of visually presented, polysyllabic non-words. For example, when RUPADKIN and YOMEFBUG appeared on the screen four correct spoken responses were possible depending on the experimental condition: rumadkin, rupafkin, rumedkin, or rupefkin. Participants' pronunciation of the 'new' item triggered a voice-key that timed the latency of their response. In Experiment 4, the task involved the rearrangement of phonemes located in either the onset or rime of the medial syllable. Results showed faster response times for extracting the consonant in an onset unit than a consonant which is part of a rime unit, indicating that subsyllabic structure exists in polysyllabic words.

Experiments by Sevald, Dell, and Cole (1995) involved explicit, audible rehearsal of the target. Participants repeatedly named a visually presented nonword for 4 s. Experimental conditions compared the production time for nonwords preceded by a nonword whose first syllable contained the same sounds as the target with one whose first syllable shared the syllable structure of the target. Results from these experiments showed faster production times when the nonwords shared the same syllable structure, and no advantage for sharing sounds without a common syllable structure.

The Sevald et al. (1995) and Fowler et al. (1993) experiments demonstrate the relevance of syllabic structure in tasks that involve the rehearsal of visually presented nonwords. Unfortunately, both also used production processes as a measure of facilitation, making it difficult to know whether it is production or rehearsal, or both, that utilise syllabic structure.

Experiments by Bruck, Treiman, and Caravolas (1995) offer a hint about the role of syllabic structure in memory rehearsal tasks that don't involve naming. Participants listened to pairs of nonwords and indicated whether they contained matching sounds in the first, middle, or last syllable by hitting a 'yes' or 'no' button. No explicit instructions about rehearsal strategies were given, but an 800 ms SOA permitted working memory rehearsal processes. Participants consistently identified a match faster when the sounds corresponded to a whole syllable, and this pattern held for all three position conditions. Faster reaction times suggest a role for syllable structure in facilitating phonological rehearsal even when naming isn't part of the task. Considering the failure of well-known monitoring experiments to find an effect of syllable structure in English (Cutler et al., 1986), Bruck et al. (1995) attributed their findings of a syllable structure effect to two main differences in these experiments. First, Bruck et al.'s comparison task required participants to hold the first word in memory, and syllable effects appear to emerge most strongly in tasks which rely on phonological memory (Treiman et al., 1995). Second, the comparison task used nonwords, so a phonological representation needed to be constructed rather than accessed in the lexicon. The process of constructing a representation might make use of articulatory codes, leading to the pre-lexical involvement of production processes.

Taken together, the English data from naming, lexical decision, and nonword experiments demonstrate effects of syllabic structure, which appear to be linked to production processes, rehearsal processes, or the assembly of phonological codes. It is not yet clear, however, whether syllable information is part of the phonological representations used during the course of normal reading or what purpose that information might serve.

Description of the present experiments

Two eye movement experiments were conducted to seek evidence for a syllable level in the phonological representations used during reading. As an on-line behavioural measure, eye movements are useful in studying cognitive processes during the reading of connected text. Eye movement data are a temporally precise (sampled each ms) and spatially accurate (within half a character) measure of reading that has contributed to our understanding of reading as it is experienced by most adults (Rayner, 1998).

Two different display change techniques were used: a fast-priming technique where a brief prime was presented foveally; and a parafoveal preview technique where the prime was presented in parafoveal view. In Experiment 1, the fast-priming technique was employed to examine the use of syllable information in word recognition when the processing of the target was delayed until the eye landed on the word. Experiment 2 used the parafoveal preview technique to examine whether syllable information was utilised when it appeared in parafoveal view, i.e., before the target word was fixated.

Display-change techniques.   While silently reading sentences, a reader typically sees the word that is in foveal view (n) and also extracts information about the following word (n+1). An eye-contingent display change (Rayner, 1975) can be used to manipulate what the reader sees foveally (n) or parafoveally (n+1). When a reader makes a saccade to get to the target word in the sentence, the eyes move across an invisible boundary and trigger a display change in the target word. Fast-priming and parafoveal preview techniques use this boundary change paradigm differently.

Fast priming.   In the fast-priming paradigm (Sereno & Rayner, 1992), the reader is prevented from seeing the upcoming target word (n+1) until it is actually fixated. Before this time, a string of xs or random letters holds the place of the target word. As the eyes move to fixate on the target word, they cross an invisible boundary just before the target region which triggers the display change. Upon fixation, the string of xs is replaced by a prime which is presented for 18–60 ms before the actual target word appears. The short prime duration suggests that fast-priming taps automatic reading processes that are not consciously controlled by the reader. Fast priming experiments have manipulated the semantic, orthographic, or phonological characteristics of the prime and measured fixation time on the target as the dependent variable (Lee et al., 1999). Generally, such experiments have shown that related primes facilitate word recognition, as indicated by shorter fixation durations in the related condition.

Experiment 1 used the fast-priming technique to examine the role of syllable structure in the phonological representations used in early word recognition processes. Because the prime and the target word did not appear until the eyes land in the target region, preview information is completely withheld from the reader. Fixation time measures, therefore, begin at the first moment any information is available from the target word location. The collected data thus describe the earliest phases of processing, some of which would normally occur parafoveally before the eyes landed on the word. For this reason, word recognition processes during fast-priming might deviate somewhat from the processes used when parafoveal information is available. However, fast-priming does offer the closest simulation of the Ferrand et al. and Schiller experiments while allowing presentation of the target in a sentence context.

Parafoveal preview.   These experiments control what information the reader gets from an upcoming word (n+1)before his or her eyes actually land on it (Rayner, 1975). Initially, a preview stimulus appears in the sentence instead of the target word. While fixating on the word (n) before the eventual target, the reader begins parafoveal processing of n+1, which is the preview stimulus. As the eyes move from n to n+1, they cross an invisible boundary and trigger the target word to replace the preview. With this paradigm, the reader generally is not aware of the display change, which indicates that parafoveal processing is automatic and beyond conscious control.

Parafoveal preview experiments manipulate the characteristics of the preview and/or the relationship of the preview to the target. The preview might share semantic, phonological, or orthographic characteristics with the target depending on the experimental question at hand. Shorter fixation times in the related preview condition show that the preview facilitated recognition of the target and suggest that the shared characteristic contributes to word recognition. Such experiments have already demonstrated that actual letter forms are not encoded parafoveally, but phonological codes and 'abstract letter identities' are perceived in the parafovea (Rayner, 1998; Liversedge & Findlay, 2000).

In Experiment 2, the parafoveal preview paradigm was used to investigate the structure of the phonological representations that facilitate word recognition during normal reading. Specifically, this experiment examined whether information about syllabic structure is available before a word is fixated, and whether that information affects the duration of fixations on the target word.

EXPERIMENT 1: FAST-PRIMING

The role of syllable structure in word recognition during silent reading was investigated using the fast priming technique (Sereno & Rayner, 1992). This experiment aimed to extend the findings from Experiments 1 and 5 by Ferrand et al. (1997) beyond the specific context of isolated word naming. Thus, the design was modelled after the Ferrand et al. experiments, such that target words with CV and CVC initial syllables were preceded by syllabically congruent, syllabically incongruent, or control primes. Stimuli were selected from the lists used in Ferrand et al. (1997), and stimuli from Finney et al. (1996) were included as well in order to increase statistical power. The target words in this experiment, however, were embedded in sentences and presentation of the prime was triggered by a saccade into the target region.

Method

Participants.   Twenty-seven students at the University of Massachusetts were paid or received experimental credit to participate in the experiment.

All were native English speakers with normal vision and all were naive as to the purpose of the experiment.

Apparatus and procedure.   The stimuli were presented on a NEC 4FG monitor through a VGA video board that was controlled by a 486 PC. An A to D converter interfaced the computer with a Fourward Technologies Generation VI Dual Purkinje eyetracker. The monitor displayed text at a 200Hz refresh rate that permitted display changes within 5 ms. The eyetracker monitored movements of the right eye, although viewing was binocular. Letters were formed from a 7 × 8 array of pixels, using the fixed-pitch Borland C default font. Participants sat 61cm away from a computer screen and silently read single line sentences while their head position was stabilised by a bite bar. At this viewing distance, 3.8 letters equalled one degree of visual angle. At the beginning of the experiment, the eye-tracking system was calibrated for the participant. At the start of each trial, a check calibration screen appeared, and participants who showed a discrepancy between where their eye fixated and the location of the calibration squares were re-calibrated before the next trial.

A trial consisted of the following events. The check calibration screen appeared and the experimenter determined that the eye-tracker was correctly calibrated. The participant was instructed to look at the calibration square on the far left of the screen, then the experimenter presented the sentence. Initially a random sequence of Greek symbols held the place of the target word. The participant read the sentence silently and at his/her own pace. The display change was initiated when the reader's eyes crossed an invisible boundary located just after the last letter of the word that preceded the target word. After the presentation of the prime was triggered during a saccade into the target region, it remained present until 40 ms after the start of the fixation in the region and then was replaced by the actual target word. When the participant finished reading the sentence, he/she clicked a response key to make it disappear. Following a quarter of the sentence trials, a comprehension question appeared on the screen. The participant responded by pressing the response key that corresponded with the position of the correct answer. Then the check calibration screen appeared before the next trial. The experiment was completed in one session of approximately 30 min.

Materials.   Ninety-six target words were embedded in single line sentences. The stimulus list consisted of 48 words with CV initial syllables and 48 words with CVC initial syllables. The list incorporated the words from Ferrand et al. (1997), which were originally compiled by Treiman and Danis (1988) and Bradley, Sanchez-Casas, & Garcia-Albea (1993), as well as a selection of words from Finney et al. (1996). Seven words from the initial stimulus list were eliminated due to their unfamiliarity to our population of readers (mean frequency = 1 per million). Of the remaining 89 target words, 43 had CV initial syllables and 46 had CVC initial syllables. On average, these CV initial words occurred 37 times per million, ranging from zero to 210, and the CVC words occurred 24 times per million, ranging from zero to 203 (Francis & Kučera, 1982). Target words ranged in length from 5 to 10 letters with a mean of 7 letters.

Design.   Each participant read every target word once, with each target preceded by one of the three possible primes (incongruent, congruent, or neutral). Experimental condition was defined by the type of prime (neutral, syllabically incongruent, or syllabically congruent) that preceded a target with either an initial CV or CVC syllable in the 2 × 3 factorial design (see Table 2). Note that in congruent conditions 3 and 6, the prime was the complete first syllable of the target. In the incongruent conditions 2 and 5, the prime consisted of one letter more (in the CV case) or less (in the CVC case) than the first syllable. Conditions 1 and 4 provided an unrelated control prime for comparison with their respective incongruent condition. Conditions 1–3 were modelled on Ferrand et al.'s Experiment 5 and Conditions 4–6 followed their Experiment 1.

All letter primes comprised either the first two or three letters of the target word and a series of dashes, so that the display of the prime and the target were of equal length. The control, non-letter prime contained only a series of dashes equal in length to the target word. Each participant read 89 experimental sentences randomly interspersed with 27 unrelated filler items that also included a fast-priming display change.

Data analysis procedures.   The purpose of the experiment was to investigate whether syllables were part of the phonological representation that accompanied lexical access. Fixation time on the target was the dependent variable, and the structure of the first syllable of the target (CV or CVC) was treated as a within participants factor and a between items factor. Prime type was treated as a within factor in both the participant and item analyses. First fixation duration and single fixation duration are the two fixation time measures reported, since these are most heavily influenced by early word recognition processes. *First fixation* is a measure of the mean time spent reading the first time the eye lands on the target word. This includes words processed in a single fixation as well as the first of multiple fixations. *Single fixation* is a measure of the time spent reading words that received only one fixation.

Consistent with most eye movement research (Rayner, 1998), pre-determined cutoffs were used to trim the data. Fixations on the target word that were under 120 ms were eliminated from the analysis since such short fixations do not seem to reflect cognitive processing of the target word (Rayner, 1998; Rayner & Pollatsek, 1987). To eliminate overly long fixations, fixations over 600 ms were excluded from the analysis. Approximately 3% of the data were lost due to these cutoffs and track losses. In addition, trials were excluded from the analyses for the following reasons: if no fixations were made on the target word before the eyes moved past it to the right, if the participant blinked while within the target region, if the eye regressed out of the target region, and, most commonly, if the display change occurred before the eyes landed in the target region. Substantial amounts of data are customarily lost in fast-priming experiments for these reasons. Following standard practice in display change experiments (Sereno & Rayner, 1992), we set a criterion to ensure that each subject contributed an adequate number of data points, deciding to analyse the data for all subjects who contributed at least 67% usable data. In addition to the 27 participants whose data were analysed, another 12 subjects were run in the experiment, but replaced because their data did not meet the 67% criterion. The usable data were subjected to analyses of variance (ANOVA) using variability due to participants (F_1) and items (F_2). In the participants analyses, target type (CV or CVC-initial syllable) and prime type were treated as within factors. In the items analyses, target type was treated as a between factor and prime type was treated as a within factor.

Results

Planned comparisons of fixation time on target words that were preceded by syllabically incongruent and congruent primes tested whether a prime

TABLE 2
Experiment 1: Example stimuli

	Prime	*Target*
Condition 1		
cv-control	- - - - - -	vagrant
Condition 2		
cv-incongruent	vag - - - -	vagrant
Condition 3		
cv-congruent	va - - - - -	vagrant
Condition 4		
cvc-control	- - - - - -	balcony
Condition 5		
cvc-incongruent	ba - - - - -	balcony
Condition 6		
cvc-congruent	bal - - - -	balcony

that included the target's first syllable boundary facilitated word recognition more than a prime that violated the syllable boundary. In the case of CVC targets, we assumed that the CVC prime would facilitate word recognition more than a CV prime, and that the separate contributions of syllabic congruency and number of letters could not be identified in these conditions. Given the difficulty that Schiller (2000) had in replicating Ferrand et al. (1997), we expected the data from the CV targets to follow any of three possible patterns. If shorter fixation times were found in the congruent than in the incongruent condition for CV targets (i.e., when a prime contained only the first two letters of the target), it would indicate that syllable information was used during word recognition. Such a result would be consistent with the results from Experiment 5 by Ferrand et al. (1997), and it would suggest that the phonological representations used in silent reading have a hierarchical structure. In contrast, finding shorter fixation times in the incongruent condition for CV targets would suggest that it is the number of shared, initial segments that influences the priming effect, per Schiller (2000). This result would support theories that propose a flat, linear structure for the phonological representations used in reading. The third possible finding would be the appearance of comparable fixation times in the incongruent and congruent conditions for CV targets accompanied by faster fixation times in the congruent than in the incongruent conditions for CVC targets. That pattern of data could reflect both syllable and segment effects, in which the cost of having one less letter in the congruent condition is offset by a benefit from syllabic congruency for the CV targets.

First fixation.   Table 3 shows the mean first fixation times on the target word in each of the prime conditions for CV and CVC target words. The main effect of prime was significant in the participants and the items analyses, $F_1(2, 52) = 16.03$, $MSe = 640$, $p < .0001$, and $F_2(2, 174) = 18.71$, $MSe = 937$, $p < .0001$. First fixations on targets that were preceded by neutral primes were 23 ms longer on average than fixations on targets

TABLE 3
Experiment 1: Measures of processing time on the target word (ms)

	Neutral prime	Incongruent prime	Congruent prime
First fixation			
CV targets	325	299	304
CVC targets	329	312	300
Single fixation			
CV targets	369	344	346
CVC targets	367	356	342

preceded by letter primes, which indicates that the fast-priming technique was operating properly. When the analysis was restricted to syllabically incongruent and congruent conditions, the main effect of prime congruency was not significant in either analysis, both $Fs < 1$. An interaction of target type and prime congruency did appear significant in both analyses, $F_1(1, 26) = 5.17$, $MSe = 412$, $p < .05$, and $F_2(1, 87) = 6.60$, $MSe = 760$, $p < .015$, such that only CVC targets were read faster when preceded by a congruent prime. Because the test for the interaction of target type and congruency is also the test for a main effect of number of letters in a prime, these results indicate that primes containing more letters provided more facilitation. The effect of number of letters in the CVC words was confirmed by simple effects tests, $F_1(1, 26) = 4.15$, $MSe = 463$, $p < .05$, $F_2(1, 45) = 5.69$, $MSe = 845$, $p < .05$. The simple effects tests were not significant for CV targets, $F_1(1, 26) = 1.02$, $MSe = 453$, $p > .3$, $F_2(1, 45) = 1.48$, $MSe = 668$, $p > .2$.

Single fixation duration. The means for targets that were read in a single fixation appear in Table 3. All participants contributed some single fixations to these means, but not all items did. Therefore, in the items analyses it was necessary to substitute in the condition mean for any items that had no single fixations, and adjust the degrees of freedom accordingly. The main effect of prime type appeared significant in the participants analyses, $F_1(2, 52) = 7.91$, $MSe = 1150$, $p < .001$, but not in the items analyses, $F_2(2, 167) = 1.61$, $MSe = 1320$, $p > .20$. Single fixations on targets that were preceded by neutral primes were 22 ms longer on average than fixations on targets preceded by letter primes, which indicates that the fast-priming technique was operating properly. When the analysis was restricted to syllabically incongruent and congruent conditions, the main effect of prime congruency was not significant in either analysis, $F_1(1, 26) = 1.19$, $MSe = 937$, $p > .25$, $F_2 < 1$. An interaction between target type and prime congruency (i.e., the effect of number of letters in a prime) was significant in the items analyses, $F_2(1, 80) = 5.07$, $MSe = 1421$, $p < .05$, but did not reach significance in the participants analysis, $F_1(1, 26) = 1.90$, $MSe = 937$, $p > .15$. Overall, these results were consistent with first fixation measures.

Discussion

Shorter first fixation times were observed for both CV and CVC syllable-initial target words which were preceded by a letter prime as compared with a prime of irrelevant symbols. This finding is consistent with the Ferrand et al. studies, and not too surprising. The absence of a syllable effect was also predicted from Ferrand et al., as they located that effect in the preparation of articulatory codes used in the naming task and no overt articulation was involved in the current experiment. The first fixation and single fixation data also indicate, however, that more letters in a prime offered more benefit, since first fixation times were 9 ms shorter on average when participants received a three letter prime as compared with a two letter prime.[1] The observation that priming effects corresponded to the number of relevant segments contained in the prime extends the findings of Schiller (2000) to word recognition in the context of silent reading. Interestingly, the effect size in this study was somewhat larger than that reported in most of Schiller's experiments.

In sum, Experiment 1 indicated that participants processed words more quickly when the target word was preceded by a three letter prime than a two letter prime, and no evidence was found for the inclusion of syllable information in the phonological representations used during reading. These results are consistent with the concept of a non-hierarchical phonological representation that includes information about individual phonemes and their sequence. However, there are at least two reasons why the results of this experiment might not accurately reflect the processing of words during natural reading.

The first reason is that the data collected with the fast-priming technique might describe only the earliest parts of the word recognition process, since processing starts from zero when the eye enters the target region. In normal reading, however, abstract letter codes and phonological information are processed while the target is in parafoveal view, i.e., processing begins well before the eye lands on the target (Rayner, 1998; Liversedge & Findlay, 2000). Second, it seems possible that the fast-priming technique itself had an effect on the word recognition processes that were observed. Since natural silent reading allows parafoveal processing of upcoming words, it is possible that being denied a parafoveal view of the target encouraged heavier reliance on foveal word recognition processes than would be expected in a normal reading situation. Therefore, Experiment 2 sought evidence for syllable structure in word recognition by collecting eye movement data using a parafoveal preview technique that is less disruptive to normal reading processes.

---

[1] The gaze duration means for the congruent and incongruent conditions followed a similar pattern. However, neither the main effect of congruency nor the interaction was significant in our analyses. Since first fixation and single fixation durations tap the earliest stages of word processing and because the effects are presumably quite subtle, we believe that these early measures are the appropriate ones. We attribute the loss of reliability to the variability associated with gaze durations due to (1) differences across participants in the frequency of additional first pass fixations on a word and (2) variability of second fixation times (Pollatsek et al., 1992).

EXPERIMENT 2: PARAFOVEAL PREVIEW

Experiment 2 was conducted with two main purposes. First, it further tested for a syllable level in the phonological representations used during reading. Alternatively, it could replicate the findings in Experiment 1 and, thereby, confirm that it is segment information alone which is used for word identification. The design here basically followed Ferrand et al. (1997), such that target words with CV and CVC initial syllables were preceded by syllabically congruent and incongruent previews. When a sentence appeared on the screen, the target region initially contained either a congruent or incongruent preview, which was replaced by the target word when the eye crossed an invisible boundary immediately before the target word.

Method

Participants. Twenty-eight students at the University of Massachusetts were paid or received experimental credit to participate in the experiment. All were native English speakers with normal vision and naive as to the purpose of the experiment.

Apparatus and procedure. The apparatus and procedure used in this experiment were the same as described in Experiment 1, with the following exceptions. Data were collected using a Fourward Technologies Generation V Dual Purkinje eyetracker. Instead of a prime, a 2 or 3 letter preview appeared in the target region when a participant began to read each sentence. Presentation of the full target word was triggered during reading by a saccade into the target region, as the eyes crossed an invisible boundary placed after the last letter of the preceding word.

Materials. Forty-eight target words were each embedded in two single line sentences. The stimulus list consisted of 24 words with CV initial syllables and 24 words with CVC initial syllables. The list mainly included words from Ferrand et al. (1997), along with a few words from Finney et al. (1996) to replace the items removed from the analysis in Experiment 1. On average, the CV initial words occurred 47 times per million, ranging from 1 to 210 per million, and the CVC words occurred 28 times per million, ranging from 0 to 203 per million (Francis & Kučera, 1982). Targets words ranged in length from 5 to 10 letters with a mean of 7 letters.

Design. As in Experiment 1 by Ferrand et al. (1997), each participant read every target word twice, once in the incongruent and once the congruent condition. Preview condition and sentence context were counter-balanced in two stimulus lists, such that 14 participants saw the target preceded by an incongruent preview in sentence context A and later saw the same target preceded by the congruent preview in sentence context B, while the other 14 participants saw the inverse. Within a stimulus list, participants were randomly assigned to a counterbalancing condition that determined whether an incongruent or congruent preview preceded the first presentation of the target. Trials were randomized in two blocks, such that all the targets were read once (preceded by either CV or CVC previews) and then read again in their alternate sentence contexts in the second block of trials.

Experimental condition (see Table 4) was defined by the type of preview (a syllabically incongruent preview or a syllabically congruent preview) that preceded either an initial CV or initial CVC target word, yielding four conditions in a 2 × 2 factorial design. Additionally, targets were presented in two different sentence contexts, which was treated as a between factor for participants and a within factor for items. Two stimulus lists were used, such that the target was read for the first time in Context A by one half of the subjects and read for the first time in Context B by the other half of the subjects. Trials were randomised for each participant and fully counter-balanced across participants. The results presented in this paper were restricted to the first presentation of each target word, for reasons discussed below. Preview conditions 1 and 2 comprised the first presentation of the CV targets and conditions 3 and 4 the first presentation of the CVC targets. In congruent condition 2, the preview was the complete first syllable of a CV-initial target (two letters), while in condition 4 the preview was the complete first syllable of a CVC-initial target (three letters). In the incongruent conditions, the preview consisted of one letter more in the CV case (three letters) or one letter less in the CVC case (two letters) than the first syllable.

All previews were comprised of either the first two or three letters of the target word followed by a placeholder (_), one Greek character (π), and a random combination of xs and ws which made the preview and the target appear to be of equal length. Each participant read 96 experimental sentences and 32 unrelated fillers, all of which included a parafoveal preview display change.

Data analysis procedures.   The data were subjected to similar proce-dures as were followed in Experiment 1, with two substantive exceptions. First, we restricted the analyses to trials in which the fixation prior to landing on the target was launched within 8 or fewer characters of the target region, so that only trials in which parafoveal processing was possible were included (Rayner, McConkie, & Zola, 1980; Rayner, Well, Pollatsek, & Bertera, 1982). Second, we found that the data from the second reading of the targets was substantially noisier than the data from

TABLE 4
Experiment 2: Example stimuli

	Preview	Target
CV-initial Target		
Incongruent Preview (1)	dev_πx	device
Congruent Preview (2)	de_πxw	device
CVC-initial Target		
Incongruent Preview (3)	ba_πxwx	balcony
Congruent Preview (4)	bal_πxw	balcony

the first reading.[2] Therefore, the analyses were restricted to the first block of data for each participant in order to avoid introducing noise from possible repetition priming effects. Approximately 2% of the data were lost due to preset cutoffs and track losses. Additionally, trials were excluded from the analyses for the following reasons: if no fixations were made on the target word before the eyes moved past it to the right, if the participant blinked while within the target region, if the display change happened before the eyes clearly fixated in the target region, or if the eye regressed out of the target region. As in Experiment 1, participants who contributed at least 67% usable data were included in the analyses. In addition to the 28 participants whose data were analysed, another 10 subjects were run in the experiment, but replaced because their data did not meet the criterion. The usable data were subjected to analyses of variance (ANOVA) using variability due to participants (F_1) and items (F_2). In the participants analysis, target type and preview congruency were treated as within factors while list was a between factor. In the items analysis, list and preview were within factors while target type was a between factor. All significant results and theoretically relevant non-significant results are reported.

Results

First fixation.   Table 5 shows the mean first fixation times on the target word in each of the prime conditions for CV and CVC target words. The main effect of syllable congruency was significant in the participants and the items analyses, $F_1(1, 26) = 5.60$, $MSe = 739$, $p < .05$, and $F_2(1, 46) = 4.06$, $MSe = 1360$, $p < .05$. First fixation time on targets that were preceded by incongruent previews was 13 ms longer on average than time spent on targets preceded by congruent previews, suggesting that information about

---

[2] No significant differences appeared in any of the four conditions during the second reading of the target words.

syllable structure was processed parafoveally and used in word recognition. The interaction of syllable type (CV or CVC) and congruency provided a test for the effect of number of letters in the preview, but that interaction was not significant in either analysis, both $Fs < 0.5$.

The effect of stimulus list also accounted for a substantial amount of the variance in the items analyses, $F_2(1, 46) = 9.60$, $MSe = 14{,}335$, $p < .003$, but not in the participants analysis, $F_1(1, 23) = 1.22$, $MSe = 5390$, $p > .25$, and did not enter into any interaction. The strength of the effect was unexpected, but probably irrelevant to the question at hand. All targets were presented in both sentence contexts with congruent and incongruent previews, and a comparable congruency effect of 11 ms appeared in both lists.

Single fixation. The means for targets that were read in a single fixation appear in Table 5. Because not all participants and not all items contributed to these means, it was necessary to substitute in the condition mean for any participants or items that had no single fixations, and adjust the degrees of freedom accordingly. The main effect of syllable congruency was significant in the participants analysis, $F_1(1, 23) = 6.22$, $MSe = 753$, $p < .05$, but did not reach significance in the items analysis, $F_2(1, 41) = 2.56$, $MSe = 2518$, $p = .11$. Single fixations on targets that were preceded by incongruent previews were 13 ms longer on average than fixations on targets preceded by congruent previews. The interaction of syllable type (CV or CVC) and congruency served as a test for the effect of number of letters in the preview, and that interaction was not significant in either analysis, $F_1(1, 23) = 1.04$, $MSe = 644$, $p > .30$, and $F_2(1, 41) < 1$.

The effect of stimulus list also accounted for a substantial amount of the variance in the items analyses, $F_2(1, 41) = 19.16$, $MSe = 1409$, $p < .0001$, but not in the participants analysis, $F_1(1, 23) = 1.19$, $MSe = 76099$, $p > .25$, and did not enter into any interaction.

TABLE 5
Experiment 2: Measures of processing time on
the target word (ms)

	Preview	
	Incongruent	*Congruent*
First fixation		
CV targets	284	271
CVC targets	287	275
Single fixation		
CV targets	300	292
CVC targets	307	289

Discussion

The data collected from measures of first fixation and single fixation time indicate a syllable congruency effect, such that shorter fixation times were observed for targets preceded by syllabically congruent previews as compared with syllabically incongruent previews.[3] This finding offers clear evidence that readers acquired syllable information parafoveally and, therefore, suggests that a syllabic level of phonological representation was activated in the early stages of word recognition. It extends the findings of Ferrand et al. (1997) to demonstrate that syllable structure is detected and represented in the early word recognition processes that occur while reading connected text. While Ferrand et al. (1997) observed a syllable effect in word naming (but not lexical decision), data from the present experiment indicate that syllable effects can arise during silent reading. This suggests that the locus of the syllable effect may not be restricted to audible, articulatory output processes. Interestingly, no effects of number of letters in the preview were found.

As in Ferrand et al. (1997), a congruency effect was found for both CV and CVC-initial target words. The data from CV-initial targets provide the strongest evidence for the representation of syllable information in word recognition. The congruent preview for the CV words had one less letter than the incongruent preview, yet it was the congruent preview that showed the most facilitation of the target.

In sum, the results from Experiment 2 indicate the salience of syllable structure in word recognition. This finding implies that the phonological representations used during silent reading have a hierarchical structure that includes syllable information, and that these representations are constructed quite early in the word recognition process.

General Discussion

The current experiments examined whether syllabically congruent primes could facilitate word recognition during silent reading in English. Whereas previous research used standard laboratory tasks to study syllable effects (e.g., naming and lexical decision), these experiments are the first to investigate whether advance syllable information can affect the time spent reading words embedded in sentence contexts. With that in mind, the findings presented here should be considered preliminary. Experiment 1 failed to find evidence for the processing of syllable information when the prime and target were presented foveally. However, Experiment 2 did

---

[3] The gaze duration means followed a similar pattern. The main effect of congruency failed to reach significance, however, in the participants analysis and the items analysis. Again, we attribute the loss of reliability to the greater variability of gaze durations.

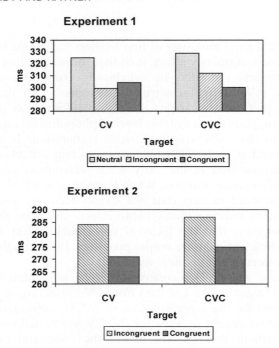

Figure 1. Experiments 1 and 2: First fixation durations for CV-initial and CVC-initial targets.

demonstrate a syllable effect, such that readers' first fixation durations on the target were shorter when the preview was syllabically congruent than when it was incongruent. The finding of a syllable effect in Experiment 2 is surprising, given past research. Syllable effects tend to appear in languages that are syllable-timed and have regular syllable structure, such as Spanish, French, and Mandarin Chinese (Carreiras & Perea, 2002; Chen, Lin & Ferrand, 2003; Ferrand, Segui, & Grainger, 1996). In stress-timed languages (such as English) syllable effects in visually presented words have appeared inconsistently, and only in tasks involving speech production (Ferrand et al., 1997; cf. Schiller, 2000). Thus, it is notable that the proficient readers in Experiment 2 did appear to represent syllable level information during silent reading.

The question of whether syllable information could facilitate word recognition was posed in order to clarify some broad issues in reading theory, such as the structure of phonological representations during reading and the similarity of those representations to the ones used for the processing of spoken language. Two views about the nature of phonological representations in silent reading were presented in the introduction. The traditional, linear view contends that phonological representations mirror the structure of the orthography from which they are built, i.e., they consist of strings of phonemes that code the individual speech sounds that the letters represent. The hierarchical view, in contrast, contends that phonological representations are multi-layered descriptions of a word's phonology with various sublexical levels that represent syllable as well as segment information. These two views of phonological representation during reading predict different patterns of experimental results. According to the linear view, the data should have indicated segment effects (such that a prime with more segments provided stronger facilitation of the target), but no syllable effects (as when a syllabically congruent prime provides stronger facilitation of the target). The hierarchical view, in contrast, predicts the appearance of syllable effects as well as segment effects. A finding of syllable effects in word recognition would, then, be incompatible with the linear view and lend support to the contention that the phonological representations in reading are very similar to those used in spoken word recognition (Berent & Perfetti, 1995). Were that the case, then a parsimonious model of reading would suggest that word recognition in reading is routinely achieved through systems used primarily for processing spoken language (Frost, 1998; Perfetti, 1999), as opposed to accessing word meaning directly from orthographic information.

The main finding of interest in these experiments was a syllable effect in word recognition during silent reading of connected text (Experiment 2), which extends the findings of Ferrand et al. (1997). Multi-syllable words were read faster when preceded by a parafoveal preview that shared the initial letters of exactly the first syllable of the target word, as compared to a preview that had one more or one less letter. This result indicates that syllable information was specified in the representations that were constructed during word recognition and, thus, supports the hierarchical view. However, when congruent and incongruent primes were presented foveally using a fast-priming technique in Experiment 1, no evidence was found for syllable effects. Rather, it appeared that primes with the greater number of segments provided more facilitation. This result extends the findings of Schiller (2000) to word recognition in silent reading and appears to support the traditional, linear view of phonological representation. Hence, the results of the two experiments seem inconsistent.

The following discussion addresses the apparent contradiction between the syllable effect found in Experiment 2 and the segment effect found in Experiment 1. A review of findings from fast-priming and parafoveal preview experiments (Rayner, 1998) suggests that the two techniques might yield different reading environments and tap different aspects of the word recognition process. Fast-priming experiments have found semantic priming effects as well as orthographic letter priming and homophone priming effects. Preview experiments, however, have found evidence for orthographic and phonological parafoveal processing of upcoming targets, but have failed to find evidence of parafoveal semantic processing. These findings suggest the possibility that the display-change techniques used in Experiments 1 and 2 gave rise to reading experiences which differed in some important ways. Understanding the contribution of those differences to the seemingly disparate findings might help identify some of the ways that phonological representations are used during word recognition.

In the fast-priming experiment (Experiment 1), nonsense characters appeared in the target region while participants read the words that preceded the target in the sentence. Since no relevant parafoveal information was available, the earliest parts of the word recognition process began at the same time as the fixation time measures for the target. In other words, eye movement data were collected from the moment readers began processing the target word, which permitted the observation of segment effects. In Experiment 2, however, readers did receive preview information about the target word. Experimental evidence suggests that abstract letter information and phonological information are processed before the eyes land on the target word, at least in reading tasks that permit a parafoveal view of the target (Hadley & Healy, 1991; McConkie & Zola, 1979; Pollatsek et al., 1992; Rayner, McConkie, & Zola, 1980). Because preview information was available, the processing of letter features and initial phonemes occurred before the eyes landed in the target region, i.e. *before* fixation time in the target region was measured. In other words, the eye movement data in this second experiment were collected later in the word recognition process and, so, would not be as likely to include early identification processes of the initial letters and phonemes. Therefore, any segment effects that might have occurred in Experiment 2 would be expected to appear while the target was in parafoveal view, i.e., before the onset of fixation time measures for the target word.

A further examination of the distinct task demands that accompany each display-change technique can also explain why syllable effects were not observed in Experiment 1. It might be useful to recall which types of tasks, discussed in the introduction, consistently yielded syllable effects. Using a variety of paradigms, research in English has found syllable effects with experimental tasks that involved speech production or storing phonological information in memory, accompanied by the assembly of phonological codes. Conversely, syllable effects appear inconsistently, or not at all, in experiments with tasks that do not require spoken output or memory storage. This pattern suggests that syllabic structure might guide the generation of articulatory codes which might, in turn, serve as the basis for a range of mental operations that require phonological coding.

Because all data were collected during silent reading, speech production was not a factor in either experiment. However, the type of display-change technique clearly affected the demands that the reading task placed on short-term memory. In Experiment 2, word identification began parafoveally. Readers needed to preserve the information from the preview during a saccade in order to integrate it with the foveally presented target word. As suggested by Pollatsek et al. (1992), this information could be held in memory in a phonological form during the 20–50 ms required to complete a saccade to the target region. In Experiment 1, however, the prime and target were presented foveally in the same location, so no memory storage was needed to preserve the form of the prime. Thus, it seems likely that a syllable effect did not appear in the fast-priming data because the phonological information in the prime did not need to be held in memory during the lexical access process.

The above discussion also holds implications for when phonological representations are constructed and for what purpose. Segment effects, which arise very early in the word recognition process, are consistent with a concept of word recognition that involves the initial letters and phonemes activating a neighbourhood of lexical candidates. In that case, a three letter preview would activate a smaller number of candidates than a two letter preview (see Schiller, 2000), which could shorten the overall time required to activate the full neighbourhood before continuing the lexical access process. A syllable level of representation must also be available early in the word recognition process, since it preserved parafoveally acquired phonological information during the saccade that brings the word into foveal view. Because syllable effects only appeared when it was necessary to hold the parafoveal information in memory, it seems possible that the representation of syllable information stems from the memory process. Once a word has been fixated, initial syllable information can be used to further restrict the number of activated candidates.

Two possible objections could be raised to the conclusion that syllable information is part of the phonological representation used during silent reading. The first point questions whether any of the effects we found are truly phonological. Admittedly, the one-to-one correspondence of phonemes to letters in our materials is a confound that raises the possibility that it was orthographic effects that were observed in these experiments. For example, the segment effects in Experiment 1 might have resulted from more orthographic overlap from a greater number of letter units, rather than from more phonological overlap from a greater number of phonemes. Unfortunately, that confound is present in the Ferrand et al. (1997) materials and the Schiller (2000) word naming experiments as well.

One might raise a similar objection to the claim that syllable effects are phonological. A reader's representation of orthography may contain information about syllable structure. After all, one purpose of orthography is to encode phonological information, which can be used to generate a representation of the word that can be held in memory for comprehension (Perfetti, 1999; Rayner, 1998; Slowiaczek & Clifton, 1980). However, there are several reasons to doubt that the syllable effects observed in Experiment 2 were solely orthographic in nature. First, the psychological reality of the syllable resides in the phonological system, as numerous studies of speech errors have clearly demonstrated. Consistent with those findings, Alvarez, Carreiras, and Perea's (2004 this issue) second experiment in Spanish offered evidence that the syllable information encoded in visually presented primes is phonological in nature. Second, behavioural research has yet to firmly establish the existence of a purely orthographic syllable in English. Although data from illusory conjunction experiments indicate that orthographically marked syllables establish perceptual boundaries within words, Prinzmetal and colleagues did not show that their syllable effect resided primarily in the orthographic system (Prinzmetal & Millis-Wright, 1984; Prinzmetal, Treiman, & Rho, 1986). Findings from these experiments were challenged by Seidenberg's (1987) experiments, which claimed that bigram troughs (e.g., low co-occurrence frequencies for intersyllabic bigrams) signalled syllable boundaries. In turn, the bigram trough hypothesis was not supported by experiments that used the Prinzmetal conjunction task to demonstrate sensitivity to syllable boundaries even in the absence of a bigram trough (Rapp, 1992). These experiments clearly suggest the presence of unspecified orthographic cues to syllable structure, but they have not established the existence of an orthographic syllable that exists independently of the phonological system. Third, cognitive neuroscience experiments have failed to find spatially distinct areas of orthographic processing (Herbster, Mintun, Nebes & Becker, 1997; Rumsey, Horwitz, Donohue, Nace, Maisog & Andreason, 1997). For example, PET data collected by Rumsey et al. (1997) during naming and lexical decision tasks with pseudowords and irregular words indicated that the phonological and orthographic systems used during reading appear active in similar brain regions. The lack of evidence for orthography-specific areas of activation poses a problem for claims that orthographic processes operate independently of phonological ones in normal readers. Thus, it seems reasonable to conclude that the syllable effects observed in Experiment 2 were primarily phonological in origin.

The second possible objection to the conclusion that syllable information is part of the phonological representation used during reading stems from the observation that this experiment delivers syllable information to readers 'on a platter', i.e., the previews were designed to convey information about the boundary of the first syllable. However, we are not claiming to demonstrate that readers routinely use syllable structure to recognise words. Rather, we think the findings from Experiment 2 indicate that *if* syllable information is available parafoveally, then the reader does encode it. Hence, there is a place in the pre-lexical phonological representation where the reader can encode syllable information. This point might be moot if such information were never available in the course of natural reading, but there are several situations in which syllable information would be available in readers' parafoveal vision. One example is when target words begin with high frequency bigrams or trigrams which could cue the reader to the first syllable boundary (RE.LATE). Processing RE as a phonological unit would facilitate lexical access by restricting the set of candidates to those words with the same first syllable, while processing RE as a morphological cue would interfere, as it does not function as a meaningful prefix in this word.[4] The high co-occurrence frequency of RE might register in the orthographic system, but the frequency rating itself is derived from the phonotactics of spoken language. Phonotactic constraints on syllable structure are also reflected in low frequency ratings for some bigrams that indicate a syllable boundary between two consonants, as in AD.MIT where /d/ is not allowed to precede a nasal (/m/) in the same syllable. Given these situations, we claim that readers use such syllable information when it is available, encoding it in a multi-layered phonological representation to facilitate processing when the word enters foveal view.

SUMMARY AND CONCLUSIONS

In sum, syllable effects appeared in the word recognition processes used during silent reading, which supports the hierarchical view of phonological representation in reading. This finding adds to a growing number of experiments in several different languages that indicate the presence of hierarchical phonological representations during reading (Berent et al., 2001; Carreiras & Perea, 2002; Chen et al., 2003; Ferrand et al., 1996). Given the mounting evidence for the specification of sublexical, syllable structure within the representation, and its appearance quite early in the word recognition process, researchers and educators might consider the implications of this information.

---

[4] In the subset of target words that have initial syllables which are also morphemes, the majority of these initial syllables functioned as pseudo-morphemes. It is unlikely that the few initial syllables which did contribute viable morphemic information were responsible for the effects observed in Experiment 2, as morphemic information does not appear to be obtained parafoveally in English (Kambe, 2004; Lima, 1987).

For example, although the dual route cascade (DRC) model (Coltheart, Rastle, Perry, Langdon, & Ziegler, 2001) is probably the most clearly elaborated model of word recognition at this time, it does not recognise the pre-lexical construction of any phonological representation, nor does it describe how a multi-layered phonological representation might arise. In that sense, there is little difference between the DRC model and PDP-type models (Seidenberg & McClelland, 1989; Seidenberg, Plaut, Petersen, McClelland, & McRae, 1994). Neither model includes a syllabic level of phonological representation, irrespective of whether it considers reading representations to be symbolic or emergent in nature. Word recognition models might be modified to include mechanisms through which syllable effects would arise, and this step could be taken well in advance of actually modelling the recognition of more complex words.

The findings presented here might also interest educators who are concerned about helping children learn to read complex, multisyllable words. Since several studies have found syllable effects in the silent reading of college students, it appears that these multi-layered phonological representations accompany proficient reading. Given that observation, it may be time to start teaching syllabification strategies, especially in the later elementary grades when Latinate words increasingly appear in content-area reading materials. Such instruction could provide students with effective tools for expanding their vocabulary through reading as well as support their comprehension of content information.

Finally, the results we presented suggest several conclusions. First, proficient adult readers routinely construct phonological representations while silently reading sentences. Second, these representations are built early in the word recognition process, since syllable effects appear during the first fixation on the target word in the second experiment. Third, these representations are multi-layered, as opposed to linear, and they specify information about word-initial segments and the organisation of those segments into syllables. Fourth, these representations are similar to those used in spoken word recognition, both in structure and in content. That similarity strongly suggests that the word recognition processes used in proficient reading are closely tied into, if not routed through, our spoken language systems.

REFERENCES

Álvarez, C.J., Carreiras, M., & Perea, M. (2004). Are syllables phonological units in visual word recognition? *Language and Cognitive Processes*, *19*, 427–452.

Besner, D. (1987). Phonology, lexical access in reading, and articulatory suppression: A critical review. *Quarterly Journal of Experimental Psychology*, *39A*, 467–478.

Berent, I., Bouissa, R., & Tuller, B. (2001). The effect of shared structure and content on reading nonwords: Evidence for a CV skeleton. *Journal of Experimental Psychology: Learning, Memory, and Cognition, 27*, 1042–1057.

Berent, I., & Perfetti, C.A. (1995). A rose is a REEZ: The two cycles model of phonology assembly in reading English. *Psychological Review, 102*, 146–184.

Berent, I., Shimron, J., & Vaknin, V. (2001). Phonological constraints on reading: Evidence from the obligatory contour principle. *Journal of Memory and Language, 44*, 644–665.

Birch, S., Pollatsek, A., & Kingston, J. (1998). The nature of sound codes accessed by visual language. *Journal of Memory and Language, 38*, 70–93.

Bradley, D.C., Sanchez-Casas, R.M., & Garcia-Albea, J.E. (1993). The status of the syllable in perception of Spanish and English. *Language and Cognitive Processes, 8*, 197–233.

Bruck, M., Treiman, R., & Caravolas, M. (1995). Role of the syllable in the processing of spoken English: Evidence from a nonword comparison task. *Journal of Experimental Psychology: Human Perception and Performance, 21*, 469–479.

Butler, B., & Hains, S. (1979). Individual differences in word recognition latency. *Memory and Cognition, 7*, 68–76.

Caramazza, A., & Miceli, G. (1990). The structure of graphemic representations. *Cognition, 37*, 243–297.

Carreiras, M., & Perea, M. (2002). Masked priming effects with syllabic neighbors in a lexical decision task. *Journal of Experimental Psychology: Human Perception and Performance, 28*, 1228–1242.

Chen, J.Y., Lin, W.C., & Ferrand, L. (2003). Masked priming of the syllable in Mandarin Chinese speech production. *Chinese Journal of Psychology, 45*, 107–120.

Clements, G.N., & Keyser, S.J. (1983). *CV Phonology.* Cambridge, MA: MIT Press.

Coltheart, M., Rastle, K., Perry, C., Langdon, R., & Ziegler, J. (2001). DRC: A dual route cascade model of visual word recognition and reading aloud. *Psychological Review, 108*, 204–256.

Cutler, A., & Clifton, C., Jr. (1984). The use of prosodic information in word recognition. In H. Bouma & D.G. Bouwhuis (Eds.), *Attention and performance X* (pp. 183–196). Hove, UK: Lawrence Erlbaum Associates Ltd.

Cutler, A., Mehler, J., Norris, D., & Segui, J. (1986). The syllable's differing role in the segmentation of French and English. *Journal of Memory and Language, 25*, 385–400.

Eriksen, C.W., Pollock, M.D., & Montague, W.E. (1970). Implicit speech? Mechanisms in perceptual encoding. *Journal of Experimental Psychology, 84*, 502–507.

Ferrand, F. (2000). Reading aloud polysyllabic words and non-words: The syllable length effect re-examined. *Psychonomic Bulletin and Review, 7*, 142–148.

Ferrand, F., & New, B. (2003). Syllabic length effects in visual word recognition and naming. *Acta Psychologica, 113*, 167–183.

Ferrand, F., Segui, J., & Grainger, J. (1996). Masked priming of word and picture naming: The role of syllabic units. *Journal of Memory and Language, 35*, 708–723.

Ferrand, F., Segui, J., & Humphreys, G.W. (1997). The syllable's role in word naming. *Memory and Cognition, 25*, 458–470.

Finney, S., Protopapas, A., & Eimas, P.D. (1996). Attentional allocation to syllables in American English. *Journal of Memory and Language, 35*, 893–909.

Forster, K.I., & Chambers, S. (1973). Lexical access and naming time. *Journal of Verbal Learning and Verbal Behavior, 12*, 627–635.

Fowler, C.A., Treiman, R., & Gross, J. (1993). The structure of English syllables and polysyllables. *Journal of Memory and Language, 32*, 115–140.

Francis, W.N., & Kučera, H. (1982). *Frequency analysis of English usage: Lexicon and grammar.* Boston: Houghton Mifflin.

Frauenfelder, U.H., & Lahiri, A. (1989). Understanding words and word recognition: Can phonology help? In W. Marslen-Wilson (Ed.), *Lexical representation and process.* Cambridge, MA: MIT Press.

Frederiksen, J.R., & Kroll, J.F. (1976). Spelling and sound: Approaches to the internal lexicon. *Journal of Experimental Psychology: Human Perception and Performance, 2,* 361–379.

Frost, R. (1998). Toward a strong phonological theory of visual word recognition: True issues and false trails. *Psychological Bulletin, 123,* 71–99.

Hadley, J.A., & Healy, A.F. (1991). When are reading units larger than the letter? A refinement of the unitization reading model. *Journal of Experimental Psychology: Learning, Memory, and Cognition, 17,* 1062–1073.

Herbster, A., Mintun, M., Nebes, R., & Becker, J. (1997). Regional cerebral blood flow during word and nonword reading. *Human Brain Mapping, 5,* 84–92.

Henderson, J.M., Dixon, P., Petersen, A., Twilley, L.C., & Ferreira, F. (1995). Evidence for the use of phonological representations during transsaccadic word recognition. *Journal of Experimental Psychology: Human Perception and Performance, 21,* 82–97.

Jared, D., & Seidenberg, M.S. (1990). Naming multisyllabic words. *Journal of Experimental Psychology: Human Perception and Performance, 16,* 92–105.

Kambe, G. (2004). Parafoveal processing of prefixed words during eye fixations in reading: Evidence against morphological influences on parafoveal processing. *Perception and Psychophysics, 66,* 279–292.

Klapp, S.T., Anderson, W.G., & Berrian, R.W. (1973). Implicit speech in reading, reconsidered. *Journal of Experimental Psychology, 100,* 368–374.

Lee, H., Rayner, K., & Pollatsek, A. (1999). The time course of phonological, semantic, and orthographic coding in reading: Evidence from the fast-priming technique. *Psychonomic Bulletin and Review, 6,* 624–634.

Lee, H., Rayner, K., & Pollatsek, A. (2001). The relative contribution of consonants and vowels to word recognition during silent reading. *Journal of Memory and Language, 44,* 189–205.

Lesch, M., & Pollatsek, A. (1998). Evidence for the use of assembled phonology in accessing the meaning of printed words. *Journal of Experimental Psychology: Learning, Memory, and Cognition, 24,* 573–592.

Lima, S.D. (1987). Morphological analysis in sentence reading. *Journal of Memory and Language, 26,* 84–99.

Liversedge, S.P., & Findlay, J.M. (2000). Saccadic eye movements and cognition. *Trends in Cognitive Sciences, 4,* 6–13.

McConkie, G.W., & Zola, D. (1979). Is visual information integrated across successive fixations in reading? *Perception and Psychophysics, 25,* 221–224.

Perfetti, C.A. (1999). Comprehending written language: A blueprint of the reader. In C.M. Brown & P. Hagoort (Eds.) *The neurocognition of language* (pp. 167–208). New York: Oxford University Press.

Perfetti, C.A., Zhang, S., & Berent, I. (1992). Reading in English and Chinese: Evidence for a "universal" phonological principle. In L. Katz (Ed.), *Orthography, phonology, morphology, and meaning* (Vol. 94, pp. 227–248). Amsterdam: Elsevier.

Pollatsek, A., Lesch, M., Morris, R.K., & Rayner, R. (1992). Phonological codes are used in integrating information across saccades in word identification and reading. *Journal of Experimental Psychology: Learning, Memory, and Cognition, 18,* 148–162.

Prinzmetal, W., & Millis-Wright, M. (1984). Cognitive and linguistic factors affect visual feature integration. *Cognitive Psychology, 16,* 305–340.

Prinzmetal, W., Treiman, R., & Rho, S.H. (1986). How to see a reading unit. *Journal of Memory and Language, 25,* 461–475.

Rapp, B.C. (1992). The nature of sublexical orthographic organization: The bigram trough hypothesis examined. *Journal of Memory and Language, 31*, 33–53.

Rayner, K. (1975). The perceptual span and peripheral cues in reading. *Cognitive Psychology, 7*, 65–81.

Rayner, K. (1998). Eye movements in reading and information processing: 20 years of research. *Psychological Bulletin, 124*, 372–422.

Rayner, K., & Balota, D.A. (1989). Parafoveal preview effects and lexical access during eye fixations in reading. In W. Marslen-Wilson (Ed.), *Lexical representation and process.* Cambridge, MA: MIT Press.

Rayner, K., McConkie, G.W., & Zola, D. (1980) Integrating information across eye movements. *Cognitive Psychology, 12*, 206–226.

Rayner, K., & Pollatsek, A. (1987). Eye movements in reading: A tutorial review. In M. Coltheart (Ed.) *Attention and performance XII: Psychology of reading* (pp. 327–362). Hove, UK: Lawrence Erlbaum Associates Ltd.

Rayner, K., Sereno, S., Lesch, M., & Pollatsek, A. (1995). Phonological codes are automatically activated during reading: Evidence from an eye movement priming paradigm. *Psychological Science, 6*, 26–32.

Rayner, K., Well, A.D., Pollatsek, A., & Bertera, J.H. (1982). The availability of useful information to the right of fixation in reading. *Perception and Psychophysics, 31*, 537–550.

Rumsey, J., Horwitz, B., Donohue, B., Nace, K., Maisog, J., & Andreason, P. (1997). Phonological and orthographic components of word recognition: A PET – rCBF study. *Brain, 120*, 739–759.

Schiller, N.O. (2000). Single word production in English: The role of subsyllabic units during phonological encoding. *Journal of Experimental Psychology: Learning, Memory, and Cognition, 26*, 512–528.

Seidenberg, M.S. (1987). Sublexical structures in visual word recognition: Access units or orthographic redundancy? In M. Coltheart (Ed.), *Attention and performance XII: The psychology of reading.* Hove, UK: Lawrence Erlbaum Associates Ltd.

Seidenberg, M.S., & McClelland, J.L. (1989). A distributed, developmental model of word recognition and naming. *Psychological Review, 96*, 523–568.

Seidenberg, M.S., Plaut, D.C., Petersen, A.S., McClelland, J.L. & McRae, K. (1994). Nonword pronunciation and models of word recognition. *Journal of Experimental Psychology: Human Perception and Performance, 20*, 1177–1196.

Selkirk, E.O. (1982). The syllable. In H. van der Hulst & N. Smith (Eds.), *The structure of phonological representations.* Dordrecht: Foris.

Sereno, S.C., & Rayner, K. (1992). Fast priming during eye fixations in reading. *Journal of Experimental Psychology: Human Perception and Performance, 18*, 173–184.

Sevald, C.A., Dell, G.S., & Cole, J.S. (1995). Syllable structure in speech production: Are syllables chunks or schemas? *Journal of Memory and Language, 34*, 807–820.

Slowiaczek, M.L., & Clifton, C. (1980). Subvocalization and reading for meaning. *Journal of Verbal Learning and Verbal Behavior, 19*, 573–582.

Treiman, R., & Danis, C. (1988). Syllabification of intervocalic consonants. *Journal of Memory and Language, 29*, 66–85.

Treiman, R., Fowler, C.A., Gross, J., Berch, D., & Weatherston, S. (1995). Syllable structure of word structure? Evidence for onset and rime units with disyllabic and trisyllabic stimuli. *Journal of Memory and Language, 34*, 132–155.

APPENDIX A

Stimulus List for Experiment 1

Experiment 1: CV-targets

The military tribunal voted to *demote* the crazy major.

The inmate hoped for a *reversal* of the judge's decision.

The military's new *covert* mission provides weapons to the rebels.

Cassie added more *vanilla* to the pudding mixture.

Alice wanted to spend a *relaxing* day walking on the sandy beach.

Arthur thought about the *dilemma* for the rest of the day.

Sam quickly stirred the *tomato* soup on the stove so that it would not burn.

Ed traveled to Maine each *November* to fish for salmon.

Mary had invented a *device* for drying large amounts of fruit.

Edith bought a silk *sarong* at the market on the tropical island.

Our family enjoyed a *delicious* dinner last night.

Ben desperately tried to *remember* the name of the book he was reading.

Phillip practiced for his *recital* during spring break.

Andrea wanted to *divorce* her husband because he was a drunkard.

John quietly leaked a *report* about the toxic spill to the press.

The inspector hoped to *reveal* the criminal's identity within twenty-four hours.

George quickly grew to *depend* on his daughter's weekly visit.

Robert wanted to *demand* his money back from the store.

The child did not express any *remorse* for his barbarous crime.

Alan obviously hoped to *remain* on the tropical island for one more week.

Mike thoroughly enjoyed his *retirement* in sunny Florida.

Dora was careful to *select* the freshest produce available.

Erin initially tried to *relate* to the traumatic experience of the refugees.

Molly wanted a japanese *pagoda* for her garden in Ohio.

The candidates agreed to *debate* on national television.

The old farmer planted *tobacco* in his field every year.

Linda regularly made a *deposit* at the local bank every Tuesday.

Thomas gradually learned to *regard* his health more since his recovery.

The friendly cousins skiied *together* in the Rockies each winter.

Adam definitely hoped to *secure* a better job within the next year.

The dead squirrel started to *decay* on the hot road.

Maggie picked her mother a *tulip* from the garden.

The symptoms of his *psychosis* were dormant until he turned thirty.

Donna attempted to *record* the rock concert without being observed.

Allison started to plan her *vacation* after she got her first pay check.

Kyle's argument tried to *negate* the evidence presented by the prosecution.

The wine store had *chablis* on sale last week.

The street was littered with *debris* after the parade.

Sandy could feel the *vibration* of the floor when the dancers jumped.

The chorus hired another *soprano* after a week of auditions.

Sam suffered from *depression* for several years after his divorce.

Todd quickly forgave the *regretful* child and gave him a cookie.

Ginger was told to *declare* the value of her new jewelry to the customs officer.

The professor posed *socratic* questions to his puzzled students.

The geese started their *migration* to Canada each spring.

Carolyn improved the *nutrition* of her diet by taking several vitamins.

Jim promised to *refrain* from eating desserts while training for the match.
The goalie lunged to *deflect* the ball and prevent a score.

Experiment 1: CVC-targets

The students sat in the *balcony* on opening night.
Mary got most of her *calcium* from dairy products.
Julia's heart started to *palpitate* from the surprise of seeing her ex-husband.
Bob intended to *salvage* the moldings from the old house.
Sally often sprinkled *talcum* powder in her tennis shoes.
Frank always wore a *helmet* when riding his motorcycle.
Last year, Agnes broke her *pelvis* when she fell in the bathtub.
Beth used an expensive *filter* to purify the water that she drank at work.
Matt enjoyed hiking in the *wilderness* during the summer.
Jennifer swam with a *dolphin* on her vacation.
The airline had to *cancel* the flight to Alaska due to bad weather.
Jasper carried a *lantern* to light his path through the woods.
Candice lost another *sandal* on the bike trail this weekend.
Mark did not bother to *mention* the stock's decline to the prospective buyer.
Cindy chewed on the *pencil* that she used for her math homework.
Dorothy polished the *pendulum* of the old clock to remove the tarnish.
Calvin rewrote the *sentence* more than a dozen times.
Most teens have a *tendency* to wear too much make-up.
Johnathan hoped to *vindicate* the memory of his father.
Adam's illness was caused by an infected *tonsil* in his throat.
Several chronic injuries *hampered* Ed's training for the Olympics.
The car just needed a *simple* adjustment to its brakes.
Sean Connery was the most *masculine* of all the Bond actors.
Leslie bought the *destitute* couple a hot lunch.
Rick reluctantly chose a new *subject* for his science report.
Father Patrick performed the *baptism* of their first child.
Meredith always enjoyed *vodka* drinks in the summer.
Lisa bought another *magnet* for the refrigerator door.
The brilliant painter added *pigment* to intensify the color.
The patrol checked every *sector* for suspicious people.
Julie tried to study *cognitive* processing during jump-rope competitions.
Joey learned how to *segment* sentences in fourth grade.
The flares helped to *signal* the search party after the accident.
Lee wanted to *dictate* a letter to his new secretary.
The ring was a *symbol* of the couple's love for each other.
Scott received a *subsidy* for his rent in the housing project.
Keith glared at the *pompous* man from across the room.
A hungry bear might *tamper* with the new trash container.
The ambassador greeted the *sultan* heartily whenever they met.
The election did not deliver a *mandate* for either candidate.
Liz had felt quite *dismal* after that long night of drinking.
A computer picks the *random* numbers for the state lottery.
The governor closed the *mental* hospital in order to save money.
Cathy gently washed the *poplin* before making the pillows for the couch.
The secretary was *seldom* seen in the office before noon.
Tom's latest movie got *splendid* reviews from the local critics.

Brett eagerly paid the *ransom* that the kidnappers demanded.
George decided to give Mary a *pendant* for her birthday.

APPENDIX B

Stimulus lists for Experiment 2

List A: Block 1, CV-targets

The prisoner hoped for a quick *reversal* of the judge's decision.
Cassie tried adding more *vanilla* to the pudding mixture.
Alice hoped to spend a few *relaxing* days walking on a sandy beach.
Arthur thought about his economic *dilemma* for the rest of the day.
Mary was designing a clever *device* for drying large amounts of fruit.
Susan learned to make really *delicious* desserts in her cooking class.
Ben desperately wanted to *remember* the name of the book he was reading.
Phillip practiced for his piano *recital* during spring break.
Andrea told a lawyer that she wanted to *divorce* her husband.
Jonathan finally submitted his *report* to the environmental journal.
George quickly grew to *depend* on his daughter's weekly visit.
Older children tend to *select* the most advertised toys.
The teenager did not appear to feel *remorse* for his barbarous crime.
Alan obviously hoped he would be chosen to *remain* on the island.
Mike thoroughly enjoyed his *retirement* in sunny Florida.
The beach was filled with smelly *debris* left by the storm.
The candidates eventually agreed to *debate* on national television.
Linda regularly made a small *deposit* at the local bank every Tuesday.
Thomas gradually learned to *regard* his health more since his recovery.
The friendly cousins played *together* every week in the summer.
Adam trained for a year in order to *secure* a better job.
The dead squirrel started to *decay* on the hot road.
Many pioneers died during their *migration* to the west coast.
Allison started to plan a spring *vacation* in Bermuda.

List A: Block 1, CVC-targets

The students sat in the top *balcony* on opening night.
Sally often sprinkled some *talcum* powder in her tennis shoes.
Frank always wore his *helmet* when riding a motorcycle.
Beth purified her water with a good *filter* to make it taste better.
The doctor failed to improve the *mental* health of his patients.
Jennifer swam in the ocean with a *dolphin* last year.
The airline needed to *cancel* the flight to Alaska due to bad weather.
Jasper carried an old *lantern* to light his path through the woods.
Candice lost her blue *sandal* on the bike trail this weekend.
The puppy happily chewed the *pencil* that Cindy used for her math homework.
Calvin quickly rewrote the long *sentence* a dozen times.
Most teenagers have a strange *tendency* to wear too much make-up.
Adam's fever was caused by a bad *tonsil* infection.
A serious car crash *hampered* Ed's training for the Olympics.

The car only needed a *simple* adjustment to its brakes.
Leslie often bought the *destitute* couple a hot lunch.
Rick reluctantly chose a new *subject* for his science report.
Brian and Meredith always drank *vodka* in the summer.
Lisa shopped for a little *magnet* for the refrigerator door.
The brilliant painter added dark *pigment* to intensify the color.
Julie wanted to study *cognitive* processing during jump-rope competitions.
Joey learned several ways to *segment* words into syllables.
George lit the flares to send a *signal* to the next camp.
Keith could easily hear the *pompous* man from across the room.

List B: Block 1, CV-targets

The surprisingly quick *reversal* of the senator's position was unfortunate.
Sheila decided to add more *vanilla* to the cookie recipe.
Alexander enjoyed a few *relaxing* hours in the pool.
The last political *dilemma* was resolved after several hours of debate.
Nathan bought a handy *device* to sharpen the kitchen knives.
Connie prepared a very *delicious* brunch for the newlyweds.
Sebastian made several attempts to *remember* his locker combination.
Abigail liked the piano *recital* that was performed by the children.
Martin was shocked by the sudden *divorce* of his parents.
The bank president gave his *report* at the last meeting.
Jack did not want to *depend* on his parents for spending money.
Dora was unusually careful to *select* the freshest produce.
The criminal did not show *remorse* at the trial.
The young couple chose to *remain* on the boat during the hurricane.
Doug started to plan for *retirement* more than ten years ago.
The street was littered with *debris* from the parade.
The Economics Club planned a *debate* about the tax reform proposal.
The company's last big *deposit* did not show up in Ed's account.
All boaters should *regard* the regulations posted on the dock.
The college students sang *together* at the candle-light vigil.
The soldiers worked all day to *secure* the new territory.
Ted noticed the slow *decay* of the old tree stump.
The geese started their *migration* to Canada each spring.
Sophie hoped to spend her winter *vacation* on a tropical island.

List B: Block 1, CVC-targets

The theater's original front *balcony* had crushed velvet seats.
Melissa carefully patted some *talcum* powder on the baby's legs.
Sally refused to wear her *helmet* when cycling in the country.
The thin walls did not seem to *filter* out the noise from the neighbors.
The governor had to close the *mental* hospital in order to save money.
Christopher patiently trained the *dolphin* to jump and roll for fish snacks.
Ellen called her travel agent to *cancel* the trip.
Jim carried the old *lantern* inside the tent.
Molly put the pretty pink *sandal* on the little girl's foot.
Laura brought a new *pencil* to school every day.
Andrew revised the long *sentence* to make it less ambiguous.
Grandparents have a common *tendency* to spoil their grandchildren.

Emily was born with only one *tonsil* in her throat.
Lisa's craving for candy *hampered* her ability to stay on a diet.
Vegetarian dishes are often *simple* to prepare and delicious to eat.
The volunteers taught a *destitute* family how to grow their own food.
Max thought for a while about the *subject* of his paper.
Most cheap brands of *vodka* taste quite similar.
The strength of the large *magnet* makes it unsafe for young children.
Boiling water helps the dark *pigment* to dissolve quickly in the dye bath.
Samantha applied to study *cognitive* problem-solving in monkeys.
The bicycle tour along the coast was the best *segment* of our trip.
The town council voted for a new *signal* to be installed next year.
The college students disliked the *pompous* teacher who didn't seem that smart.

LANGUAGE AND COGNITIVE PROCESSES, 2004, *19* (3), 427–452

Are syllables phonological units in visual word recognition?

Carlos J. Álvarez and Manuel Carreiras

Universidad de la Laguna, Tenerife, Spain

Manuel Perea

Universitat de València

A number of studies have shown that syllables play an important role in visual word recognition in Spanish. We report three lexical decision experiments with a masked priming technique that examined whether syllabic effects are phonological or orthographic in nature. In all cases, primes were nonwords. In Experiment 1, latencies to CV words were faster when primes and targets shared the first syllable (*ju.nas-JU.NIO*) than when they shared the initial letters but not the first syllable (*jun.tu-JU.NIO*). In Experiment 2, this syllabic overlap could be phonological + orthographical (*vi.rel-VI.RUS*) or just phonological (*bi.rel-VI.RUS*). A syllable priming effect was found for CV words in both the phonological + orthographical and the phonological condition. In Experiment 3 we compared a "phonological-syllable" condition (*bi.rel-VI.RUS*) with two control conditions (*fi.rel-VI.RUS* and *vir.ga-VI.RUS*). We found faster latencies for the phonological-syllabic condition than for the control conditions. These results suggest that syllabic effects are phonological in nature.

One important issue in visual word recognition is to determine the role played by sublexical units such as the syllable. It has been claimed that words are not processed as a whole, but rather the lexical processor routinely uses the syllable as a sublexical unit (Lima & Pollatsek, 1983; Millis, 1986; Prinzmetal, Treiman, & Rho, 1986; Rapp, 1992; Spoehr &

Correspondence should be addressed to Carlos J. Álvarez, Departamento de Psicología Cognitiva, Facultad de Psicología, Universidad de La Laguna, 38201– Tenerife, Spain. Email: calvarez@ull.es

Preparation of this article was supported by grant BSO2002-03286 (Spanish Ministry of Science and Technology) to Manuel Perea, and by grants BSO2000-0862 and PI2001/058 (Spanish Ministry of Science and Technology, and Canary Islands Government) to Manuel Carreiras.

Smith, 1973; Taft & Forster, 1976; Tousman & Inhoff, 1992). Among these proposals, several authors have characterised the syllable in orthographic terms (Prinzmetal et al., 1986) or have argued for syllable-type processing units that include morphological and orthotactic restrictions (Taft, 1979). Nonetheless, because the syllable is a co-articulatory and a phonological structure in speech, syllabic effects in visual word recognition have usually been interpreted as involving phonological processing (Grainger & Ferrand, 1996; Spoehr & Smith, 1973).

Evidence in favour of syllabic processing during visual word recognition has been mostly obtained in Romance languages with clear syllable boundaries (e.g., Spanish or French) rather than in English. In Spanish, a number of experiments have found that positional token syllable frequency influences response times to words (Álvarez, Carreiras, & de Vega, 2000; Álvarez, Carreiras, & Taft, 2001; Álvarez, de Vega, & Carreiras, 1998; Carreiras, Álvarez, & de Vega, 1993; Carreiras & Perea, 2002; Marín & Carreiras, 2002; Perea & Carreiras, 1995, 1998). The main result is that words with high-frequency syllables produce longer response times than words with low-frequency syllables in lexical decision and progressive demasking tasks (see also Conrad & Jacobs, 2003; Mathey & Zagar, 2001, for evidence of this effect in German and in French, respectively). This inhibitory effect of syllable frequency has been interpreted in terms of competition at the word level: If the syllables are of high frequency, they will activate more word units than the syllables of low frequency. Hence, unique word identification will be delayed for words with larger syllabic neighbourhoods. This interpretation readily captures the fact that the number of higher frequency syllabic neighbours (i.e., words of higher frequency that share the first syllable with the target word) has an inhibitory effect in lexical decision (Perea & Carreiras, 1998; see also Álvarez et al., 2001). It is important to note that a number of other potential explanatory factors of the syllable-frequency effect have been discarded. It has been previously shown that bigram frequency (Carreiras et al., 1993), orthographic neighbourhood density/frequency (Perea & Carreiras, 1998; see also Álvarez et al., 2001), or morpheme frequency (Álvarez et al., 2001) cannot account for the previous findings. Furthermore, recent evidence seems to suggest that the first syllable of the word is more prominent in the process of activation of lexical units than the other syllables (Álvarez et al., 1998, 2000). This bias towards the initial syllable is in accordance with the view that word beginnings play a privileged role in visual word recognition (e.g., see Briihl & Inhoff, 1995; Grainger, O'Regan, Jacobs, & Segui, 1992; Inhoff & Tousman, 1990; O'Regan & Jacobs, 1992; Perea, 1998; Rayner, 1979).

Of particular relevance for our research goals is the evidence obtained with the masked priming technique (see Forster & Davis, 1984; Forster,

Mohan, & Hector, 2003), which is the technique used in the present experiments. In this technique, a forward-masked, lowercase prime is presented briefly (for around 40–66 ms) and is subsequently replaced by the uppercase target. In a direct antecedent of the present research, Carreiras and Perea (2002) conducted four masked priming experiments that showed syllabic priming effects using disyllabic words. In Experiment 1, using primes of higher frequency than the target words, Carreiras and Perea found slower response times to target words when prime-target pairs shared the first syllable (e.g., *bo.ca-BO.NO*) than when the prime-target pairs were unrelated (*ca.ja-BO.NO*). (A dot marks the syllable boundary throughout this article, although the stimuli presented did not contain the dots.) In Experiment 2, in which they used nonwords as primes, the priming effects were facilitative. The different pattern of results with high-frequency words and nonwords as primes is consistent with previous results in which orthographic neighbours were used as primes (e.g., Forster & Veres, 1998; Perea & Rosa, 2000; Segui & Grainger, 1990). However, it could be argued that the syllabic neighbours in the Carreiras and Perea (2002) experiments not only shared the first syllable but also the first two letters, so that the observed effects could be also attributed to orthographic overlap. To disentangle orthographic from syllabic overlap, Carreiras and Perea (2002) employed both monosyllabic (*zinc*) and disyllabic words (*ra.na*) as targets in Experiment 3. Monosyllabic words could be primed by monosyllabic pseudowords, either sharing the first two letters with the target: Related condition (*ziel*) or by unrelated pseudowords (*flur*). In addition, disyllabic words were preceded by a related pseudoword (*ra.jo*) or by an unrelated pseudoword (*cu.fo*). Thus, in the two related conditions, primes and targets shared the two first letters, but only in the case of disyllabic words did these letters form the first syllable. The results showed a facilitative priming effect only for disyllabic targets, suggesting that syllabic activation plays a role in the early stages of word recognition (see Carreiras & Perea, 2002).

Taken together, these results are consistent with an activation-based model in which sublexical input phonology is structured syllabically (see Ferrand, Segui & Grainger, 1996). As indicated by Carreiras and Perea (2002), it is not clear how visual word recognition models such as the original version of the interactive-activation model (McClelland & Rumelhart, 1981), the Dual-Route Cascaded [DRC] model (e.g., Coltheart et al., 2001), or PDP models (Plaut et al., 1996; Seidenberg & McClelland, 1989) could account for the observed syllabic effects without explicitly adding a syllabic level of processing. (Note for instance, that the computational version of the DRC model only applies to monosyllabic words.) However, although syllabic effects could be readily explained in activation-based models with a syllabically structured sublexical input phonology (e.g., Ferrand et al., 1996), it is important to gather empirical evidence on whether syllabic effects arise from a sublexical phonological level or from a sublexical orthographic level. This is the main aim of the present research.

It is important to bear in mind that the fact that syllables are phonological units in speech does not necessarily imply that any syllabic effects observed in visual word recognition experiments are due to the activation of phonological codes. Most readers in Spanish have learned to read via a syllabic method, taking advantage of the fact that Spanish has clear syllable boundaries. Accordingly, it could be the case that phonological syllables in speech turn out to be phonological processing units in the development of reading skills. However, there is a possibility that, because most Spanish readers learn to read "syllabically", they segment the visual input into units that correspond to syllables, but that these syllables may remain orthographic units (i.e., without a mandatory involvement of phonological coding). We will call these hypothetical orthographic units "orthographic syllables". Indeed, in other languages (e.g., in English), it has been claimed that readers can segment words according to orthographic sublexical units that do not necessarily correspond to phonological syllabic units. For instance, it is possible that orthographic processing ignores the spoken structure and simply tries to maximise the size of the initial unit of orthographic processing (Taft, 1979, 1992). Specifically, Taft indicated that words in English could be segmented according to the spoken syllable by maximising the onset (e.g., *mur-der* or *si-ren*), or according to the Basic Orthographic Syllabic Structure (BOSS) which maximises the coda (e.g., *murd-er* or *sir-en*), and Taft empirically supported the idea that the coda of the first syllable is maximised. More recently, Taft (2001, 2002) modified his conclusion that the BOSS is always preferred as an orthographic structure to the syllable; this would only be true for better readers. Consequently, it is debatable whether the syllabic effects reported in Spanish are phonological in nature.

In sum, there is a growing body of evidence supporting the role of the syllable as a relevant sublexical unit in reading words, at least in Spanish. However, the orthographic/phonological status of the syllable has not been systematically studied. In addition, it is uncertain if the phonological codes are structured syllabically (as proposed for instance by Ferrand et al., 1996). To disentangle the effect of phonological syllables from the effect of orthographic syllables, we used prime-target pairs that shared the phonological, but not the orthographical first syllable. We chose a lexical decision task rather than a naming task as the naming task may have an intrinsic phonological component independent of lexical access.

The paradigm used in the present series of experiments, the masked priming paradigm, has proved to be effective in studying the possible early activation and use of phonological information without the intervention of conscious processing (see Ferrand & Grainger, 1992, 1993, 1994; Frost, Ahissar, Gottesman, & Tayeb, 2003; Grainger & Ferrand, 1996; Lukatela, Frost & Turvey, 1999; Lukatela, Savič, Urosevič, & Turvey, 1997; but see Shen & Forster, 1999). By using pseudohomophones as primes, phonological priming effects have been found at very short stimulus-onset asynchronies (SOAs) in lexical decision. For instance, Lukatela, Frost, and Turvey (1998) found that a target word such as *CLIP* was responded to more quickly in a lexical decision task when preceded by its pseudohomophone *klip* than when it was preceded by the orthographic control *plip* (see also Drieghe & Brysbaert, 2002; Frost et al., 2003; Lukatela, Eaton, Lee, Carello, & Turvey, 2002, for similar results and discussion).

To summarise, the present lexical decision experiments examined whether syllables are used as phonological units during reading in Spanish. To test the presence of syllabic priming effects with the masked priming technique, target words in Experiment 1 were preceded by nonword primes that always shared the first three letters, but only half of the cases shared the first syllable (e.g., *ju.nas-JU.NIO* vs. *jun.tu-JU.NIO*). The goal of Experiments 2 and 3 was to ascertain whether phonological syllables play an important role in the early stages of the process of visual word recognition. To that end, participants in Experiment 2 were presented with target words (e.g., *BA.LÓN*) preceded by nonwords primes that shared phonological syllables (*va.lis*), orthographical syllables (*ba.lis*), or did not share any syllable (*bal.ti*, *valti*). In Experiment 3, besides comparing a phonological-syllable condition (e.g., *va.lis-BA.LÓN*) and its nonsyllabic orthographic control (e.g., *val.ti-BA.LÓN*), we examined the role of a rime-only condition (e.g., *fa.lis-BA.LÓN*) on the basis that rimes may play an important role as a sublexical representation between the letter and word levels. The SOA in all three experiments was 64 ms (see Carreiras & Perea, 2002).

EXPERIMENT 1

Before examining the issue of whether syllables are phonological or orthographic in nature, it is relevant to replicate the presence of the involvement of the syllable in the early stages of word recognition. Experiment 1 was designed to disentangle syllabic overlap from segmental overlap with the masked priming technique. As stated in the Introduction, Carreiras and Perea (2002; Experiment 3) found that disyllabic prime-target pairs that shared the first syllable (and the initial two letters; e.g., *ra.jo-RA.NA*) produced an advantage over an unrelated condition (*cu.fo-RA.NA*), whereas monosyllabic pairs that shared the initial two letters (e.g., *ziel-ZINC*) did not produce an advantage over an unrelated condition (*flur-ZINC*). However, this result should be treated with some caution, since the unrelated condition differed from the related condition in terms of the number of shared letters (two letters in common vs. zero letters in common). To avoid this potential problem, we now used pairs of disyllabic items of five letters with a CV or a CVC initial syllable: One condition involved primes and targets that shared the first three letters and the first syllable (e.g., *ju.nas-JU.NIO*) and the other condition involved primes and targets that also shared the first three letters but not the first syllable (e.g., *jun.tu-JU.NIO*). We employed pseudowords as primes, and the targets had a CV or a CVC syllabic structure in the first syllable. According to a syllabic parsing account, faster reaction times should be found for those pairs that shared the first syllable (see Ferrand et al., 1996).

Method

Participants.   Forty students from introductory psychology courses at the University of La Laguna took part in the experiment to fulfil a course requirement. All were native speakers of Spanish.

Materials.   Forty-four disyllabic Spanish words, all of them consisting of five letters, were selected from the Spanish word pool (Alamada & Cuetos, 1995; Cobos et al., 1995). Twenty-two words had a CV structure in the first syllable, and the other twenty-two words had a CVC structure in the first syllable. The mean frequency of the CV words was 18 (range: 7–45) per one million words and the average number of orthographic neighbours was 8.4 (range: 0–16). The mean frequency of the CVC words was 14 (range: 8–27) per one million words and the average number of orthographic neighbours was 6.3 (range: 1–12). In all cases, primes were pseudowords of five letters (the mean number of orthographic neighbours across conditions varied from 1.4 to 3.0). Primes and targets shared the first three letters. Word targets were preceded by a prime that either shared the first syllable or did not. For instance, the CVC word *mon.ja* could be preceded either by *mo.nis* or *mon.di*, whereas the CV word *ju.nio* could be preceded either by *ju.nas* or *jun.tu*. In addition, we used forty-four disyllabic nonwords in order to perform a lexical decision task, twenty-two of them with a CV structure in the first syllable and the other twenty-two with a CVC structure in the first syllable. Similarly to word targets, nonword targets were preceded by CV nonword primes or CVC nonword primes.

Design.   Type of prime (CV vs. CVC structure in the first syllable) and type of target (CV vs. CVC structure in the first syllable) for words was varied within participants. Each participant was given a total of

88 experimental trials: 44 nonword-word trials and 44 nonword-nonword trials.

Procedure. Participants were tested individually in a quiet room. Presentation of the stimuli and recording of reaction times were controlled by PC-compatible microcomputers. Reaction times were measured from target onset until participants' response. On each trial, a forward mask consisting of a row of five hash marks (#####) was presented for 500 ms on the centre of the screen. Next, a centred lowercase prime nonword was presented for 64 ms. Primes were immediately replaced by an uppercase target item. Participants were instructed to press one of two buttons on the keyboard to indicate whether the uppercase letter string was a legitimate Spanish word or not. This decision had to be taken as quickly and as accurately as possible. When the participant responded, the target disappeared from the screen. After an inter-trial interval of 1 second, the next trial was presented. Participants were not informed of the presence of lowercase nonwords. Both nonword-word pairs and nonword-nonword pairs were counterbalanced across two experimental lists so that if the pair *ju.nas-JU.NIO* was in one list, *JU.NIO* would be preceded by *jun.tu* in the other list. Stimulus presentation was randomised, with a different order for each participant. Each participant received a total of 20 practice trials (with the same manipulation as in the experimental trials) prior to the 88 experimental trials. The whole session lasted approximately 13 min.

Results and discussion

Incorrect responses for words (4.6%) were excluded from the latency analysis.[1] In addition, reaction times less than 300 ms or greater than 2000 ms (less than 0.5% of the data for words) were excluded in a first pass, and all reaction times more than 2.0 standard deviations above or below the mean for that participant in all conditions were also excluded. The percentage of trials that were removed due to the screening procedure was similar in the syllabic and the orthographic conditions. For CVC target words, these percentages were 4.7% and 6.1% for the syllabic and the orthographic conditions, respectively; whereas for CV target words these percentages were 3.6% and 5.2% for the syllabic and the orthographic conditions. Mean reaction times on words were submitted to separate

---

[1] For brevity's sake, we will only report the results for the word targets since it is difficult to make any strong conclusions on the basis of "no" responses in a masked priming paradigm. Please bear in mind that negative responses are usually thought to be made via a temporal deadline (see Forster, 1998; Grainger & Jacobs, 1996).

TABLE 1
Mean lexical decision times (in ms) and percentage of errors
(in parentheses) on target words in Experiment 1

	Syllabic structure of the prime		
	CV	CVC	CVC-CV
Words			
CV structure	702 (3.3)	744 (2.2)	42 (−1.1)
CVC structure	724 (5.5)	733 (7.3)	9 (1.8)

ANOVAs, with Type of prime, Type of target, and List as factors.[2] The mean lexical decision time and the error rate on the stimulus words in each experimental condition are shown in Table 1.

The ANOVA on the latency data showed that the effect of type of target was not statistically significant, both $Fs < 1$. The main effect of type of prime was statistically significant, $F_1(1, 38) = 18.30, p < .001; F_2(1, 39) = 15.30, p < .001$: On average, participants responded faster when the prime had a CV structure than when the prime had a CVC structure. More importantly, the interaction between Type of prime and Type of target was significant, $F_1(1, 38) = 11.69, p < .002; F_2(1, 39) = 4.69, p < .04$. This interaction reflected that CV target words were responded to faster when the prime has a CV structure in the first syllable than when the prime had a CVC structure, $F_1(1, 38) = 31.54, p < .001; F_2(1, 39) = 18.07, p < .001$. However, there was no effect of type of prime for CVC targets, $F_1(1, 38) = 1.44; F_2(1, 39) = 1.56$.

The ANOVA on the error data only showed a significant effect of type of target, $F_1(1, 38) = 10.72, p < .001; F_2(1, 39) = 4.22, p < .05$; participants made more errors for CVC targets than for CV targets.

The results showed a substantial priming effect for CV target words that shared the first three letters and the first syllable (*ju.nas-JU.NIO*) relative to CV target words that shared the first three letters but not the first syllable (*jun.tu-JU.NIO*). This finding is in agreement with the results reported by Carreiras and Perea (2002), and it supports the view that syllabic priming effects can be obtained in the lexical decision task with brief SOAs (Carreiras & Perea, 2002). Rather surprisingly, we did not obtain any syllabic priming effects for CVC target words (i.e., faster recognition of the target word in the pair *ver.bu-VER.JA* than in the pair *ve.rus-VER.JA*). It is important to note that other recent studies using different tasks (e.g., picture naming, illusory conjunctions, and stem completion) and languages (Spanish and French) have also found distinct

---

[2] Because of a typing error in the input file, the word *LÁPIZ* was discarded from the data analysis.

patterns of results for CV and CVC words (e.g., see Costa & Sebastián, 1998; Marín & Carreiras, 2002; Peretz, Lussier, & Beland, 1998). One possible explanation for the advantage of CV primes is that the CV syllable is by far the most frequent syllabic structure in Spanish. As the CV syllable can be considered the canonical syllable, it could always be processed by default even if the processor finds a CVC structure in the first syllable. (We discuss this issue further in the General Discussion.)

EXPERIMENT 2

Experiment 1 provided further empirical evidence of the involvement of the syllable in the early stages of visual word recognition. However, it cannot be used to tease apart phonological and orthographic accounts of the syllabic effects. In the architecture proposed by Ferrand and Grainger, (1994); (Ferrand et al., 1996; Ferrand & Segui, 1998), sublexical phonological representations are coded syllabically. In contrast, in Taft's (1991) model, syllable-size orthographic representations intervene between letter units and whole-word representations.

The process of translating print into sound in Spanish is unambiguous. Each letter of the alphabet receives a unique pronunciation, but some graphemes map onto the same sound. Specifically, the letters which map onto the same sound are the following: "j" and "g" when followed by "i" and "e" are pronounced /x/; "b" and "v", which are mapped onto the phoneme /b/; "k" and "c" when followed by "a", "o" and "u" map onto the sound /k/. Finally, in the Canary Islands (as well as in Southern Spain and Latin America) the letters "z", "s", and "c" when followed by "e" and "i" are pronounced /s/.

In the present experiment, we take advantage of the fact that some consonant letters share the same pronunciation, in order to investigate whether syllabic effects are phonological or orthographical in nature. In particular, to examine whether syllable-size units are represented in the phonological input, we include nonword primes that share the same orthographic and phonological initial syllable (e.g., *vi.rel-VI.RUS*) or only the same phonological initial syllable with the target (e.g., *bi.rel-VI.RUS*; "v" and "b" share the same sound in Spanish, /b/). We also used control primes that shared the same number of letters with the targets as with the experimental primes, but did not share the initial syllable (e.g., *vir.ga-VI.RUS* and *bir.ga-VI.RUS*). If syllables are phonological units of processing, priming effects should be observed either as a result of orthographic overlap or phonological overlap in the syllabic conditions. If the advantage of the syllabic over the non-syllabic control conditions is similar in the orthographic + phonological condition and in the phonological-only condition, this could be taken as favouring a phonological representation of the syllable—as proposed by Ferrand et al. (1996).

Method

Participants.   Forty students from introductory psychology courses at the University of La Laguna took part in the experiment to fulfil a course requirement. None of them had participated in the previous experiments. All were native Spanish speakers of the Canary Islands. We would like to stress that, in this region of Spain, the graphemes "s" and "z", as well as the grapheme "c" (before "i" and "e") correspond to the same sound /s/.

Materials.   Ninety-six disyllabic Spanish words, all of them consisting of five letters, were selected from the Spanish word pool (Alamada & Cuetos, 1995; Cobos et al., 1995). Forty-eight words had a CV structure in the first syllable, and the other forty-eight words had a CVC structure in the first syllable. The mean frequency of the CV words was 18 (range: 1–110) per one million words and the average number of orthographic neighbours was 5.9 (range: 0–15). The mean frequency of the CVC words was 20 (range: 2–70) per one million words and the average number of orthographic neighbours was 5.8 (range: 0–15). The average number of orthographic neighbours for the target nonwords was 2.6 (range: 0–11). In all cases, primes were pseudowords of five letters (the mean number of orthographic neighbours across conditions varied from 0.6 to 2.3). Of these 96 disyllabic pseudowords, half had a CV structure in the first syllable and the other half had a CVC structure in the first syllable. As in Experiment 1, in the orthographic + phonological condition word and nonword targets were preceded by a prime that either shared the first orthographic and phonological syllable or did not. However, in the phonological condition, word and nonword targets were preceded by a prime that either shared the first phonological syllable or did not. Orthographic + phonological syllables differed from the phonological syllables in their initial letters, but not in their pronunciation. For instance, the CVC word *GES.TA* could be preceded in the orthographic + phonological condition by *ge.ser* or *ges.po*, and in the phonological condition by *je.ser* or *jes.po*. The CV word *VI.RUS* could be preceded in the orthographic + phonological condition either by *vi.rel* or *vir.ga*, and in the phonological condition by *bi.rel* or *bir.ga*. In addition, we used 96 disyllabic nonwords, 48 of them with a CV structure in the first syllable and the other 48 with a CVC structure in the first syllable. Similarly to word targets, nonword targets were preceded by CV nonword primes (either orthographic + phonological or only phonological) or CVC nonword primes (either orthographic + phonological or only phonological).

Design.   Type of prime (CV vs. CVC prime), type of target (CV vs. CVC target) and orthographic-phonological relation of primes and targets (orthographic + phonological vs. only phonological) was varied within participants. The design was the same for words and nonwords. Each participant was given a total of 192 experimental trials: 96 nonword-word trials and 96 nonword-nonword trials.

Procedure.   The procedure was the same as in Experiment 1.

Results and discussion

Incorrect responses for words (7.0%) were excluded from the latency analysis. A preliminary analysis revealed that five words provoked a high error rate (over 40%): *cirio* = 42.5%, *zares* = 85%, *visor* = 52.5%, *visir* = 80%, *vulgo* = 87.5%. These five items were therefore excluded from the analyses reported below. (The ANOVAs yielded the same results with and without these five items.) In addition, reaction times less than 300 ms or greater than 2000 ms (less than 0.7% of the data for words) were excluded in a first pass, and all reaction times more than 2.0 standard deviations above or below the mean for that participant in all conditions were also excluded. The percentage of trials that were removed due to the screening procedure was similar in the syllabic and the orthographic conditions. For CVC target words, these percentages were 4.3% and 4.6% for the syllabic and the orthographic conditions, respectively; whereas for CV target words these percentages were 5.7% for both the syllabic and the orthographic conditions. Mean reaction times on words were submitted to ANOVAs by subjects and by items, with the Type of prime, Type of target, Orthographic-phonological relation between primes and targets, and List as factors. The mean lexical decision time and the error rate on the stimulus words in each experimental condition are shown in Table 2.

The ANOVA on the latency data showed that the effect of orthographic-phonological relation was significant, $F_1(1, 36) = 12.93$, $p < .001$ $F_2(1, 83) = 8.13$, $p < .01$: participants responded faster when the prime-target relation was orthographic + phonological (719 ms) than when it was only phonological (733 ms). The main effect of type of prime was also statistically significant, $F_1(1, 36) = 15.30$, $p < .001$; $F_2(1, 83) = 16.12$, $p < .001$: On average, participants responded more quickly when the prime had a CV structure than when the prime had a CVC structure. Although the interaction between Type of prime and Type of target was not significant, $F_1(1, 36) = 1.95$; $F_2(1, 83) = 1.49$, CV target words were responded to faster when the prime had a CV structure than when the prime had a CVC structure, $F_1(1, 36) = 11.87$, $p < .01$; $F_2(1, 85) = 6.65$, $p < .02$, as in Experiment 1. In contrast, the effect of type of prime for

TABLE 2
Mean lexical decision times (in ms) and percentage of errors (in parentheses) on target words in Experiment 2

	Syllabic structure of the prime		
	CV	CVC	CVC-CV
Words			
Orthographic + phonological			
CV structure	705 (9.5)	738 (10.0)	33 (0.5)
CVC structure	709 (6.3)	726 (6.1)	17 (−0.2)
Phonological			
CV structure	722 (6.8)	757 (6.6)	35 (−0.2)
CVC structure	717 (4.5)	737 (6.1)	20 (1.6)

CVC targets was significant only in the analysis by participants, $F_1(1, 36) = 6.52, p < .02; F_2(1, 85) = 2.03, p < .15$ but in the same direction as for the CV words: an advantage of the CV primes. The other interactions were not significant (all *ps* > .15).

The ANOVA on the error data also showed that the effect of orthographic-phonological relation was significant, $F_1(1, 36) = 8.94, p < .005; F_2(1, 83) = 5.10, p < .05$. Participants made more errors when the prime-target relation was orthographic + phonological (8.0%) than when it was only phonological (6.0%). The main effect of type of target was also significant, but only in the analysis by participants, $F_1(1, 36) = 8.39, p < .01; F_2(1, 83) = 1.98$. The other effects and interactions were not significant (all *ps* > .15).

The main results of this experiment can be summarised as follows: first, CV words were responded to more quickly when they were preceded by a nonword with the same initial syllable than when they were preceded by a nonword with a different initial syllable. Although, similarly to Experiment 1, CVC words showed faster response times when preceded by CV primes, this effect was far from significant in the analysis by items (we defer a discussion of this issue until the General Discussion). Second, the fact that the syllabic structure of the prime (CV prime vs. CVC prime) yielded similar effects for the orthographic + phonological condition and for the phonological condition suggests that syllabic priming effects are phonological in origin. This outcome implies that phonological syllabic activation is taking place in addition to pure orthographic processing: A priming effect is observed as a result of orthographic overlap as well as a result of a pure-phonological (but syllabic) overlap. Finally, we would like to note that although participants were faster in the orthographic + phonological condition than in the phonological condition—which may suggest that orthography plays a role over and above phonology in the process of visual word recognition, this advantage is compromised by a speed-accuracy trade-off. Finally, it is important to note that these results cannot be explained simply in terms of orthographic overlap, since in the phonological conditions (syllabic and non-syllabic), primes and targets shared only the same two letters (the second and the third).

EXPERIMENT 3

The results obtained in Experiment 2 indicate that the syllable priming effect for CV target words occurs when primes and targets share the first phonological syllable. However, one could argue that the advantage of the phonological + orthographic condition over the phonological-only condition in the response times was due to the fact that the former condition, primes and targets shared more letters. Moreover, the syllabic priming effect in the phonological-only condition could also have been produced by the prime-target pairs sharing the rime/body, rather than the whole first syllable. Indeed, several studies have shown priming effects independently of whether prime and targets shared onsets in lexical decision tasks (e.g., Grainger & Ferrand, 1996). Likewise, it has been claimed that subsyllabic units such as rimes play an important role as a sublexical representation between the letter and word levels (see Forster & Taft, 1994; Grainger & Ferrand, 1996; Treiman & Chafetz, 1987).

The main aim of Experiment 3 was to examine if the phonological effects found in Experiment 2 were indeed caused by the first phonological syllable rather than the rime/body. To test this hypothesis, a phonological-syllable priming condition (e.g., *va.lis-BA.LÓN*) was compared with a rime-only condition (e.g., *fa.lis-BA.LÓN*). For comparison purposes with Experiment 2, we also included a phonological control condition in which primes and targets shared the first three phonemes, but not the initial syllable (e.g., *val.ti-BA.LÓN*). An advantage of the phonological-syllable condition over the two control conditions (rime-only and phonological control) would reinforce the notion of the syllable as a sublexical phonological processing unit.

Method

Participants. Thirty-six undergraduate students from the University of La Laguna took part in the experiment, receiving course credits for their participation. None of them had participated in the previous experiments. All were native Spanish speakers from the Canary Islands.

Materials and design. Forty-five disyllabic Spanish words, all of them consisting of five letters, were selected from the Spanish word pool (Alameda & Cuetos, 1995; Cobos et al., 1995). Words had a CV structure in the first syllable and a CVC structure in the second one (e.g., *BA.LÓN*). The mean frequency was 63 (range: 1–637) per one million words and the average number of orthographic neighbours was 3.7 (range: 0–13). In all cases, primes were pseudowords of five letters with very few orthographic neighbours (from 0.6 to 1.1 orthographic neighbours across conditions). Primes and targets always shared the second and the third letters. Word targets were preceded by three prime conditions: (1) a prime that shared the first phonological syllable, but not the orthographic one (e.g., *va.lis-BA.LÓN*); (2) a prime that shared only the rime or body (*fa.lis-BA.LÓN*); and (3) a prime that shared the first three phonemes but not the first syllable (*val.ti-BA.LÓN*). In addition, we used forty-five disyllabic nonwords preceded by nonwords primes with the same manipulation as that for the word targets.

Procedure.   The procedure was the same as in Experiments 1 and 2.

Results and discussion

Incorrect responses for words (4.6%) were excluded from the latency analysis. In addition, reaction times less than 300 ms or greater than 2000 ms (less than 0.5% of the data for words) were excluded in a first pass, and all reaction times more than 2.0 standard deviations above or below the mean for that participant in all conditions were also excluded (3.4%). Mean reaction times and error rates for words were submitted to separate ANOVAs, with Type of prime and List as factors. The mean lexical decision time and the error rate on the stimulus words in each experimental condition are shown in Table 3.

The ANOVA on the response times to word stimuli showed a significant effect of type of prime, $F_1(1, 33) = 6.49$, $p < .05$; $F_2(1, 42) = 4.52$, $p < .05$. The ANOVA on the error data did not show a significant effect of type of prime (both $ps > .1$).

Planned comparisons on the response times showed that target words were responded to faster when preceded by primes that shared the phonological-syllable than when preceded by primes that only shared the rime/body (695 vs. 755 ms), $F_1(1, 33) = 4.87$, $p < .05$; $F_2(1, 42) = 8.34$, $p < .05$. In addition, target words preceded by primes that shared the

TABLE 3
Mean lexical decision times (in ms) and percentage of errors (in parentheses) on target words in Experiment 3

Priming condition	Phonological syllable	Rime/body	Phonological control
	695 (5.6)	755 (4.1)	740 (4.0)

phonological-syllable were responded to faster than when preceded by primes that shared the first three phonemes but not the initial syllable (695 vs. 740 ms, respectively), $F_1(1, 33) = 6.49$, $p < .05$; $F_2(1, 42) = 4.71$, $p < .05$. The difference between the rime/body condition and the phonological control phonemes was not significant (both $ps > .1$).

The results of the present experiment are straightforward: response times to target words were substantially faster when primes and targets shared the first phonological syllable than when primes and targets only shared the first three phonemes (but not the first syllable) or when they only shared the rime/body of the initial syllable. That is, leaving aside the finding of an advantage of the phonological syllable against the phonological control (replicating Experiment 2),[3] we also found a superiority of the phonological syllable over the rime-only condition. We should note that there is empirical evidence that shows that the rime of the syllable acts as a relevant processing unit in English, and possibly this evidence is even stronger than the evidence which supports the syllable as a sublexical unit (Jared, 1997; Forster & Taft, 1994; Treiman & Chafetz, 1987; Treiman & Zukowski, 1988; Treiman, Mullennix, Bijeljac-Babic, & Richmond-Welty, 1995). However, this does not seem to be the case in Spanish: we found a clear superiority of the syllable over the rime. Thus, our data reinforce the results obtained in Experiment 2 and provide further evidence that syllabic effects are phonological in origin. This pattern suggests that phonological input phonology may be structured syllabically (Ferrand et al., 1996).

Finally, and even though we are not dealing with the time course of the phonological effects, the present results are in accordance with previous studies that have found phonological priming with similar (or even shorter) SOAs (e.g., Ferrand & Grainger, 1992, 1993; Frost et al., 2003; Lukatela & Turvey, 1994; Lukatela et al., 1998).

---

[3] The goal of Experiments 2 and 3 was to investigate whether the syllabic effects obtained in previous research (including Experiment 1 in the present paper) could be of phonological nature. Indeed, Experiments 2 and 3 show that there is an advantage for CV target words when primes and targets share the first syllable relative to when they do not, even when all items share the three first letters/phonemes. A different question is to ask whether it is possible to obtain phonological effects for disyllabic words when there is no syllabic compatibility between primes and targets, but different degrees of phonological overlap. This question has not been systematically addressed in the present study, and the answer may depend on the differential degree of overlap between primes and targets across conditions. It may be worth noting that, in an unpublished experiment in which primes and targets differed in syllabic structure, we failed to find any reliable differences when prime-target pairs shared three out of five phonemes (e.g., *val.ja-BA.LAS*) and when prime-target pairs shared two out of five phonemes (e.g., *ral.ja-BA.LAS*).

GENERAL DISCUSSION

The present findings add further empirical support to the general notion that syllables are fundamental units of processing in this language, and they also extend previous research that suggested that syllabic effects are phonological in nature (Álvarez et al., 1998, 2000, 2001; Carreiras & Perea, 2002; Carreiras et al., 1993; Dominguez, de Vega, & Cuetos, 1997; Perea & Carreiras, 1998).

We found syllabic priming effects at very brief SOAs in all three experiments. In Experiments 1 and 2 we found syllabic priming effects for CV words when letter overlap between primes and targets was perfectly controlled. In particular, CV targets preceded by pseudoword primes that shared the first three letters with the target were recognised faster when primes and targets shared the first CV syllable than when they did not. Experiment 2 studied phonological syllabic priming effects by using an orthographic + phonological condition (e.g., *vi.rel-VI.RUS*) pitted against a purely phonological condition (e.g., *bi.rel-VI.RUS*; note that "b" and "v" sound the same in Spanish). Syllabic priming effects were obtained in both conditions for CV targets; that is, the syllabic priming effects of Experiment 1 were also found when primes and targets shared only the first phonological (but not orthographic) syllable. We consider this result remarkable, since we found an advantage of the syllabic primes not only when prime and target shared the first "orthographic" syllable (both sounds and letters) but also when prime and target shared just the first phonological syllable. We are not implying, however, that orthographic processing plays a secondary role in the process of visual word recognition. What we argue is that the computation of the phonological units at a syllable level can facilitate the recognition of the word target. This can be deduced from the fact that a syllabic priming effect can be observed when some orthographic information is omitted (the first letter), while the first phonological syllable is intact. It could be argued that this conclusion may be problematic because equivalent syllabic priming effects were obtained in both in the orthographic + phonological condition and in the phonological-only condition (note that, in the former case, more information is shared by prime and targets). However, this argument only stands if we accept that orthographic and phonological priming effects combine additively, an issue that has been challenged recently (e.g., in terms of morphological and form priming; see Forster & Azuma, 2000).

In Experiment 3, we replicated the syllabic priming effect when primes and targets shared the initial phonological syllable (e.g., *va.lis-BA.LÓN*) relative to when primes and targets only shared the first three phonemes (e.g., *val.ti-BA.LÓN*). Furthermore, we found an advantage of the phonological-syllable condition (*va.lis-BA.LÓN*) relative to a rime/body condition (e.g., *fa.lis-BA.LÓN*) hence ruling out an account of syllable priming effects in terms of rime/body overlap. Taken together, these results indicate that the codes produced or generated from masked primes are structured syllabically, as proposed by Carreiras and Perea (2002; see also Ferrand et al., 1996). More importantly, they also suggest that these syllabic priming effects (when they do arise) are phonological in nature and cannot be attributed to purely orthographic factors or some initial (non-syllabic) phonemic overlap.

One possible objection to this conclusion, however, is to argue that a grapheme-grapheme conversion mechanism is at work, as proposed by Taft (1982), instead of a grapheme-phoneme mechanism—as we have assumed. According to Taft (1982), orthographic similarity may be dictated by phonological similarity. Thus, the consonant letters "b" and "B" are always perceived as graphemically equivalent because they are pronounced the same way. What is more, one could argue that for instance, the b/v alternation in Spanish could work in a similar way to case alternation. There is, however, one important difference between case alternation and the change of consonants that map onto the same sound (e.g., b/v): In a masked priming paradigm, case alternation always implies a repeated access to the same lexical entry, whereas change of consonants like b/v or z/s may result in two different lexical items (e.g., pairs such as *va.ca-ba.ca*, *ca.bo-ca.vo*, *ca.za*, and *ca.so*, etc., have different meanings in Spanish).

Most of the research focused on the influence of phonology in visual word recognition, in particular studies using priming paradigms and pseudohomophones (or homophones) as primes, has employed mono-syllabic words and nonwords, maximising phonological similarity between primes and targets. In Experiment 3 we used disyllabic prime-target pairs in which the orthographic similarity between the phonological-syllable prime (*va.lis-BA.LÓN*) and the rime/body prime (*fa.lis-BA.LÓN*) was the same: In both conditions, the first letters of the primes (the onsets) were different compared with the first letters of the targets. Likewise, primes and targets shared the same syllabic structure. The finding of robust phonological syllable priming effects under conditions in which letter and sound overlap between primes and targets is relatively low provides additional support for the view that readers are able to represent words in terms of phonological syllables. Additionally, the results in Experiment 3 do not corroborate the common finding in English that subsyllabic units such as rimes play an important role in visual word recognition (Forster & Taft, 1994; Grainger & Ferrand, 1996; Treiman & Chafetz, 1987). Instead, at least in a Romance language like Spanish, the syllable (rather than the rime) seems to act as the most relevant sublexical unit of processing. Further research is needed to examine whether the present findings can be generalised to other languages, especially all other syllable-timed languages. Studies comparing the role of the syllable (and other sublexical units) across languages offer a promising way of examining this issue. For instance, Álvarez, Taft, and Carreiras (1998), using English-Spanish homographic in a lexical decision task with split stimuli (e.g., *fi.nal*), found that Spanish readers produced faster responses to stimuli segmented after the syllable boundary (*fi//nal*) than segmented after the BOSS (*fin// al*). However, English good readers produced the opposite pattern, suggesting the presence of different segmentation strategies across languages during reading. Indeed, unlike the mixed evidence in English on the role of the syllable in visual word recognition, the syllable seems to be a relevant unit in visual word processing in French (e.g., Colé, Magnan, & Grainger, 1999; Mathey & Zagar, 2001; Taft & Radeau, 1995).

One unexpected result in both Experiments 1 and 2 that deserves comment refers to the results with the CVC targets. As indicated above, we found that CV words such as (*JU.NIO*) were responded to faster when they were preceded by a prime nonword with the same initial syllable (*ju.nas*), than when they were preceded by a prime nonword with a different initial syllable (*jun.tu*). However, lexical decision responses to CVC words (e.g., *VER.JA*) were not modulated by the presence of nonword primes that shared the first initial syllable with the target item.[4] A replication of Experiments 1 and 2 with a different set of materials (i.e., six-letter items) found a similar pattern: A syllabic priming effect for CV target words but not for CVC target words. Thus, this divergence between CV and CVC words seems to be real and, indeed, it has always been documented in the literature: Previous studies have also found a different pattern of results for CV and CVC words (Costa & Sebastián, 1998, in a speech production study; Peretz et al., 1998, in an implicit visual/auditory task; Marín & Carreiras, 2002, in visual word recognition in Spanish using perceptual discrimination tasks). Peretz et al. (1998) suggested that these asymmetrical syllabic effects for CV and CVC are related with distributional organisation for the lexicon, because there are more French words starting with CV than with CVC segments. A tentative explanation for this pattern of results is that the CVC word structure is a much less frequent pattern in Spanish and French (e.g., CVC syllables are three times less frequent than CV syllables in Spanish; see Sebastián-Gallés, Martí, Carreiras, & Cuetos, 2000). Thus, unlike CV syllables—the canonical syllable for Spanish, CVC syllables might not give rise to an optimal level of sublexical activation and/or the activation they produce may not be

---

[4] A combined analysis of Experiments 1 and 2 failed to find any signs of syllabic priming effects for CVC target words in the analyses by items ($p > .20$).

quick enough to influence target recognition. For instance, Marín and Carreiras (2002) found robust syllabic effects employing an illusory conjunction paradigm. However, in the case of words with initial CVC syllables, both the CVC syllable and the embedded (illicit) CV syllable (illicit because it was not the current syllable) showed a similar number of illusory conjunctions. They concluded that CV and CVC segments collaborate rather than compete in the process of word segmentation: When processing a CVC syllable, the embedded CV syllable is also processed. This would explain an advantage for CV primes, if anything, for CVC targets. Clearly, the fact that CV and CVC words sometimes behave differently is a puzzling finding that needs further research. Nonetheless, it is important to stress that this issue does not undermine our claim that syllabic effects, when they do arise (as was the case in the CV target words in all three experiments), are phonological in nature. In addition, current computational models of visual word recognition are either restricted to monosyllabic words (DRC models) or do not include a syllabic level of processing (multiple read-out model) and as such cannot accommodate the observed syllabic effects. One would need to implement a quantitative model of visual word recognition with a syllabic level to examine whether or not this model can capture the divergence between CV and CVC targets.

Finally, the present results have important implications for visual word recognition models. The observed (phonological) syllabic priming effects are consistent with the proposals of an early and mandatory activation of phonology in (monosyllabic) word reading (Frost, 1998; Lukatela & Turvey, 1994; Lukatela et al., 1998, 2002; Pollatsek, Lesch, Morris, & Rayner, 1992; Van Order, 1987; Van Order, Johnston, & Hale, 1988). The empirical support for these proposals comes mainly from studies using monosyllabic homophones and pseudohomophones. As such, they do not address whether phonological processing is syllabically structured. To accommodate the present findings, an implement model should include a syllable-based phonological level. Alternatively, there are models in which words can be identified via an orthographic code without necessarily resorting to the computation of phonology (e.g., the DRC model; Coltheart et al., 2001; see also Coltheart, 1978; Coltheart, Curtis, Atkins, & Haller, 1993; Coltheart & Rastle, 1994; Rastle & Coltheart, 1999). The current implementation of the DRC model is restricted to monosyllabic words, and as such, it does not include syllabic processing in the phonological route either. We believe that future implementations of the DRC model need to take into account the early activation of phonological codes (see also Frost et al., 2003) in multisyllabic words. In addition, the fact that similar syllabic priming effects were obtained when prime and target shared either the phonological-only syllable or the orthographic (and phonological) syllable can be explained by the entry-opening model (Forster & Davis, 1984; Forster et al., 2003). In this model, priming occurs when the prime has accessed the entry of the target word (e.g., when the prime is a close match for the target). Our results seem to suggest that both phonological-only syllabic overlap and orthographic and phonological syllabic overlap are establishing a closer match between the two stimuli than a non-syllable condition.

Our data can be readily accommodated within a model of multisyllabic word reading that incorporates a syllabic level of processing connected with a word level of representation. Specifically, they can be captured by the bimodal interactive activation model (Ferrand et al., 1996; Grainger & Ferrand, 1996; Grainger & Jacobs, 1996), which is a theoretical framework for word recognition and naming. Performance in tasks such as lexical decision is based not only on activity in the orthographic lexicon (composed by a level with sublexical orthographic units and another level with whole-word orthographic units) but also in the phonological lexicon (with a level of sublexical phonological units or sublexical input phonology and a word phonological level). The bi-directional connections between orthographic and phonological units allow the model to handle the early effects of phonology found in lexical decision. Ferrand et al. (1996) suggested that the sublexical input phonology would be organised syllabically. This notion is clearly supported by the present findings. Computer simulations with an implemented version of this model would, however, be necessary to examine whether this model can accommodate the observed discrepancy in syllabic priming effects for CV and CVC words.

In sum, the present findings strengthen the view that syllables are phonological sublexical units in visual word recognition. This notion can be accommodated in an activation-based model in which phonological syllables mediate between letter and word levels (e.g., the model proposed by Ferrand et al., 1996). Whether this theoretical proposal must be restricted to Spanish or can be generalised to other syllable-timed languages or to most languages is a question that merits further empirical research.

REFERENCES

Alameda, J.R., & Cuetos, F. (1995). *Diccionario de frecuencia de las unidades lingüísticas del castellano* [*Dictionary of frequency of Spanish words*]. Oviedo: Servicio de publicaciones de la Universidad de Oviedo.

Álvarez, C.J., Carreiras, M., & de Vega, M. (2000). Syllable-frequency effect in visual word recognition: Evidence of a sequential-type processing. *Psicológica, 21*, 341–374.

Álvarez, C.J., Carreiras, M., & Taft, M. (2001). Syllables and morphemes: Contrasting frequency effects in Spanish. *Journal of Experimental Psychology: Learning, Memory and Cognition, 27*, 545–555.

Álvarez, C.J., de Vega, M., & Carreiras, M. (1998). La Sílaba como unidad de activatión léxica en la lectura de palabras trisílabas. *Psicothema, 10*, 371–386.

Álvarez, C.J., Taft, M., & Carreiras, M. (1998, November). *The role of syllables and BOSSes in reading cognate words in English and Spanish.* Paper presented at the First International Workshop on Written Language Processing, Sydney, Australia.

Briihl, D., & Inhoff, A.W. (1995). Integrating information across fixations during reading: The use of orthographic bodies and of exterior letters. *Journal of Experimental Psychology: Learning, Memory and Cognition, 21*, 55–67.

Carreiras, M., & Perea, M. (2002). Masked priming effects with syllabic neighbors in a lexical decision task. *Journal of Experimental Psychology: Human Perception and Performance, 28*, 1228–1242.

Carreiras, M., Álvarez, C.J., & de Vega, M. (1993). Syllable frequency and visual word recognition in Spanish. *Journal of Memory and Language, 32*, 766–780.

Cobos, P.L., Domínguez, A., Álvarez, C.J., Alameda, J.R., Carreiras, M., & de Vega, M. (1995). Diccionario de frecuencia silábica. In J.R. Alameda & F. Cuetos (Eds.), *Diccionario de frecuencia de las unidades lingüísticas del castellano* [*Dictionary of frequency of Spanish words*] (Vol. 2). Oviedo: Servicio de Publicaciones de la Universidad de Oviedo.

Colé, P., Magnan, A., & Grainger, J. (1999). Syllable-sized units in visual word recognition: Evidence from skilled and beginning readers of French. *Applied Psycholinguistics, 20*, 507–532.

Coltheart, M. (1978). Lexical access in simple reading tasks. In G. Underwood (Ed.), *Strategies of information processing.* London: Academic Press.

Coltheart, M., & Rastle, K. (1994). Serial processing in reading aloud: Evidence for dual route models of reading. *Journal of Experimental Psychology: Human Perception and Performance, 20*, 1197–1211.

Coltheart, M., Curtis, B., Atkins, P., & Haller, M. (1993). Models of reading aloud: Dual-route and parallel-distributed-processing approaches. *Psychological Review, 100*, 589–608.

Coltheart, M., Rastle, K., Perry, C., Langdon, R., & Ziegler, J. (2001). DRC: A dual route cascaded model of visual word recognition and reading aloud. *Psychological Review, 108*, 204–256.

Conrad, M., & Jacobs, A. (2003). *Replicating syllable frequency effects in Spanish in German: One more challenge to computational models of visual word recognition.* Submitted for publication.

Costa, A., & Sebastián, N. (1998). Abstract phonological structure in language production: Evidence from Spanish. *Journal of Experimental Psychology: Learning, Memory, and Cognition, 24*, 886–903.

Domínguez, A., de Vega, M., & Cuetos, F. (1997). Lexical inhibition from syllabic units in Spanish visual word recognition. *Language and Cognitive Processes, 12*, 401–422.

Drieghe, D., & Brysbaert, M. (2002). Strategic effects in associative priming with words, homophones, and pseudohomophones. *Journal of Experimental Psychology: Human Perception and Performance, 28*, 951–961.

Ferrand, L., & Grainger, J. (1992). Phonology and orthography: Evidence from masked nonword priming. *Quarterly Journal of Experimental Psychology, 45A*, 353–372.

Ferrand, L., & Grainger, J. (1993). The time course of orthographic and phonological code activation in the early phases of visual word recognition. *Bulletin of the Psychonomic Society, 31*, 119–122.

Ferrand, L., & Grainger, J. (1994). Effects of orthography are independent of phonology in masked form priming. *Quarterly Journal of Experimental Psychology, 47A*, 365–382.

Ferrand, L., Segui, J. (1998). The syllable's role in speech production: Are syllables chunks, schemas, or both? *Psychonomic Bulletin and Review, 5*, 253–258.

Ferrand, L., Segui, J., & Grainger, J. (1996). Masked priming of words and picture naming: The role of syllabic units. *Journal of Memory and Language, 35*, 708–723.

Forster, K.I. (1998). The pros and cons of masked priming. *Journal of Psycholinguistic Research, 27*, 203–233.

Forster, K.I., & Davis, C. (1984). Repetition priming and frequency attentuation in lexical access. *Journal of Experimental Psychology: Learning, Memory, and Cognition, 10*, 680–698.

Forster, K.I., Mohan, K., & Hector, J. (2003). The mechanics of masked priming. In S. Kinoshita & S.J. Lupker (Eds.), *Masked priming: State of the art*. Hove, UK: Psychology Press.

Forster, K.I., & Azuma, T. (2000). Masked priming for prefixed words with bound stems: Does *submit* prime *permit*? *Language and Cognitive Processes, 15*, 539–561.

Forster, K.I., & Veres, C. (1998). The prime lexicality effect: Form priming as a function of prime awareness, lexical status, and discrimination difficulty. *Journal of Experimental Psychology: Learning, Memory, and Cognition, 24*, 498–514.

Forster, K.I., & Taft, M. (1994). Bodies, antibodies, and neighborhood density effects in masked form priming. *Journal of Experimental Psychology: Learning, Memory and Cognition, 20*, 844–863.

Frost, R. (1998). Towards a strong phonological theory of visual word recognition: True issues and false trails. *Psychological Bulletin, 123*, 71–99.

Frost, R., Ahissar, M., Gottesman, R., & Tayeb, S. (2003). Are phonological effects fragile? The effect of luminance and exposure duration on form priming and phonological priming. *Journal of Memory and Language, 48*, 346–378.

Grainger, J., & Ferrand, L. (1996). Masked orthographic and phonological priming in visual word recognition and naming: Cross-task comparisons. *Journal of Memory and Language, 35*, 623–647.

Grainger, J., & Jacobs, A.M. (1996). Orthographic processing in visual word recognition: A multiple read-out model. *Psychological Review, 22*, 696–713.

Grainger, J., O'Regan, J.K., Jacobs, A.M., & Segui, J. (1992). Neighborhood frequency effects and letter visibility in visual word recognition. *Perception and Psychophysics, 51*, 49–56.

Inhoff, A.W., & Tousman, S. (1990). Lexical priming from partial-word previews. *Journal of Experimental Psychology: Learning, Memory and Cognition, 16*, 825–836.

Jared, D. (1997). Spelling-sound consistency affects the naming of high frequency words. *Journal of Memory and Language, 36*, 505–529.

Lima, S.D., & Pollatsek, A. (1983). Lexical access via orthographic code: The Basic Orthographic Syllabic Structure (BOSS) reconsidered. *Journal of Verbal Learning and Verbal Behavior, 22*, 310–332.

Lukatela, G., & Turvey, M.T. (1994). Visual lexical access is initially phonological: 1. Evidence from associative priming by words, homophones and pseudohomophones. *Journal of Experimental Psychology: General, 123*, 107–128.

Lukatela, G., Eaton, T., Lee, C.H., Carello, C., & Turvey, M.T. (2002). Equal homophonic priming with words and pseudohomophones. *Journal of Experimental Psychology: Human Perception and Performance, 28*, 3–21.

Lukatela, G., Frost, S.J., & Turvey, M.T. (1998). Phonological priming by masked nonword primes in the lexical decision task. *Journal of Memory and Language, 39*, 666–683.

Lukatela, G., Frost, S.J., & Turvey, M.T. (1999). Identity priming in English is compromised by phonological ambiguity. *Journal of Experimental Psychology: Human Perception and Performance*, 25, 775–790.

Lukatela, G., Savič, M., Urosevič, Z., & Turvey, M.T. (1997). Phonological ambiguity impairs identity priming in naming and lexical decision. *Journal of Memory and Language*, 36, 360–381.

Marín, J., & Carreiras, M. (2002, September). *Syllable processing upon illusory conjunction paradigm.* Paper presented at the 8th Annual Conference on Architectures and Mechanisms for Language Processing. Tenerife, Spain.

Mathey, S., & Zagar, D. (2001, September). *Lexical similarity in visual word recognition: The effects of sublexical units in French.* Paper presented at the XII Conference of the European Society for Cognitive Psychology, Edinburgh, UK.

McClelland, J.L., & Rumelhart, D.E. (1981). An interactive activation model of context effects in letter perception: Part 1. An account of basic findings. *Psychological Review*, 88, 375–407.

Millis, M.L. (1986). Syllables and spelling units affect feature integration in words. *Memory and Cognition*, 14, 409–419.

O'Regan, J.K., & Jacobs, M. (1992). Optimal viewing position effect in word recognition: A challenge to current theory. *Journal of Experimental Psychology: Human Perception and Performance*, 18, 185–197.

Perea, M. (1998). Orthographic neighbours are not all equal: Evidence using an identification technique. *Language and Cognitive Processes*, 13, 77–90.

Perea, M., & Carreiras, M. (1995). Efectos de frecuencia silábica en tareas de identificación. *Psicológica*, 16, 483–496.

Perea, M., & Carreiras, M. (1998). Effects of syllable frequency and syllable neighborhood frequency in visual word recognition. *Journal of Experimental Psychology: Human Perception and Performance*, 24, 134–144.

Perea, M., & Rosa, E. (2000). Repetition and form priming interact with neighborhood density at a brief stimulus-onset asynchrony. *Psychonomic Bulletin and Review*, 7, 668–677.

Peretz, I., Lussier, I., & Beland, R. (1998). The differential role of syllabic structure in stem completion for French and English. *European Journal of Cognitive Psychology*, 10, 75–112.

Plaut, D.C., McClelland, J.L., Seidenberg, M.S., & Patterson, K. (1996). Understanding normal and impaired word reading: Computational principles. *Psychological Review*, 103, 56–115.

Pollatsek, A., Lesch, M.F., Morris, R.K., & Rayner, K. (1992). Phonological codes are used in integrating information across saccades in word identification and reading. *Journal of Experimental Psychology: Human Perception and Performance*, 18, 148–162.

Prinzmetal, W., Treiman, R., & Rho, S.H. (1986). How to see a reading unit. *Journal of Memory and Language*, 25, 461–475.

Rapp, B.C. (1992). The nature of sublexical orthographic organization: The bigram trough hypothesis examined. *Journal of Memory and Language*, 31, 33–53.

Rastle, K., & Coltheart, M. (1999). Lexical and nonlexical phonological priming in reading aloud. *Journal of Experimental Psychology: Human Perception and Performance*, 25, 461–481.

Rayner, K. (1979). Eye guidance in reading: Fixation locations within words. *Perception*, 8, 21–30.

Sebastián-Gallés, MN., Martí, M.A., Carreiras, M., & Cuetos, F. (2000). *LEXESP: Una base de datos informatizada del español* [LEXESP: A computerized database of Spanish]. Universitat de Barcelona, Spain.

Segui, J., & Grainger, J. (1990). Priming word recognition with orthographic neighbors: Effects of relative prime-target frequency. *Journal of Experimental Psychology: Human Perception and Performance, 16,* 65–76.

Seidenberg, M.S., & McClelland, J.L. (1989). A distributed developmental model of word recognition and naming. *Psychological Review, 96,* 523–568.

Seidenberg, M.S. (1989). Reading complex words. In G. Carlson & M. Tanenhaus (Eds.), *Linguistic structure in language processing.* Dordrecht: Kluwer Academic Publishers.

Shen, D., & Forster, K.I. (1999). Masked phonological priming in reading Chinese words depends on the task. *Language and Cognitive Processes, 14,* 429–459.

Spoehr, K.T., & Smith, E.E. (1973). The role of syllables in perceptual processing. *Cognitive Psychology, 5,* 71–89.

Taft, M. (1979). Lexical access via an orthographic code: The BOSS. *Journal of Verbal Learning and Verbal Behavior, 18,* 21–39.

Taft, M. (1982). An alternative to grapheme-phoneme conversion rules? *Memory and Cognition, 10,* 465–474.

Taft, M. (1991). *Reading and the mental lexicon.* Hove, UK: Lawrence Erlbaum Associates Ltd.

Taft, M. (1992). The body of the BOSS: Subsyllabic units in the lexical processing of polysyllabic words. *Journal of Experimental Psychology: Human Perception and Performance, 18,* 1004–1014.

Taft, M. (2001). Processing of orthographic structure by adults of different reading ability. *Language and Speech, 44,* 351–376.

Taft, M. (2002). Orthographic processing of polysyllabic words by native and non-native English speakers. *Brain and Language, 81,* 532–544.

Taft, M., & Forster, K.I. (1976). Lexical storage and retrieval of polymorphemic and polysyllabic words. *Journal of Verbal Learning and Verbal Behavior, 15,* 607–620.

Taft, M., & Radeau, M. (1995). The influence of the phonological characteristics of a language on the functional units of reading: A study in French. *Canadian Journal of Experimental Psychology, 49,* 330–346.

Tousman, S., & Inhoff, A. (1992). Phonology in multisyllabic word recognition. *Journal of Psycholinguistic Research, 21,* 525–544.

Treiman, R., & Chafetz, J. (1987). Are there onset and rime-like units in printed words? In M. Coltheart (Ed.), *Attention and Performance XII* (pp. 281–298). Hove, UK: Lawrence Erlbaum Associates Ltd.

Treiman, R., & Zukowski, A. (1988). Units in reading and spelling. *Journal of Memory and Language, 27,* 466–477.

Treiman, R., Mullennix, J., Bijeljac-Babic, R., & Richmond-Welty, E.D. (1995). The special role of rimes in the description, use, and aquisition of English orthography. *Journal of Experimental Psychology: General, 124,* 107–136.

Van Orden, G.C., Johnston, J.C., & Hale, B.L. (1988). Word identification in reading proceeds from spelling to sound to meaning. *Journal of Experimental Psychology: Learning, Memory and Cognition, 14,* 371–385.

Van Orden, G.C. (1987). A ROWS is a ROSE: Spelling, sound and reading. *Memory and Cognition, 15,* 181–198.

APPENDIX
Prime-target pairs in Experiment 1

The items are arranged in triplets in the following order: CV prime, CVC prime, target word.

balir; balta; BALDE; banar; bante; BANDO; basus; bascu; BASTO; caler; calta; CALDO; casur; caste; CASCO; cinus; cincu; CINTA; colir; colsa; COLMO; curor; curla; CURSI; finel; fintu; FINCA; honir; honru; HONDA; maris; marti; MARZO; monis; mondi; MONJA; pales; palca; PALMO; parer; partu; PARDO; pasur; pasca; PASMO; pesis; pesmo; PESTE; salin; salge; SALDO; senis; sento; SENDA; tenur; tenge; TENSO; torri; torca; TORPE; venes; vengi; VENTA; verus; verbu; VERJA; basun; bascu; BASES; camiz; campu; CAMAS; casis; cascu; CASAR; celir; celte; CELOS; cosus; costi; COSER; curon; curvi; CURAS; genir; genta; GENES; hones; honta; HONOR; junas; juntu; JUNIO; lapes; lapse; LÁPIZ; marir; marzu; MARES; moner; montu; MONOS; palir; palmi; PALOS; pesir; pestu; PESOS; pisel; pisti; PISOS; recer; rectu; RECIO; salin; saldu; SALAS; secal; secti; SECOS; tenel; tensu; TENAZ; toral; torpa; TOROS; tumas; tumbi; TUMOR; venil; vendu; VENAS

Prime-target pairs in Experiment 2

The items are arranged in quintuplets in the following order: CV prime (orthographic + phonological), CVC prime (orthographic + phonological), CV prime (phonological-only), CVC prime (phonological-only), target word.

balis; balta; valis; valta; BALDE; balir; balco; valir; valco; BALSA; bamin; bampe; vamin; vampe; BAMBU; banis; banfe; vanis; vanfe; BANCO; baner; banso; vaner; vanso; BANDA; banil; bansa; vanil; vansa; BANDO; barel; barle; varel; varle; BARBA; baren; barfo; varen; varfo; BARCA; basir; baspo; vasir; vaspo; BASTA; beliz; belte; veliz; velte; BELGA; binur; binte; vinur; vinte; BINGO; bolir; bolte; volir; volte; BOLSA; bolud; bolma; volud; volma; BOLSO; bomes; bompo; vomes; vompo; BOMBA; bomar; bompe; vomar; vompe; BOMBO; boras; borta; voras; vorta; BORDE; bules; bulma; vules; vulma; BULTO; burin; burto; vurin; vurto; BURLA; caluz; calta; kalux; kalta; CALCO; calir; calcu; kalir; kalcu; CALDO; caler; calde; kaler; kalde; CALMA; caloz; calmi; kaloz; kalmi; CALVO; canar; canri; kanar; kanri; CANTO; carun; carto; kaun; karto; CARGA; casur; caspi; kasur; kaspi; CASCO; casin; caslo; kasin; kaslo; CASPA; casor; casmo; kasor; kasmo; CASTA; celer; celto; seler; selto; CELDA; celur; celmo; selur; selmo; CELTA; cenur; cente; senur; sente; CENSO; ceril; cerma; seril; serma; CERCO; ceral; cerla; seral; serla; CERDO; cesur; cesmo; sesur; sesmo; CESTA; cinir; cindo; sinir; sindo; CINTA; cires; cirta; sires; sirta; CIRCO; colas; colta; kolaz; kolta; COLMO; corar; corma; korar; korma; CORTE; cosez; cosmi; kosez; kosmi; COSTA; culaz; culma; kulaz; kulma; CULTO; curer; curte; kurer; kurte; CURVA; geser; gespo; jeser; jesop; GESTA; vasud; vasla; basud; basla; VASCO; venor; vento; benor; bento; VENDA; venil; venso; benil; benso; VENTA; verel; vergo; berel; bergo; VERJA; verul; verma; berul; berma; VERSO; vular; vulme; bular; bulme; VULGO; zuril; zurma; suril; surma; ZURDO; balun; balte; valun; valte; BALAS; baliz; balma; valiz; valma; BALÓN; banor; bante; vanor; vante; BANAL; baral; barlo; varal; varlo; BARES; baser; basmo; vaser; vasmo; BASAL; bason; basli; vason; vasli; BASES; besun; besgo; vesun; vesgo; BESAR; bolen; bolto; volen; volto; BOLAS; bonar; bonta; vonar; vonta; BONOS; canis; cansi; kanis; kansi; CANAL; capel; capti; kapel; kapti; CAPÓN; comiz; combu; komix; kombu; COMER; carin; carle; karin; karle; CAROS; casiz; caste; kasiz; kaste; CASAR; celan; celma; selan; selma; CELOS; cenis; censi; senis; sensi; CENAR; cesol; cesme; sesol; sesme; CESAR; cinor; cinti; sinor; sinti; CINES; siras; cirla; siras; sirla; CIRIO; coler; colmi; koler; kolmi; COLAS; coper; copte; koper; kopte; COPIA; corun; corme; korun; korme; CORAL; corad; corfe; korad; korfe; COROS; cosil;

cosmo; kosil; kosmo; COSER; cunel; cunto; kunel; kunto; CUNAS; curol; curla; kurol; kurla; CURAR; gemal; gembo; jemal; jembo; GEMIR; genor; genta; jenor; jenta; GENES; genas; gensa; jenas; jensa; GENIO; girol; girte; jirol; jirte; GIRAR; valos; valca; balos; balca; VALER; vasel; vasma; basel; basma; VASOS; velor; velto; belor; belto; VELAS; velin; velta; belin; belta; VELOZ; vener; venfe; bener; benfe; VENAS; venos; venlo; benos; benlo; VENIR; verer; vermo; berer; bermo; VERAZ; vinar; vinla; binar; binla; VINOS; viros; virto; biros; birto; VIRIL; virel; virga; birel; birga; VIRUS; visal; visma; bisal; bisma; VISIR; viser; visga; biser; bisga; VISÓN; visus; vispa; bisus; bispa; VISOR; volon; volce; bolon; bolce; VOLAR; voril; vorgo; boril; borgo; VORAZ; zarir; zarga; sarir; sarga; ZARES; zonel; zonto; sonel; sonto; ZONAS; zumal; zumpa; sumal; sumpa; ZUMOS

Prime-target pairs in Experiment 3

The items are arranged in quadruplets in the following order: phonological prime, rime-only prime, control prime, target word.

valol; ralol; valja; BALAS; valis; falis; valti; BALÓN; vasun; fasun; vastu; BASES; vesel; fesel; vesde; BESOS; volen; folen; volme; BOLAS; kalud; lalud; kalfo; CALOR; kaner; maner; kange; CANAL; kasun; ñasun; kascu; CASOS; senud; penud; sengo; CENAR; sesol; jesol; sespo; CESAR; kolel; folel; koldo; COLAS; kolud; zolud; kolga; COLOR; komor; pomor; kombo; COMÚN; korez; vorez; kortu; CORAL; kosun; dosun; kosgo; COSAS; kosuz; gosuz; kosda; COSER; kuron; buron; kurgo; CURAR; jired; pired; jirco; GIRAR; zalen; galen; zalpa; SALAS; zaler; raler; zalul; SALÓN; zanel; tanel; zande; SANOS; zecod; becod; zecto; SECAR; zenin; fenin; zente; SENOS; zoled; joled; zolfo; SOLAR; zolin; nolin; zolpi; SOLOS; zonod; donod; zonte; SONAR; bacin; pacin; bactu; VACAS; basul; pasul; basmu; VASOS; becin; mecin; becna; VECES; elon; lelon; belge; VELAS; velud; melud; veldu; VELOZ; benol; penol; bensu; VENAS; benaz; zenaz; benti; VENIR; berun; serun; berpo; VERAZ; binul; rinul; binca; VINOS; boled; noled; volte; VOLAR; sonel; conel; sonde; ZONAS; zimue; pimue; zimbe; SIMIO; sumul; fumul; sumbe; ZUMOS; benol; tenol; benge; VENUS; balod; jalod; baltu; VALER; biroz; firoz; birno; VIRIL; saled; raled; zalne; SALIR; zerei; terei; zerto; SERIO; jenal; ñenal; jenca; GENIO

LANGUAGE AND COGNITIVE PROCESSES, 2004, *19* (3), 453–471

Sublexical units and supralexical combinatorics in the processing of interfixed Dutch compounds

Andrea Krott

University of Birmingham, Birmingham, UK

Peter Hagoort

F.C. Donders Centre for Cognitive Neuroimaging, the Netherlands

R. Harald Baayen

University of Nijmegen, Nijmegen, the Netherlands

This study addresses the supralexical inferential processes underlying wellformedness judgements and latencies for a specic sublexical unit that appears in Dutch compounds, the interfix. Production studies have shown that the selection of interfixes in novel Dutch compounds and the speed of this selection is primarily determined by the distribution of interfixes in existing compounds that share the left constituent with the target compound, i.e. the "left constituent family". In this paper, we consider the question whether constituent families also affect wellformedness decisions of novel as well as existing Dutch compounds in comprehension. We visually presented compounds containing interfixes that were either in line with the bias of the left constituent family or not. In the case of existing compounds, we also presented variants with replaced interfixes. As in production, the bias of the left constituent family emerged as a crucial predictor for both acceptance rates and response latencies. This result supports the hypothesis that, as in production, constituent families are (co-)activated in comprehension. We argue that this co-activation is part of a supralexical inferential process, and we discuss how our data might be interpreted within sublexical and supralexical theories of morphological processing.

Correspondence should be addressed to Andrea Krott, School of Psychology – Hills Building, University of Birmingham, Edgbaston, Birmingham B15 2TT, UK. Email a.krott@bham.ac.uk

This study was financially supported by the Dutch National Research Council NWO (PIONIER grant to the third author), the University of Nijmegen (the Netherlands), and the Max Planck Institute for Psycholinguistics (Nijmegen, the Netherlands). We want to thank Dominiek Sandra and an anonymous reviewer for their comments on an earlier version of this paper.

http://www.tandf.co.uk/journals/pp/01690965.html   DOI: 10.1080/01690960344000251

INTRODUCTION

This study investigates a specific kind of sublexical unit, the interfix, that occurs in compounds in a range of Germanic languages including German, Swedish, Danish, and Dutch. Dutch interfixes are enigmatic in several respects. First, the form of Dutch interfixes suggests that they might be suffixes. For instance, the interfix *-en-* in *boek-en-kast*, "book case", is similar to the plural *-en* in *boek-en*, "books", and Schreuder, Neijt, Van der Weide, and Baayen (1998) have shown that this interfix may elicit plural semantics for *boek* "book" in *boekenkast*. But in *pann-en-koek*, "pancake", the *-en-* does not contribute a plural meaning. While a bookcase is a case for books, a pancake is not a kind of food made in several pans. This example illustrates that, unlike normal affixes, the semantics of interfixes are underdetermined. Second, the distribution of the interfixes is underdetermined as well. A given noun may appear with no interfix at all in some compounds, and with interfixes in other compounds. For instance, *rund-vlees*, "beef" has no interfix, but *rund-er-gehakt*, "minced beef", contains the interfix *-er-*. There are no clear syntagmatic rules governing the distribution of the interfixes. To complicate matters, some words appear both with and without interfix. Thus, *spelling-regel* "spelling rule" coexists side by side with *spelling-s-regel*. Third, even though semantically and distributionally underdetermined, speakers of Dutch have clear intuitions about whether an interfix is appropriate for a given compound, and if so, which interfix is the preferred choice.

These enigmatic properties of interfixes raise the question of how interfixes are produced and understood. What guides a speaker of Dutch to say *asielzoeker-s-centrum* more often than *asielzoeker-centrum*? Why is it that to a Dutch reader or listener, *asielzoeker-s-centrum* intuitively feels somewhat more appropriate than the form without the interfix *-s-*?

A series of recent studies have addressed the production of interfixes. These studies have shown that the distribution of Dutch and German interfixes is primarily determined by paradigmatic analogy (Krott, Baayen, & Schreuder, 2001; Krott, Schreuder, & Baayen, 2002a, 2002b). The notion of paradigmatic analogy can be made precise in terms of the probability distributions of interfixation in the constituent families of the left and right constituents of a given compound. The left constituent family of a noun such as *boek-en-kast* consists of all compounds in Dutch that share the modifier *boek* as the left constituent. Similarly, the right constituent family of *boek-en-kast* is the set of compounds sharing the head *kast* as the right constituent. Lexical statistics, experimentation, and computational modelling all show that the probability distributions of interfixation in these constituent families, primarily the left constituent family, but also to some extent the right constituent family, guide the selection of the interfix in production. The greater the probabilistic support for an interfix given the left and right constituents, the more likely it is to be selected, and the shorter the time required to select the interfix is. Conversely, an interfix with little paradigmatic support is hardly ever selected, and when it is selected, selection times are long (Krott et al., 2002b). When the probability distributions of interfixation in the constituent families are uniform, i.e., all interfixation possibilities are equally plausible within a given constituent family, participants are unsure about what interfix to select, and the choices made are variable within and across speakers.

The observed effects of paradigmatic analogy can be understood as arising from activation spreading within the left and right constituent families. A computational model is formulated in Krott et al. (2002a). Reformulated within the general framework of Levelt, Roelofs, and Meyer (1999), the conceptualisation process would lead to the activation of the lemma of, e.g., *boek-en-kast* ("book case"). This lemma would in turn activate the lemmas of its constituents *boek* ("book"), *kast* ("case"), and that of the interfix *-en-*. When activation is allowed to spread from *boek* (strongly) and *kast* (weakly) to the lemmas of the compounds in their left and right constituent families, with these compounds in turn co-activating their own interfixes, the pattern of activation of the interfixes will come to reflect the weighted sum of the probability distributions of the left and right constituent families. Combined with a thresholding mechanism, the observed patterns of interfix selection and the corresponding selection latencies result, as shown by Krott et al. (2002a).

Thus far, the possible role of paradigmatic analogy for interfixes in language comprehension has not been studied. The present study addresses this issue for the visual modality. In order to understand how paradigmatic analogy might arise, it is useful to consider briefly the two main theories of morphological processing in visual word recognition.

According to "sublexical" theories of morphological processing, morphological structure is already detected during the early stages of visual processing, before lexically stored information is accessed. Sublexical effects, such as the longer rejection latencies obtained for Italian pseudo-affixed words by Burani, Dovetto, Thornton, and Laudanna (1997) or the equivalent effect of masked priming obtained by Longtin, Segui, and Hallé (2003) for French opaque derived words and pseudo-derived simplex words, can be accounted for by assuming that affixes are sublexical units with their own visual access representations. Frequency effects for complex words can be explained by assuming that complex words also have access representations with activation levels proportional to frequency of use (Sereno & Jongman, 1997; Baayen, Dijkstra, & Schreuder, 1997; Bertram, Laine, Baayen, Schreuder, & Hyönä, 1999).

According to "supralexical" theories, however, morphological structure does not leave traces at prelexical levels of processing (Giraudo & Grainger, 2001, 2003). Instead, morphological effects are constrained to occur after access to the lexicon has been completed. Frequency effects for compounds can be explained by assuming that co-occurrence probabilities are available for combinations of word constituents. Effects suggesting the presence of access representations for affixes have to be explained in terms of inferential processes generalising over stored lexical representations of affixed words.

In this study, we will remain agnostic as to whether morphology has a sublexical component. In what follows, we will build on the minimal assumptions that, upon visual presentation of a Dutch compound, (1) the modifier and head lemma representations will be activated, (2) that a lemma representation for the interfix will be activated, either through bottom-up activation from a dedicated access representation, or by an inferential lexical process, and (3) that in the case of existing words, the lemma representation for the compound will be activated, either through a corresponding access representation, or through lexical tracking of the co-occurrence likelihood of head and modifier.

These assumptions lead to a number of predictions. First, it follows from assumption (1) that the constituent families of the head and modifier might be activated during reading, thanks to activation spreading from the head and the modifier into their respective constituent families. Second, assumption (2) predicts that changing the interfix in existing words, and using different interfixes in novel compounds, should be detected and affect lexical processing. Third, given assumption (3), frequency effects for the compound as a whole are expected that might interact with changing the interfix in existing words.

Note that within this framework, paradigmatic analogy, if present, would arise as a purely supralexical effect. Consequently, the theoretical goal of the present paper can be viewed as showing how inferential processes of the kind required by supralexical theories of morphology might work in the case of the – sublexical – interfixes of Dutch.

There is one line of research suggesting that an effect of paradigmatic analogy may well be present in reading, namely, the work by Gagné and colleagues on the semantic interpretation of compounds (Gagné, 2001; Gagné & Shoben, 1997). These authors show that the interpretation of a compound is guided by the probability distribution of the semantic relations entertained by the modifier constituent. Given that paradigmatic analogy constrains and guides semantic interpretation, we expect paradigmatic analogy to likewise guide and constrain the interpretation of the interfixes.

On the other hand, the possibility of an effect of paradigmatic analogy is called into question by the results reported by De Jong, Feldman, Schreuder, Pastizzo, and Baayen (2002) for Dutch compounds without interfixes. De Jong et al. manipulated the type count of both left and right constituent families, i.e., the morphological family size of the modifier and the head. The morphological family size has been shown to co-determine response latencies in lexical decision experiments for both mono-morphemic words (e.g., De Jong, Schreuder, & Baayen, 2000; Schreuder & Baayen, 1997) and derived words (Bertram, Schreuder, & Baayen, 2000). Like the effect of the constituent family on the selection of interfixes, the effect of family size has been interpreted as indicating co-activation of family members during lexical processing (e.g., Schreuder & Baayen, 1997). De Jong et al. (2002) reported a facilitatory family size effect for both the modifier and the head. However, post-hoc analyses suggested that a correlated variable, the summed frequency of the compounds of the families sharing either the head or the modifier, is the crucial predictor. This suggests that the probability of a noun to be modifier or head in a compound might be the crucial predictor. While these findings support our assumption (1), namely, that the constituents of a compound are detected, it is unclear whether type-based analogical effects should be expected when moving from compounds without interfixes to compounds with interfixes.

In order to study the possible effect of paradigmatic analogy, we made use of a variant of the lexical decision task, namely, a wellformedness decision task. Instead of having to decide whether a letter string is a word of Dutch in a list containing both words and pseudo words, we asked participants to decide whether letter strings were well-formed words of Dutch in a list containing compounds with conventional and non-conventional interfixes and correct as well as incorrect plural suffixes. The use of wellformedness decision instead of lexical decision has several advantages. First, in lexical decision, the semantic interpretability of a compound co-determines response latencies. By directly tapping into grammaticality judgements, we hope to reduce semantic paradigmatic analogy as a source of variation in our experiment. Second, replacing the conventional interfix may result in a word that feels more grammatical, or in a word that feels less grammatical, depending on whether the change goes with or against the probabilistic bias. Since both the original form and the manipulated form are legitimate words of the language, lexicality decisions are inappropriate for the question at hand. Third, in order to study the reading of novel interfixed compounds, neologisms were included in the experiment. Such neologisms are likely to elicit no-responses in lexical decision, an understandable response that, however, is of no use for the understanding of paradigmatic analogy in comprehension of new possible Dutch words.

A disadvantage of the wellformedness decision task, that it shares to some extent with visual lexical decision, is that it is unclear to what extent strategic processes might be involved, and hence, to what extent it reflects normal reading of continuous text. Although wellformedness latencies are somewhat longer than lexical decision latencies, they are far too short for strategic effects involving the left and right constituent families—speakers of Dutch are completely unaware of why they find some interfixed compounds more acceptable than others. Further research using, e.g., eye-movement recordings, will have to clarify to what extent the effects obtained with this task in vitro generalise to reading in vivo.

In what follows, we therefore present a wellformedness decision experiment addressing the question of whether the analogical effect of the left constituent family that has been observed in production experiments can also be attested for wellformedness decisions of novel and existing Dutch compounds.

EXPERIMENT

To study the role of paradigmatic analogy in comprehension, we made use of an incomplete factorial design with three factors. The first factor of interest is the Existence of the compound (levels Existing and Novel). The critical manipulation, however, is the support for a given interfix provided by the bias of the left constituent family. The bias of the left constituent family with respect to a given interfix is the probabilistic support that this interfix receives. A positive bias indicates that the interfix is the maximum likelihood choice, a negative bias indicates that it is dispreferred. For this experiment, we defined two levels for the factor Left Bias: Support (the interfix is the maximum likelihood choice) versus No Support (there is little or no support for the interfix). We expect faster response latencies when the interfix is supported by the bias than when it is not supported. In case of novel compounds, we also expect participants to accept a compound more often as well-formed if its interfix is supported by the bias. In the case of existing compounds, a third variable comes into play: whether the interfix is the conventional choice in current use. Since existing compounds usually have a single conventional interfix, we can replace the conventional interfix by another, non-conventional one. This leads us to the third factor in our experiment, the factor Replacement with two levels, Normal and Replaced. We expect that participants rarely accept a replaced interfix since this leads to an unusual form of a known compound, and to find rejections even if a replaced interfix is supported by a large part of the constituent family. However, we expect that an interfix will be less often rejected if it is supported by the bias.

Method

Materials.   We determined frequencies and constituent families for all compounds that we used in our experiment on the basis of the CELEX database (Baayen, Piepenbrock, & Gulikers, 1995). We first constructed a list of 160 novel compounds in the plural form (List 1) using interfixes that were supported by the Left Bias. Support by the Bias was quantified as the percentage of family members containing the interfix of the target compound. Across the items in our experiment, the mean percentage was 96.7% (range 70.6–100%). The mean number of such supporting compounds was 10.5 (range 1–78). An example of a compound with a Left Bias is *mosterdzielen* "mustard souls". (For ease of exposition, we will describe the absence of an overt interfix as the presence of a zero-interfix. Thus, *mosterd* is described as having a strong positive bias for the zero interfix.) The bias of the right constituent family for the chosen interfix varied, but was neutral on average (average bias: 45.1% (3.2 family members), range 0–95.5% (0–90 family members)). For each compound of List 1, we constructed three additional variants. List 1a contained compounds in which the interfix was replaced by an interfix that is not supported by the Left Bias (new left bias: mean 1.7% (0.2), range 0–29.4% (0–14)) new right bias: mean 31.1% (2.6), range 0–78.9% (0–22); example: *mosterdszielen* "mustards souls"). The second and third variants (Lists 1b and 1c) mirrored Lists 1 and 1a with respect to the interfix, but used an ungrammatical plural suffix (*mosterdziels* "mustard souls", *mosterdsziels* "mustards souls"). These words served as targets for an experiment not reported here, and served as fillers for the present experiment. For the sake of comparability with this other experiment, the target items for the present study were also presented in their plural form.

In addition, we selected two lists of existing compounds from the CELEX database: List 2 contained 160 compounds in the plural form with interfixes that were supported by the Left Bias (bias strength: mean 98.3% (23.1), range 80–100% (4–200); example: *filmtheaters* "film theaters" with a bias for the zero interfix), while List 3 contained plural compounds with interfixes that were not supported by the Left Bias (*vruchtbomen* "fruit trees" with bias for *-en-*). Since the latter type of compounds is rare, the size of List 3 was smaller (62 compounds, bias strength: mean 14.7% (2.4), range 0–29.4% (0–15)). The bias of the right constituents in both Lists 2 and 3 usually preferred the same interfix as the bias of the left constituents (List 2: bias strength: mean 56.5% (6.9), range 0–100% (0–46); List 3: bias strength: mean 27.1% (6.1), range 0–91.3% (0–52)). Thus, the right bias was in line with the left bias. For each compound of Lists 2 and 3, we constructed a variant (Lists 2a and 3a) by replacing the normal interfix with another one, such that for List 2 the new interfixes were not supported by the Left Bias (new left bias: mean 0.9% (0.2), range 0–20% (0–8); new right bias: mean 24.3% (3.1), range 0–77.8% (0–28); example: *filmen-theaters* "films theaters"), while for List 3 the new interfixes were supported by the Left Bias (new left bias: mean 84.3% (15.7), range 70–100% (4–72); new right bias: mean 55.6% (11.8), range 0–100% (0–50)); *vruchtenbomen* "fruits trees"). For the compounds of List 2 and List 2a, we again constructed the corresponding filler plural compounds with incorrect plural suffixes (*filmtheateren* "film theaters"; *filmentheateren* "films theaters"). We did not create a corresponding list for List 3 since this list is too small (62 compounds) to be split up into more than 2 groups for a between-subject design.

The compounds of Lists 1 to 3 were matched for length, the compounds of Lists 2 and 3 were also matched for frequency (List 1: length: mean 12.2 letters = 4.5 cm, range 3.2–5.4 cm; List 2: length: mean 12.0 letters = 4.5 cm, range 3.1–5.0 cm; compound frequency (per 42 million wordforms): mean 21.7, range 0–342; List 3: length: mean 12.5 letters = 4.4 cm, range 3.3–5.2 cm; compound frequency (per 42 million wordforms): mean 23.4, range 0–258).

We distributed the items over four experimental lists such that each experimental list contained a compound stem only once (abstracting away from plural suffix and interfix). This ensured that no participant saw a compound stem twice. Thus, a given participant was exposed to 160 novel compound stems (40 stems with support for interfix and correct suffix, 40 stems with support for interfix and incorrect suffix, 40 stems with unsupported interfix and correct suffix, and 40 stems with unsupported interfix and incorrect suffix), to 160 existing compounds with a strong left bias for the conventional interfix (40 stems with conventional interfix and correct suffix, 40 stems with conventional interfix and incorrect suffix, 40 stems with replaced interfix and correct suffix, and 40 stems with replaced interfix and incorrect suffix), to 62 compounds with no left bias for the conventional interfix (31 with the conventional interfix, and 31 with a non-conventional one). We also presented to each subject a set of 160 additional plural compounds with normal plural endings, which served the purpose of increasing the number of wellformed compounds (from 151 to 311), given the high number of illformed compounds for each subject (231). In all, a participant responded to 542 trials, preceded by 25 practice items.

Procedure.   Participants were tested in a noise-attenuated experimental room. We asked them to decide as quickly and as accurately as possible whether a compound appearing on the screen is a wellformed Dutch compound, by pressing either a "yes" or a "no" button. We illustrated what they should treat as wellformed by means of an example of an existing compound. We presented an "illformed" (= replaced) interfix and an "illformed" (= replaced) suffix. We instructed them to treat existing and novel compounds equally, i.e., to judge the wellformedness, not the existence of the compound. Each trial started with a fixation mark remaining on the screen for 500 ms. After another 500 ms., the Dutch definite article for plural noun forms, *de* (Engl. "the"), appeared on the screen and remained for 200 ms. The presentation of the article was inserted for the analysis of the fillers. For the present analysis, it has no other effect than being an additional fixation point. After another 200 ms, the stimulus compound appeared at the same position for 1500 ms. The maximum time span allowed for response was 2000 ms from stimulus onset of the compound. Stimuli were presented on Nec Multicolor monitors in white lowercase 21 point Helvetica letters on a dark background. The experiment was interrupted by three breaks and lasted approximately 40 mins.

Participants.   Forty students of the University of Nijmegen were paid to participate in the experiment. All were native speakers of Dutch.

Results

Due to coding errors, we had to exclude from the analysis the responses to three existing compounds, two containing an interfix that was supported by the Left Bias, one containing an interfix that was not supported by the Left Bias. In addition, responses outside the maximum time span were counted as errors. Figure 1 and Table 1 summarise the mean percentages and the mean response latencies broken down by Left Bias and Existence. Note that in the case of existing compounds, the presented word either contained a normal or a replaced interfix and that the support by the Left Bias refers to the support of the interfix presented.

A by-item logistic regression analysis of the response decisions (wellformed or not wellformed) revealed signicant main effects of the Left Bias (more rejections when the interfix is not supported by the bias), $F(1, 756) = 639.0$, $p < .0001$, and Existence (more rejections for non-existing constituent combinations), $F(1, 757) = 35.6$, $p < .0001$, and no interaction between these factors, $F(1, 755) < 1$. Thus, existing compounds were accepted as being wellformed more often than novel compounds. More importantly, participants accepted a compound more often when the interfix was supported by the Left Bias than when it received no such support.

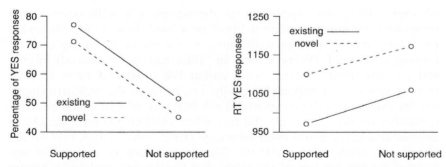

Figure 1. Mean percentage and mean response latency (RT in ms) of "yes" responses to existing and novel compounds with interfixes that are supported or not supported by the Left Constituent Family Bias.

Since we know from production studies that the bias of the right constituent family also has an effect on the decisions, we included it as a covariate. The covariance analysis supported the main effects of Left Bias, $F(1, 756) = 639.0, p < .0001$, and Existence, $F(1, 757) = 35.6, p < .0001$, and revealed an additional effect of the Right Bias (a higher acceptance rate as the support from the right constituent family increases), $F(1, 755) = 26.6, p < .0001$. None of the factors interacted with each other. We conclude that the wellformedness decisions are based not only on the bias of the left constituent family, but also on the right constituent family, just as observed previously for the production of interfixes.

We also examined the counts of wellformedness decisions for the novel compounds and the existing compounds separately, as this allows us to

TABLE 1
Percentage of yes responses, no responses, and errors as well as mean response latencies (RT in ms, standard deviations in parentheses) when deciding on the wellformedness of novel (3200 responses) and existing compounds (5620 responses) containing interfixes that are supported by the Left Constituent Family Bias versus interfixes that are not supported by the Left Constituent Family Bias

Compound type	Response	Supported		Not supported	
		%	RT	%	RT
existing	yes	77.0	971 (275)	51.5	1059 (304)
existing	no	20.6	1121 (280)	45.5	1131 (267)
existing	error	2.4		3.0	
novel	yes	71.2	1099 (284)	45.1	1172 (291)
novel	no	27.0	1216 (301)	51.9	1175 (303)
novel	error	1.8		3.0	

include various frequency measures as covariates, including the frequency of the compound as a whole (available only for the existing compounds) and the frequency of the constituents as independent nouns.

First consider the novel compounds. The bottom half of Table 1 and Figure 1 summarise the pattern of results broken down by Left Bias. A logistic analysis of covariance revealed a main effect of Left Bias (no support by Left Bias implies more rejections), $F(1, 318) = 222.37, p < .0001$, and an interaction of Right Bias and the frequency of the right constituent as an independent noun (a greater Right Bias combined with a greater right frequency leads to a higher acceptance rate), $F(1, 317) = 26.18, p < .0001$.

Next consider the existing compounds. Table 2 and Figure 2 show the cell means broken down by Replacement and Left Bias. A logistic analysis of covariance revealed main effects of Replacement (replacing the conventional interfix led to more rejections), $F(1, 438) = 614.62, p < .0001$, and Left Bias (support by the bias led to fewer rejections), $F(1, 437) = 335.78, p < .0001$, as well as three interactions. The interaction of Replacement by Compound Frequency showed that a higher frequency led to higher acceptance rates for compounds with the conventional interfix, and to higher rejection rates for compounds with a non-conventional interfix, $F(2, 435) = 36.33, p < .0001$, as expected. The interaction of Right Bias by the Right Constituent Family Frequency shows that a high right bias combined with a head constituent that is very frequent as a head in compounds led to higher acceptance rates, $F(1, 432) = 11.66, p = .0006$. This suggests a cumulative effect of the lexicality of the head on the wellformedness of the interfix. The third interaction, Replacement by Right Bias, is enigmatic, as it suggests that a greater Right Bias led to more

TABLE 2

Percentage of yes responses, no responses, and errors as well as mean response latencies (RT in ms, standard deviations in parentheses) when deciding on the wellformedness of existing compounds with normal and replaced interfixes that are either supported by the Left Constituent Family Bias or not supported by the Left Constituent Bias

		Supported		Not supported	
Interfix	Response	%	RT	%	RT
normal	yes	83.9	967 (273)	73.7	1023 (294)
normal	no	14.1	1120 (288)	23.1	1162 (270)
normal	errors	2.0		3.2	
replaced	yes	68.1	977 (278)	34.4	1119 (312)
replaced	no	29.0	1121 (277)	63.0	1122 (266)
replaced	errors	2.6		2.9	

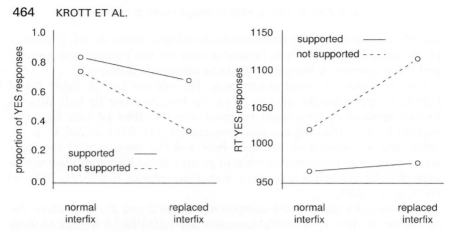

Figure 2. Proportion and response latencies (RT in ms) of yes responses to existing compounds with normal and replaced interfixes that are either supported or not supported by the Left Constituent Family Bias.

rejections for the compounds with the conventional interfix, $F(2, 433) = 10.61$, $p < .0001$, instead of less rejections.

The results for replaced interfixes are remarkable. We expected that participants would rarely accept a replaced interfix since a replacement leads to an unusual form of the compound. This expectation turned out to be wrong. Compounds containing replaced interfixes were accepted very often when the replaced interfix was supported by the Left Bias (844 out of 1240 compounds). In other words, when the conventional interfix is exceptional given the probability distribution of the interfixes in the left constituent family, our replacement manipulation amounted to a form of regularisation that made the compound more wellformed.

Considered jointly, these analyses document the importance of the left and right bias for wellformedness decisions for novel and existing compounds. The combined presence of frequency effects of the compound as a whole and of its constituents provide further support for the (supra)lexical basis of the wellformedness decisions, as expected given our spreading activation model developed for the production of interfixes.

We now turn to consider the decision latencies in our experiment. A multi-level analysis of covariance with log response latency as dependent variable, and Existence, Left Bias and type of Response (positive versus negative wellformedness judgements) as predictor variables, with Right Bias as covariate, and with Subject as error stratum (see, e.g., Pinheiro & Bates, 2000) revealed main effects for Left Bias, Right Bias, and Response, as well as various interactions between these variables and Existence (all p values less than .02). We therefore analysed the yes and no responses separately for the subsets of novel and existing compounds.

First consider the response latencies for the novel compounds judged to be wellformed. We carried out a multi-level analysis of covariance with log response latency as dependent variable, Left Bias as predicting factor, and various frequency measures pertaining to the two constituents of the compound as covariates. (The logarithmic transformation of the response latencies changes a skewed, non-normal distribution into a nearly normal distribution, thereby bringing the dependent variable more in line with the normality assumptions of linear modelling and analysis of variance.) Of these measures, the frequency of the right constituent, as well as the family frequency of the right constituent, turned out to be relevant. After stepwise removal of irrelevant predictors, we observed a main effect for the frequency of the right constituent (compounds with a higher-frequency right constituent were responded to faster, $t(1819) = -2.39, p = .0169$), as well as two interactions, one of the frequency of the right constituent by Left Bias (compounds with an interfix not supported by the Left Bias were responded to more slowly for increasing frequency of the right constituent, $t(1819) = 6.12, p < .0001$), and one of the Right Bias by the Right Constituent Family Frequency (a higher Right Bias combined with a higher Right Constituent Family Frequency led to faster response latencies, $t(1819) = -5.12; p < .0001$). These main effects and interactions all remained highly significant in a sequential analysis of variance. (This also holds for all analyses to follow below.) The standard deviation of the Subject random effect was estimated at 0.1651, and that of the residual error at 0.2111. In sum: higher frequency counts for the right constituent led to faster positive responses for novel compounds, except when there is a conflict between an interfix not supported by the Left Bias (requiring a no-response) and a high right constituent frequency (requiring a yes-response). The latter suggests that the Right Bias might only influence response times when the compounds of the right family have sufficiently strong representations. Note that there was no independent contribution of the Left Bias to the response times. The large difference in Table 1 is due to the interaction of Left Bias and frequency of the right constituent. Assuming that left constituents are processed before right constituents, the strong effects of frequency measures of the right constituent might have masked any effects of the left constituent.

A similar analysis was carried out for the response latencies of the novel compounds judged to be not well-formed. For this subset of trials, we observed a main effect of Left Bias (lack of Left Bias support led to shorter rejection latencies, $t(1221) = -2.40, p = .0165$), as well as a main effect of Right Bias (a greater Right Bias led to faster rejection latencies, $t(1221) = -2.20, p = .0278$). Interestingly, the interaction between Left and Right Bias, $t(1221) = 2.8655, p = .0042$, showed that for compounds with an interfix not supported by the Left Bias, the effect of Right Bias was inhibitory. In other words, novel compounds with an interfix that is not supported by the Left Bias are easy to reject, except when there is a conflict with the Right Bias. The standard deviation of the subject random effect was 0.1343, and that of the residual error 0.2211.

Turning to the analysis of response latencies of existing compounds, we first consider the positive responses. We studied two factors, Replacement (is the interfix the conventional one or not), and Left Bias (is the interfix supported by the Left Bias or not). Covariates that turned out to be important in this analysis were Right Bias, Right Constituent Family Frequency, Compound Frequency, and the frequency of the left constituent. Main effects were observed for Left Bias [response latencies are longer when the Left Bias is small, $t(3604) = 2.09, p = .0365$], the Right Bias [a higher right bias led to longer response latencies, $t(3604) = 3.36, p = .0008$], and Compound Frequency [higher-frequency compounds are accepted faster, $t(3604) = -10.40, p < .0001$]. In addition, there were three interactions: an interaction between Replacement and Left Bias showed that a replaced interfix led to slower responses when there was no support of the Left Bias, $t(3604) = 5.63, p < .0001$. Note that a replaced interfix with a high Left Bias was accepted as fast as a conventional interfix with high Left Bias. An interaction between Right Bias and Right constituent family frequency indicated that for right constituents with non-negligible right family frequency, the right bias is facilitatory, $t(3604) = -5.79, p < .0001$. Finally, we observed an interaction between left constituent frequency and right constituent family frequency [compounds with left constituents that are frequent nouns and right constituents that occur in compounds that are frequent have shorter responses, $t(3604) = 4.75, p < .0001$]. Thus, for existing compounds, various measures of frequency of occurrence, the Left and Right Bias as well as Replacement of the interfix emerge as crucial determinants of response speed. The standard deviations of the subject random effect and the residual error were 0.1591 and 0.2306 respectively for the fitted multilevel model.

Finally, we consider the rejection latencies for the existing compounds. The only main effects for this subset of the data were Right Bias [a higher right bias led to shorter response latencies, $t(1838) = -3.79, p = .0002$] and Compound Frequency [higher frequency compounds were rejected faster, $t(1838) = -4.38, p = .0001$]. There was a significant interaction between Right constituent family frequency and Left constituent frequency [compounds with left constituents that are frequent nouns and right constituents that occur in compounds that are frequent elicited shorter responses, $t(1838) = 2.64, p = .0084$]. The prominent role of frequency suggests that the non-conventional use of an interfix is more easy to detect in higher frequency compounds and in compounds with more frequent constituents. For the multilevel model fit to this subset of the data, the standard deviation of the subject random effect was approximately 0.1099, and that of the error 0.2090.

DISCUSSION

This study addressed the supralexical combinatorics underlying perceived wellformedness of a particular sublexical unit, the interfix in Dutch compounds. All experimental research carried out thus far on interfixes has studied the production of interfixes in novel compounds. This study addresses the perceived wellformedness of interfixes, broadening the scope from production to comprehension, and studying not only novel compounds, but also existing compounds. We made use of a well-formedness decision task requiring participants to indicate, by means of a button box, as quickly and accurately as possible, whether a visually presented compound was a well-formed word of Dutch. We analysed both the wellformedness decisions themselves and the time (in ms) required to reach these decisions. The main pattern in the data is that, as in the production of interfixes, the probability distribution of interfixation in the left constituent family of a compound is a crucial predictor of both wellformedness decisions and of the corresponding response latencies. A stronger bias, i.e., stronger probabilistic support, leads to a higher incidence of positive wellformedness decisions and to shorter response latencies.

The pattern of results for the existing compounds is especially revealing. For these compounds, we observed a strong effect of compound frequency. Not surprisingly, a greater familiarity with a compound gives rise to more positive wellformedness decisions and to reduced response latencies. Replacement of the conventional interfix in a compound by another interfix was detected more often for higher-frequency compounds, and led to a reduction in the number of positive decisions, as expected. Interestingly, a strong left bias led to more positive wellformedness decisions, and to shorter response latencies, independently of the frequency of the compound, and also independently of whether the interfix in the compound was the conventional one or an experimental replacement. Although replacing the interfix by a non-conventional interfix led to lower acceptance rates, it reduced the speed of acceptance only if the interfix was not supported by the left bias. This shows that the processing of existing compounds is not merely a matter of activating the lemma of the compound. If that were the case, no effect of the left bias would be present, contrary to fact. Apparently, the left bias is effective "on-line", independently of whether the compound exists or not, supporting congruent interfixes and exerting regularisation pressure on incongruent interfixes.

Our experimental work on the production of interfixes revealed a small but consistent effect of the bias of the right constituent family in addition to the strong effect of the left constituent family (e.g., Krott et al., 2002a). The present comprehension experiment also revealed such an effect for the right bias, sometimes as a main effect, but often in interaction with other frequency measures such as the right constituent family frequency. Like the left bias, a right bias supporting the interfix leads to more positive decisions and to shorter response latencies.

In this study, we included various frequency measures as covariates that have been reported in the literature as affecting visual lexical processing, such as the frequencies and the positional family frequencies of the left and right constituent families. Of special interest is the finding that in many of our analyses the positional family frequency of the right constituent emerged as a significant predictor. This statistic was first observed to be relevant for visual lexical processing by De Jong et al. (2002). However, while these authors observed a positional family frequency effect for both the right and the left constituent, we see such an effect only for the right constituent. We suspect this is due to the presence of compounds with incorrect plural endings in our filler materials, attracting attention to the right side of compounds, and due to the presence of nonword compounds with an existing left (or right) constituent in the materials of De Jong et al., spreading attention equally over both constituents.

Considered jointly, our results provide strong evidence for a supralexical inferential process underlying intuitions of the wellformedness of Dutch compounds. Krott et al. (2002a) documented the feasibility of such a supralexical inferential process by means of a simulation study for the production of interfixes in novel compounds. The present results suggest that a similar spreading activation model might be appropriate for comprehension.

First consider novel compounds. Upon presentation of a novel compound, the access representations of its head and modifier constituents are activated, which in turn activate their corresponding lemma representations. Subsequently, activation flows into the constituent families, leading to co-activation of the compounds in these constituent families. The co-activated compounds in turn provide support for the different interfixes, resulting in a distribution of lemma activation levels for the interfixes that mirrors the probability distribution of the interfixes in the constituent families.

In sublexical theories of morphological processing, an access representation for the interfix would also be activated, which in turn would activate a corresponding lemma representation. The percept of wellformedness of the compound would then depend on the degree of convergence or divergence between the bottom-up support and the inferential lexical support from the constituent families. In supralexical theories of morphological processing, no access representations for sublexical units such as interfixes are permitted. In order to explain the dependence of wellformedness on the Left Bias of the interfix in novel compounds, some mechanism is required that allows the form of the presented compound to be checked against the form of the compound that would be synthesised for production. The most likely representational level for such a comparison would be the level of phonological form. The degree of mismatch between the phonological form that arises from bottom-up visual processes and the synthesised phonological form that arises from inferential analogical processes would then determine the percept of wellformedness.

For exisiting compounds, the sublexical and supralexical explanations would proceed along similar lines, with the addition of a lemma representation for the compound itself enhancing the bottom-up support proportional to its frequency.

Given that the current experimental literature is ambiguous as to whether the sublexical or the supralexical account is to be preferred (compare, e.g., Longtin et al., 2003, with Giraudo & Grainger, 2001, 2003), and given that the present experiment documents supralexical aspects of comprehension but has nothing to say about possible sublexical effects of interfixes, we will remain agnostic as to which account is to be preferred.

In the present study, as in the preceding studies, the bias of the constituent families is based on a type count of the compounds in these constituent families supporting the interfixes of Dutch. We saw in several of our analyses that right family frequencies also influence decisions and response latencies. This raises the question of whether the probabilistic support for the interfixes should not be weighted by the frequencies of the compounds in the constituent families. The weight of a single high-frequency, well-known compound in the constituent family might be stronger than the combined contribution of several less-frequent compounds. Along the lines of the traditional concept of analogy found in linguistics, such a single influential exemplar might drive analogical inference (e.g., Anshen & Aronoff, 1988). As a first step towards a more refined probability measure, we therefore included the frequency of the compound with the highest frequency in the left constituent family as a predictor. A multi-level analysis of covariance revealed this frequency measure to be an additional significant predictor ($p < .0001$): the higher this maximum frequency, the higher the wellformedness. The fact that this maximum frequency measure does not render the bias superfluous as a predictor shows that the traditional linguistic concept of analogy is too restricted. On the other hand, the fact that it is a significant predictor shows that a principled way of weighting by token frequency needs to be developed.

Summing up, we conclude that the analogical sets of the left and right constituent families are highly involved in wellformedness decisions of novel and existing Dutch compounds. Our study has thus broadened the evidence for an effect of the constituent family from the domain of language production to the domain of visual lexical processing. There are two lines of research that are required to strengthen these results. First, it will be necessary to clarify whether and to what extent analogical inferential processes take place when we move from wellformedness decisions on isolated compounds to the reading of compounds in running text. Second, further research is required on the nature of the probability distributions in the constituent families, which thus far have been calculated on a type basis but for which weighting by token frequencies is clearly required.

REFERENCES

Anshen, F., & Aronoff, M. (1988). Producing morphologically complex words. *Linguistics, 26,* 641–655.

Baayen, R.H., Dijkstra, T., & Schreuder, R. (1997). Singulars and plurals in Dutch: Evidence for a parallel dual route model. *Journal of Memory and Language, 36,* 94–117.

Baayen, R.H., Piepenbrock, R., & Gulikers, L. (1995). *The CELEX lexical database* [CD-ROM]. Philadelphia, PA: Linguistic Data Consortium, University of Pennsylvania.

Bertram, R., Laine, M., Baayen, R.H., Schreuder, R., & Hyönä, J. (1999). Affixal homonymy triggers full-form storage even with inflected words, even in a morphologically rich language. *Cognition, 74,* B13–B25.

Bertram, R., Schreuder, R., & Baayen, R.H. (2000). The balance of storage and computation in morphological processing: The role of word formation type, affixal homonymy, and productivity. *Journal of Experimental Psychology: Learning, Memory, and Cognition, 26,* 419–511.

Burani, C., Dovetto, M., Thornton, A.M., & Laudanna, A. (1997). Accessing and naming suffixed pseudo-words. In G.E. Booij & J. Van Marle (Eds.), *Yearbook of morphology 1996* (pp. 55–73). Dordrecht: Kluwer.

De Jong, N.H., Feldman, L.B., Schreuder, R., Pastizzo, M., & Baayen, R.H. (2002). The processing and representation of Dutch and English compounds: Peripheral morphological, and central orthographic effects. *Brain and Language, 81*(1/2/3), 555–567.

De Jong, N.H., Schreuder, R., & Baayen, R.H. (2000). The morphological family size effect and morphology. *Language and Cognitive Processes, 15,* 329–365.

Gagné, C. (2001). Relation and lexical priming during the interpretation of noun-noun combinations. *Journal of Experimental Psychology: Learning, Memory, and Cognition, 27,* 236–254.

Gagné, C., & Shoben, E.J. (1997). The influence of thematic relations on the comprehension of modifier-noun combinations. *Journal of Experimental Psychology: Learning, Memory, and Cognition, 23,* 71–87.

Giraudo, H., & Grainger, J. (2001). Priming complex words: Evidence for supralexical representation of morphology. *Psychonomic Bulletin and Review, 8,* 127–131.

Giraudo, H., & Grainger, J. (2003). On the role of derivational affixes in recognizing complex words: Evidence from masked priming. In R. Baayen & R. Schreuder (Eds.), *Morphological structure in language processing* (pp. 211–234). Berlin: Mouton.

Krott, A., Baayen, R.H., & Schreuder, R. (2001). Analogy in morphology: Modeling the choice of linking morphemes in Dutch. *Linguistics, 39*(1), 51–93.

Krott, A., Schreuder, R., & Baayen, R.H. (2002a). Linking elements in Dutch noun-noun compounds: constituent families as predictors for response latencies. *Brain and Language, 81*(1–3). 708–722.

Krott, A., Schreuder, R., & Baayen, R.H. (2002b). Analogical hierarchy: Exemplar-based modeling of linkers in Dutch noun-noun compounds. In R. Skousen, D. Londsdale, & D.B. Parkinson (Eds.), *Analogical modeling: An exemplar-based approach to language* (pp. 181–206). Amsterdam: John Benjamins.

Levelt, W.J.M., Roelofs, A., & Meyer, A.S. (1999). A theory of lexical access in speech production, *Behavioral and Brain Sciences, 22*, 1–38.

Longtin, C., Segui, J., & Hallé, P. (2003). Morphological priming without morphological relationship. *Language and Cognitive Processes, 18*, 313–334.

Pinheiro, J.C., & Bates, D.M. (2000). *Mixed-effects models in S and S-PLUS*, Statistics and Computing. New York: Springer.

Schreuder, R., & Baayen, R.H. (1997). How complex simplex words can be. *Journal of Memory and Language, 37*, 118–139.

Schreuder, R., Neijt, A., Van der Weide, F., & Baayen, R.H. (1998). Regular plurals in Dutch compounds: linking graphemes or morphemes? *Language and Cognitive Processes, 13*, 551–573.

Sereno, J., & Jongman, A. (1997). Processing of English inflectional morphology. *Memory and Cognition, 25*, 425–437.